Citizenship Education and the Modern State

Edited by

Kerry J. Kennedy

 The Falmer Press

(A member of the Taylor & Francis Group)

London • Washington, D.C.

UK	Falmer Press, 1 Gunpowder Square, London
USA	Falmer Press, Taylor & Francis Inc., 1900 Frost Road, Suite 101, Bristol, PA 19007

First published in 1997

A catalogue record for this book is available from the British Library

Library of Congress Cataloging-in-Publication Data are available on request

ISBN 0 7507 0704 6 cased
ISBN 0 7507 0647 3 paper

Jacket design by Caroline Archer

Typeset in 10/12pt Times by
Graphicraft Typesetters Ltd., Hong Kong.

Printed in Great Britain by Biddles Ltd., Guildford and King's Lynn on paper which has a specified pH value on final paper manufacture of not less than 7.5 and is therefore 'acid free'.

Contents

Contents

Preface

As a graduate student in the School of Education at Stanford University in the late 1970s and early 1980s I worked under Professor Richard E. Gross in the Curriculum and Teacher Education Program taking a specialization in Social Studies Education. When he indicated to me that I would need to take a course in Citizenship Education to meet requirements I argued that such a course would be of little use to me since in Australia we did not teach citizenship education. Fortunately his wisdom prevailed, as it so often did, and I took the course. Just to reinforce his point, he presented me with a copy of his co-authored book, *Educating Citizens for Democracy* on the day I completed my PhD orals. I returned from Stanford with little doubt that citizenship education should play a role in the curriculum of Australian schools but somewhat perplexed as to why it didn't.

Citizenship education has been an important feature of the school curriculum in the United States from the time of Hamilton and Jefferson when it was argued that 'educating people for citizenship was . . . a means of assuring the establishment and maintenance of the republic' (Dynneson and Gross, 1991, p. 2). In Australia, however, citizenship education did not have such an impetus and I offered the following explanation:

> There has not been the historical need in Australia to create and reinforce a rationale for a 'new' democracy. Australians in general have settled for a democracy based on their colonial heritage. For the most part, the issue of how a democratic culture might actively be manifested in Australia has remained unaddressed (Kennedy, 1993, p. 1)

This is not to say that there was no citizenship education in Australia at all. I carried out a study on early twentieth Australia (Kennedy, 1995) to find that there was a very active civics education movement (the distinction between citizenship education and civics education is an important one — the latter refers largely to formal programs of instruction while the former is broader and encompasses the multiple ways in which citizens are encouraged to pursue their roles in a democratic society). These early civics programs sought to develop an intelligent citizenry that had its roots firmly in its colonial past. There were no 'Australian' citizens until 1949 — there were British subjects forging a new society in a land many thousands of kilometres from Great Britain. Of course, there were other groups as well such as the indigenous people who were not formally Australian citizens until 1967, yet little was heard of them in the early civics texts. The comparison between the revolutionary spirit that shaped civics and citizenship education in the United

States and the colonial spirit that shaped Australian developments led me to look further to see how different political and social contexts influenced educational programs directed at shaping citizens of the future.

Into this somewhat academic exercise came a brand new initiative of the Australian government when it announced in June 1994 the establishment of a Civics Expert Group 'to provide the Government with a strategic plan for a non-partisan program of public education and information on the Australian system of government, the Australian constitution, Australian citizenship and other civic issues' (Civics Expert Group, 1994, p. 1). Work started in June 1994. The Prime Minister had his report by December and three months were allowed for public responses, with the Prime Minister announcing the Government's response in June 1995.

Both the public and government response to the report were overwhelmingly positive:

> The Commonwealth's proposed civics and citizenship education program will ensure that Australians have the opportunity to become informed about our system of government, our Constitution, and other civics and citizenship issues ... the program will aim to improve our understanding of what citizenship means in a modern society, and thereby encourage practical participation in our nation's civic life ... (Office of the Prime Minister, 1995, p. iii)

Such an initiative was welcomed by the educational community especially since it brought with it some $25 million of new money. Yet it was also clear to me that there were significant dangers in launching a new program of civics and citizenship education without understanding the contexts, theoretical, political and social, that could shape such programs in the late 1990s. Thus was born the idea for this book — an attempt to place those contexts up front and to provide a background against which new ideas and suggestions for civics and citizenship education could be tested.

It soon became clear that such a task could not be completed by one person and that it could not focus only on Australia. Citizenship education has been both an implicit and explicit objective of governments for a very long time. Philosophers, historians, political scientists, educators as well as politicians have all had something to say about it at one time or another. Andy Green and Victoria Foster, delivering papers at the AERA meeting in San Francisco in 1994, provided voices that I thought were important to hear. David Hogan, back in Australia after a long period in the US, was able to traverse the ancients and moderns in a way that brought important issues to bear on current issues in citizenship education. Rob Gilbert has always provided a strong voice from a postmodernist perspective and it seemed important to include that as well. Writing from specific country perspectives, Murray Print has been at the forefront of civics and citizenship education in Australia in recent times. Paul Morris has written extensively about curriculum issues in east Asia in general and Hong Kong in particular. It was good to have him at the University of Canberra for a brief time while he was on leave. Haris Jadi I first met at the PCC Conference in Vancouver in 1994 and I was keen to get a Malaysian perspective. Sherry Field became known to me through the Society for the Study of Curriculum History and this was an ideal perspective to have in such a volume. Ken Fogelman I have only met virtually, through his writing and the internet, but given recent developments in England, I was anxious to have his unique perspective. I am grateful to all these people for giving generously of their time and their intellect. They have brought together in the one place significant ideas about a phenomenon that characterizes the modern state in a postmodern world. The tensions, the disagreements and the conflicting views are deliberate: citizenship education is a highly contested area of endeavour.

I believe that the contestation can and must be worked through if we are to have a future in which there will be no impediments for individuals or groups to participate and contribute to the common good in a constructive way. Without such a hope, I believe there will be little in the future for celebration.

This is a volume of its time in more ways than the saliency of the subject matter. Most of the correspondence and interaction between contributors has been carried out by email across four continents. Documents have been attached to email correspondence in London, Penang and Georgia and sent to Canberra. Miraculously it has all worked and the text has unfolded 'little by little into the full light'. What did we do before the internet?

I am particularly grateful to The Australian National University where this work was started and to the University of Canberra where it has been finished. I want to thank Kaye Simmonds who has been responsible for putting together the final manuscript — her patience, diligence and technical expertise were essential ingredients to seeing a final product emerge. I want also to thank my wife and her generosity of spirit that has characterized our years together.

Kerry J. Kennedy
Faculty of Education,
University of Canberra

List of Acronyms

AEC	Australian Education Council
AI	Advisory Inspectorate
APEC	Asian Pacific Economic Cooperation
CCESMP	Civics and Citizenship Education School Curriculum Material Project
CDC	Curriculum Development Council
CDI	Curriculum Development Institute
DES	Department of Education and Science
EC	European Community
ED	Education Department
EPA	European Productivity Agency
EU	European Union
GATT	General Agreement on Tariffs and Trade
GPA	Government and Public Affairs
HK	Hong Kong
IMF	International Monetary Fund
NAFTA	North American Free Trade Association
NCC	National Curriculum Council
OTL	Opportunity to Learn
OFSTED	Office for Standards in Education
PCC	Pacific Circle Consortium
PRC	People's Republic of China
SCAA	Schools Curriculum Assessment Authority
SGLRC	Senate Le Gal and Constitutional References Committee
SSCEET	Senate Standing Committee on Employment, Education and Training
UN	United Nations

Citizenship Education in Review: Past Perspectives and Future Needs

Kerry J. Kennedy

If government policy development were at all rational, it might be expected that educators could influence the process by contributing theoretical and practical advice that could help to shape new policies. Yet educational theory often seems of little avail — policy development marches onward despite the concerns of educators embedded in theoretical positions that are often seen to be irrelevant by policy makers. This situation has serious implications for which conceptions of citizenship education will be advanced and supported, for there is no single unitary construct that will suit everyone. As this volume demonstrates, educators have much to offer policy makers to assist them in making wise decisions.

In suggesting that there are different conceptions of citizenship education I want to suggest that citizenship education is capable of being constructed in multiple ways and that it is important to be aware of how those constructions take place. Musgrave recently conducted a study of commonly used textbooks in Australian schools from 1895–1965 and identified five main strands that highlighted implicit values that supported citizenship formation in this period:

1 *Citizenship was for some not all*: Aboriginal people, other non-white people and non-Anglo-Celtic migrants were excluded from consideration.

2 *Citizenship was based on an assumption of a single dominant religion*: While sectarianism was excluded from texts used in state schools, there was nevertheless the assumption that Australia was a Christian country.

3 *Citizenship was conceived of in monolingual terms*: English, especially written English that reflected the values of Great Britain, was promoted although local variants were accepted gradually.

4 *Citizenship promoted the values of a capitalist economic system*: Exhortations seeking to enhance the productive capacity of Australia and Australians have been with us for a long time.

5 *Citizenship was based on a view of the world seen largely through British eyes*: The acceptance of international responsibilities has come later for Australia with the first signs appearing only after 1945. (Musgrave, 1994, pp. 15–16)

The lesson here is that either knowingly or unknowingly images of citizenship can be conveyed and reinforced in simple instructional material. When the images are exclusive they automatically support exclusive notions of citizenship with some individuals and groups being 'in' and others being 'out'. We can thus construct citizenship to suit our needs. In a democratic society citizenship should be inclusive rather than exclusive but we must deliberately set out to make it so, otherwise it can fall into exclusivism.

There can also be very limiting views of citizenship education. As part of the work of the Australian government's Civic Expert Group's work, Australian National Opinion Poll's (ANOP) Research Services were asked to conduct 'a benchmark study into the Australian community's knowledge about governmental, constitutional, citizenship and civic issues' (Civics Expert Group, 1994, p. 130). The outcomes of this study revealed a 'a high level of community ignorance about Australia's system of government and its origins' (Civics Expert Group, 1994, p. 132), with people in the 15–19 years age group described as having a 'level of ignorance (that) is striking' (p. 134). Stuart Macintyre (1995, p. 4), Chair of the Civics Expert Group, has raised the spectre of a 'a civic deficit' by which is meant a deficit in civic knowledge. The ANOP polling indicated that there were important facts that Australian citizens, young and old, did not know. For example, '87 per cent of Australians have only the sketchiest knowledge of the Constitution, 78 per cent lack knowledge of the functions of the High Court 70 per cent do not understand the historical basis of the federal system' (Macintyre, 1995, p. 7).

The concept of a 'civic deficit' or a deficit in civic knowledge is a deceptively simple one for it suggests that the remedy is simply to ensure that young people, and indeed all people, know more facts about the political system. Now the rationale for knowing more facts might well be important as Macintyre has pointed out:

> How can these citizens, whether as republicans or monarchists, follow the current constitutional debate? How many of those who, in various public opinion polls, say they would prefer a directly elected head of state to one appointed by parliament appreciate that the present arrangements for appointing the head of state are even less participatory than either of these alternatives? (Macintyre, 1995, p. 7)

Yet facts alone will not deliver a more intelligent and active citizenry and in an instructional context might well turn students off civics education all together. Citizenship education is about more than facts. There are at least two broad aspects that have to be considered.

First, paralleling a deficit in civic knowledge, there are civic issues the understanding of which demand much more than simple recitation of a predigested body of knowledge. Macintyre (1995, p. 1) has identified three such issues: 'multiculturalism, the recognition of ethnic and cultural diversity; reconciliation, the recognition of the special status of the indigenous peoples of this country; and republicanism, the recognition of constitutional self-sufficiency'. While these issues have a particular Australian context, many of them are also relevant internationally. Writing prior to the report of the Civics Expert Group, I also identified these issues but included the recognition of the changing status of women and pointed to a range of international events and activities that had the potential to shape Australia's future: APEC, the globalization of the economy, the impact of communications technology and the changing role of the United Nations (Kennedy, 1995). From an international perspective, EU, NAFTA and the GATT also have the potential to change the way we think about citizenship education since the focus moves away from the needs of individual nations to more global needs and interests.

These very broad influences and issues might best be understood as 'civic megatrends' — complex issues demanding a response that is at once knowledge based and values based. The kind of knowledge required is interdisciplinary and integrated while the values must be firmly embedded in a vision that focuses on the good of all rather than the selfish demands of individuals. These megatrends have the potential to define who citizens are at the end of the twentieth century and shape whom they shall become in the next millennium. They must be an essential part of any citizenship education program in any country.

Second, it would be easy to draw links between the so-called civic deficit and civic megatrends to show how the two might be related. What kind of knowledge is needed if communities are to understand and actively contribute to shaping their own future? Yet it is as simple as that. There are also what are best described as the civic realities of everyday life — living and working in a democratic society. Civic realities do not always show our towns and cities at their best irrespective of the national context. Drug taking is on the increase, violence is becoming an increasingly common feature of urban life, homelessness is not uncommon, alcohol consumption and gambling amongst young people is a fact of life and youth unemployment continues to soar. Given this context, it seems bizarre to lament the fact that young people do not know the names of government officials and local representatives or cannot name the houses of parliament. This is not the world of young people — it is the world of adults, of the past, of those who have failed to make adequate provision for the future. Civics and citizenship education therefore, must also be about civic realities — the things that matter to young people, the things that can help them understand their reality and give them a stake in the future that rightly belongs to them.

The challenge for civics and citizenship education is to somehow meld together civic knowledge, civic megatrends and civic realities in a way that will meet young people where they are. Disembodied facts, unrelated to everyday life and real needs, will not solve any of our current problems and will not connect young people to a future that should be full of hope and promise. To be successful, civics education must speak to young people — to use Stuart Macintyre's (1995, p. 16) sentence, 'we must connect young Australians with the substance of their citizenship' — and the same can be said for all young people irrespective of their national location.

There has developed a vast literature on civics and citizenship and it is not confined to education. The breadth of the issues as they are outlined below gives an indication of the complexities facing those charged with delivering civics and citizenship education programs.

There has been a range of views expressed on the nature and purpose of citizenship. One set of differences centres on the relative emphasis to be placed on the public or common interest as distinct from private interests. The question is raised as to whether civics education should promote one at the expense of the other. Macintyre (1996), Kennedy (1995), Crittenden (1995), Saunders (1996), Hill (1996) and Thompson (1996) support the notion of a common citizenship under-pinned by a set of common values. It follows from this position that one task of civics education is to engender support for what all citizens share in common, including values, political structures and a willingness to participate actively in democratic processes. Equally strong arguments are made to highlight the import-ance of individual interests and the need to safeguard these in a democratic soci-ety (Hogan, 1996; Gilbert, 1993; Singh, 1993; Wyn, 1995; Watts, 1995). Diamond (1994) has pointed out that the tension between these two positions might be resolved if it is kept in mind that individual interests can only be safeguarded by a political and legal system that guarantees freedom of thought and action. Thus civics education can highlight the importance of individual interests while seeking support for those institutions and the values that allow individual interests to flourish.

The tension between public and private interests is nowhere better demon-strated than in the way different groups prefer to see themselves depicted as cit-izens. Foster (1996b) has pointed to the inadequacies of *Whereas the people*, (Civics Expert Group, 1994) in relation to women. She argues that the role of women as citizens has not been adequately conceptualized or understood. In the same way, Woods (1996) points to the complexities of citizenship for Aboriginal and Torres Strait Islander people. She does not want to be subsumed into a common citizen-ship but rather seeks to maintain an identity that has the potential to contribute to new understandings about modern citizenship. Civics education, therefore, must recognize the contribution of difference and diversity in modern society and not seek to submerge them.

Support for private interests has been criticized for overemphasizing the rights of citizens at the expense of their responsibilities. Rights have been described broadly to mean social, political and economic rights (Gilbert, 1992; Watts, 1995; Pixley, 1993). Musgrave (1994) regards this as a consumer approach to citizen-ship by which rights and entitlements are amassed in the interest of individuals. He argues strongly that young people ought to be made aware of their duties and responsibilities as citizens. For civics education it is not one or the other: rights and responsibilities are both important parts of learning about citizenship. The issue is establishing the relationship between rights and responsibilities so that they are seen as complementary rather than mutually exclusive.

The issue of rights and responsibilities as aspects of civics and citizenship education raises more direct questions about the knowledge base of civics educa-tion. There are strong advocates for History as providing the knowledge base for civics education (Civics Expert Group, 1994; Young, 1996) while others point to the strengths of the principles and concepts underlying Studies of Society and the Environment (Hogan et al., 1996a). Woods (1996) argues strongly for grounding civics in Aboriginal and Torres Strait Islander Studies. Saunders (1996) sees the need for citizens to have an understanding of the system of government if they are to participate effectively in democratic decision making. Lepani (1996) focuses on the needs of the knowledge economy and highlights the importance of developing systems thinking and information literacy as necessities for effective citizenship.

Other writers come at the issue from a different perspective. Brennan (1996) talks in terms of pedagogies (group work and group based assessment), school governance and the meaningful involvement of students and community based research projects involving students. Wyn (1995) agrees with the experiential approach advocated by Brennan (1996) and argues that young people need to be equipped with the means to overcome the unequal power relationships that characterize modern society and that impact on youth in particular. Watts (1995) echoes a similar view by calling for civics and citizenship education to be an empowering process that will result in young people having a real sense of social agency.

The range of views expressed above is symptomatic of the field itself. In the articles that follow, these themes are taken up in different ways. Rather than try to summarize them here, it is better to let the authors speak for themselves in their individual contributions. This is not to say that the issues raised should be left without resolution. They should not. Citizenship education is not a field for academic speculation: it is about the lives of people who live and work from day to day. It is true that citizenship education, or education of any kind, cannot solve all the problems which people face in their daily lives. Yet it can ensure that people are able to live their lives based on principles of peace, harmony, respect and tolerance and that they will know when these principles are being violated. They will also be aware of their responsibilities and how they can exercise them. In this sense, citizenship education provides the foundations on which a truly democratic society can be built. Hopefully, this collection of articles will provide directions that will not only enhance the debates but will also contribute to the development of durable and stable foundations.

Part 1:

Frameworks for Citizenship Education

1 Education and State Formation in Europe and Asia

Andy Green

The historical role of education in the process of state formation or 'nation-building' is now widely accepted. The development of national education systems in nineteenth-century Europe, Japan and the North Americas, though occurring at different times, invariably overlapped with the process of nation-building, both contributing to it and as a function of it. The leading role which the state apparatus, or political state, played in this process in many countries is also widely, if not universally, accepted as an historical fact (Bendix, 1964; Boli, 1989; Curtis, 1988; Green, 1990; Melton, 1988).

However, if the links between education and state formation are fairly common currency for historians, the same cannot be said for analysts of contemporary education, particularly in the English-speaking world. In many countries, both Anglophone and otherwise, there is now considerable scepticism regarding the role of the state in education and the role of education in the process of state formation. There are a number of reasons for this.

The first, and most obvious, is that the resurgence of neo-liberal politics and *laissez-faire* economics has decisively undermined the leading role which Keynesian welfarism formerly assigned to the state in the direction and regulation of economies and societies (Harvey, 1990). The second is that a combination of economic globalization and growth of supra-national and regional political organization has problematized the role of nation state and possibly reduced the powers of the state apparatus within it, at least in certain areas (Held, 1989; Hobsbawm, 1990; Reich, 1991). Thirdly, and not least, the increasingly plural and heterogeneous character of modern advanced societies has provided a challenge to the concept of national identity and, even, to the concept of society itself. It is not only to Margaret Thatcher that 'there is no such thing as society'. To postmoderns such as Baudrillard societies have been replaced by the hyper-reality of virtual cities and imagined communities (Green, 1994), and this perception has spread way beyond the Anglo-Saxon heartlands of deconstructionism.

In almost all countries politicians and others accord education and training an important role in economic development, and this has become increasingly evident as globalization has heightened international economic competition. However, there is now much less confidence in the ability of education systems to perform other developmental functions such as the cultivation of social solidarity, democratic citizenship and national identity. These classic functions were the essence of national education to nineteenth-century thinkers such as Durkheim but they are seen as increasingly problematic today (Durkheim, 1956). To some educational analysts such aims have become positively anachronistic in the postmodern world with its increasing social fragmentation and cultural diversity. According to Rust (1991) and Usher and Edwards (1994), postmodernism fundamentally questions the relevance today of the whole 'modernist' education project where schools were universalizing institutions which aimed to assimilate and integrate diverse populations and promote unifying national cultures. In the extreme postmodern vision education becomes a matter of individualized consumption in a market of differentiated educational products. Information technology replaces the school and college with the virtual classroom individually customized for each office and living room (Usher and Edwards, 1994). Education as a public, collective and social process disappears.

The argument in this chapter, however, is that such a view is not universally shared in these countries and is certainly not yet the dominant belief outside of the Anglophone world. There are other paradigms which continue to assert the primacy of education in the processes of social integration and citizen-building, and other conceptions of the 'learning society' which go beyond the purely economic and instrumental (Ranson, 1994). There are also models of development which continue to stress the importance of the leading role of the state. One such model is the concept of the 'developmental state'.

This chapter seeks to explore the relationship between education and state formation in a number of countries, and particularly those which may be defined as 'developmental states'. Various countries might qualify for this description and those considered here are not a methodologically rigorous sample; rather they consist of a number of countries from the Asian Pacific and western Europe which have been defined as 'developmental states' at different periods and which have coincidentally gone through rapid periods of educational growth. The chapter thus deliberately crosses centuries and continents in order to ask whether there is anything common about the role of education in state formation in certain types of 'developmental state', even where these are manifested in diverse geopolitical and historical contexts.

The hypothesis here is that education has played a particularly important role in the so-called 'developmental' states and that its rapid growth in certain periods has been closely linked with the intensive process of state formation engendered by the developmental ambitions of the state. Rapid educational advance is both a product of the developmental state and an important vehicle for its work. The argument so stated might seem unexceptional, as merely a restatement of a human capital theory of development given a *dirigiste* twist. However, what is suggested here is somewhat more controversial since it specifically relates economic development with the broader aspects of state formation which concern the cultivation of social cohesion and national identity.

State Formation and the Developmental State

It is useful to start by defining some concepts. The term 'nation state' is used in the classical nineteenth-century sense of sovereign or citizen states, even where these include a diversity of 'nations' or 'peoples' (Gellner, 1993; Hobsbawm, 1990). It is not a very helpful term conceptually since it is sometimes taken to imply the existence within the territorial political state of a culturally homogeneous 'nation', which is rarely the case. Nevertheless, it is employed here as a concession to common usage and because it usefully serves to distinguish the idea of nation state as citizen population plus political state, from the idea of the 'state' as simply the state apparatus, which is how the latter is sometimes used.

State formation is taken here to refer to the historical process by which 'states' or 'nation states' are formed or reformed. In its broad sense 'state formation' encompasses the achievement and maintenance of national/state sovereignty; the construction of national public institutions and economic infrastructures; and also the popularization of the notions of citizenship, statehood and national identity which bind it together. The term is deliberately bi-vocal: it connotes both the process by which 'states' are formed and the active role played by the state apparatus in this process, particularly in states which may be termed 'developmental'.

The term 'developmental state' was first used by Chalmers Johnson in his classic study of Japan's post-war economic transformation (Johnson, 1982) and has since been adopted by Manuel Castells and others to define the mode of development of the four 'Asian tigers': Taiwan, South Korea, Singapore and Hong Kong. David Marquand has also used the same term to describe certain post-war European states such as France, Sweden, Germany and Austria, as well as nineteenth-century Prussia and Meiji Japan (Marquand, 1988, p. 106).

The defining characteristic of the developmental state is the dynamic, shaping role played by the state leadership and bureaucracy in relation to civil society. According to Castells a 'state is developmental when it establishes as its principle of legitimacy its ability to promote and sustain (economic) development' (1992, p. 56). Marquand understands the role of the developmental state more broadly to encompass both political and economic modernization (Marquand, 1988). He describes this process in post-war France in the period of state planning and the *économie concertée*: 'the state', he writes, 'acting in close collaboration with large, private sector firms, prodded, bullied, bribed, cajoled and argued a predominantly private-owned economy into a more advanced and more competitive shape' (1988, p. 106). Both authors note that rapid educational advance was an inherent part of the developmental process in these states. This can be traced historically in a number of instances.

The Developmental State and the Formation of National Education Systems in the Nineteenth Century

National or public education systems developed in most major European states during the course of the nineteenth century as well as in the northern states of the

USA and in Japan. They were distinctly new forms of public education involving state-funded networks of elementary schools and later secondary schools; teacher training and accreditation provided by the state; the inspection and licensing of schools and state control over curricula and examinations (Green, 1990). These new systems represented a decisive break with the family- church- and apprentice-based forms of education which prevailed in early modern Europe. They replace the particularistic and essentially clerical educational forms of the earlier period with a new universalistic mission of schooling to serve the interests of the individual and, above all, the state. The national education systems were the precursors of modern state schooling.

Whilst the national systems developed in most major states at some point between 1770 and 1900, they did not develop at the same rate or in quite the same forms in different countries. The first systems were pioneered by eighteenth-century absolutist monarchs like Frederick the Great in Prussia and Maria Theresa in Austria. They were consolidated during the first three decades of the nineteenth century along with the systems in the other German states and in France. Holland, Sweden and the northern states in the USA were not far behind, consolidating their public systems in the 1830s and 40s. In other areas, however, national systems were much slower to develop. The Catholic Mediterranean states developed public education considerably later, led by Italy's pioneering regional initiatives after unification in 1870. Japan laid the foundations of its system in the 1880s as part of the reforming efforts of the Meiji restoration, and the southern states of the USA delayed implementing public education until the decades after the Civil War. England was the most tardy of the major states, delaying the development of a public system of elementary schools until after 1870 and not instituting a national system of secondary schools until 1902, almost a hundred years after Napoleon had created the state lycées in France. On the whole the pioneer education systems in France and the German states tended to be more comprehensive and coherent in their forms than those in states like Britain, which long clung to the earlier voluntarist forms and only reluctantly brought the state into education (Archer, 1979).

Exactly why these new systems developed, and why they developed faster and more completely in some states than others, has long been a subject of historical debate (Archer, 1979; Boli, 1989; Green, 1990; Melton, 1988). Many of the traditional theories of educational change cannot explain the uneven development of these systems (Archer, 1979). Theories linking educational development with industrialization and urbanization cannot explain why national systems developed first in countries like Prussia and France when they were predominantly pre-industrial and rural societies, whilst Britain, the most industrialized and urbanized nation, was relatively slow to develop its national system. Equally, Whiggish historical accounts, which link educational advance with Protestantism and the steady progress of reason and democracy, cannot explain why educational development occurred more rapidly in the more authoritarian states like Prussia and Austria than in liberal Britain, and why there were major exceptions to the general rule of Protestant ascendancy in education, as provided by the relative advance of the Catholic areas of France and Austria (Green, 1990).

A more satisfactory explanation of the uneven rise of national education systems would seem to lie in the theory of state formation. In essence what the argument suggests is that educational advance was an integral part of the general process of state formation and was most apparent in states and at times when this process was most intensive and most accelerated, as was the case in France and Prussia after the French Revolution and in the northern USA during the Early Republic. In states like Britain and Italy, where, for various reasons, the process of state formation was relatively gradual, protracted or delayed, the pressure for educational development seems to have been less insistent, despite other attendant factors, like British economic and urban development, which might otherwise have seemed conducive towards educational reform.

What gave rise to these accelerated periods of state formation? In each case it would appear to have been a concerted drive towards national development led by the state and prompted by crises in state viability. These crises usually resulted from protracted territorial conflicts and foreign invasion, as in Prussia; revolution, as in France; or struggles for independence, as in the USA. Powerful popular nationalisms which, as Tom Nairn has noted, are often products of historical conditions such as these, were also evident in each case, although necessarily in different forms (Nairn, 1981). In each case economic and technological backwardness, relative at least to some other rival powers, appear to have been attendant features although not necessarily at this stage the overriding motivation. Each of these conditions left the countries concerned with major tasks of national reconstruction, usually involving widespread political and constitutional reforms, accelerated economic development, and extensive cultural and ideological transformations to establish and popularize new notions of national identity.

Countries involved in domestic and international wars and conflicts generally experience a centralization of power and the efforts of reconstruction after such conflicts also, typically, necessitate enhanced activity on the part of the state. Likewise, countries determined to catch up economically with other more advanced states generally find that this requires exceptional state activity since the efforts of individual entrepreneurs are unlikely to be sufficient for this task. As Eric Hobsbawm and Paul Bairoch have both noted, *laissez-faire* economics and free trade generally favour the already strong, as Britain well knew in the mid nineteenth century (Bairoch, 1993; Hobsbawm, 1969). It is not surprising, therefore, that reconstruction and modernization in France and Prussia in the early nineteenth century was largely driven and directed by the central state. Barrington Moore describes the Prussian experience, like that of Meiji Japan at the end of the century, as 'revolution from above' (Moore, 1967). In the Early Republic of the USA, constituted in reaction against the overweening centralism of the old Europe, this was less obviously the case since, as both Marx and de Tocqueville noted, here the central state tended to underplay and mask its presence (de Tocqueville, 1956). However, even in the land of democratic localism, nationalism was a most powerful force and the local state was intensely active in building the foundations of the new republic (Kaestle, 1983).

The importance of education in this process of state formation is evident. The major impetus for the creation of national education systems lay in the need to provide the state with trained administrators, engineers and military personnel; to spread the dominant cultures and inculcate popular ideologies of nationhood; to forge the political and cultural unity of the burgeoning nation-states; and to cement the ideological hegemony of their dominant classes. In all countries there was a need to promulgate popular literacy and to generalize the use of the dominant language or dialect as part of the process of fostering national identity. In new nations, such as the USA, education also had to play a major part in assimilating immigrant cultures (Kaestle, 1983), just as in France under Jules Ferry it was used to assimilate the patois-speaking peasant populations of the underdeveloped rural areas to the new citizen ideals of the Third Republic (Weber, 1979).

Schooling, as Hobsbawm has written, was 'the most powerful weapon for forming . . . nations' (Hobsbawm, 1977, p. 120). National education helped to construct the very subjectivities of citizenship, justifying the ways of the state to the people and the duties of the people to the state. Furthermore, if state formation involved using schooling to create new subjects or citizens, it was also about creating new gendered social roles for these subjects. As Davey and Miller have shown (1993), notions of rights, citizenship and social contract rarely included women as equals. Rousseau's plans for the education of Sophie were very different from his plans for Emile, and even Jacobins like Lepelletier, who wanted girls educated alongside boys, thought girls needed less education than boys (Archer and Vaughan, 1971). Typically, schools were entrusted with making boys into useful citizens and girls into wives and mothers who would rear the next generation of male citizens.

The role of the developmental state in this process of accelerated state formation and educational development can be seen most clearly in Prussia, France and Japan. Each of these countries experienced intensive periods of state formation, following either revolution, foreign invasion, or, in Japan's case, the threat of foreign invasion. Each was a pioneer educational state in their region; Japan somewhat after France and Prussia, but certainly precocious for its geo-political context and for a scarcely post-feudal state. In each case social transformation was essentially state-led, with the political powers and the state bureaucracies playing crucial roles. Other countries, like England and Canada, followed different paths and could not be considered as examples of the developmentalist state in action. However, in these countries, no less than in the developmentalist states, education was still integral to the process of state formation.

Prussia

The consolidation of a full national education system in Prussia dates from the first three decades of the nineteenth century. It occurred during the 'era of reforms' which followed the Napoleonic occupation of Prussia and represented part of the process by which the Prussian state was regenerated in the wake of military defeat and national humiliation. The immediate causes of those subsequent educational developments, which were to so impress foreign observers, lay in that historic moment of state formation when the Prussian Junker class, pumped up by fierce nationalistic reaction to French occupation, re-established its power after the abolition of serf-dom through a reformed state apparatus and the imposition of new social relations amongst its subjects (Anderson, 1974).

The characteristic forms of Prussian education were clearly rooted in its his-torical origins in the absolutism of the eighteenth century. The right of the state to impose compulsory schooling on the masses and the patriotic duty of the latter to conform to this had been well established in the earlier period and required no major cultural revolution to be made effective in the following century. The drive for military power and bureaucratic efficiency which had prompted educational development earlier was still a motive force and continued to provide the shaping spirit behind educational innovation. What was added to this in the subsequent period was a virulent nationalistic impulse, epitomized in the writings of Johann Fichte, and a desire to use education to promote the reform of the Prussian state and later to galvanize industrial development through technical expertise. Educational development was to become one of the most active ingredients in a process of compacted and forced state formation that transformed a society based on serfdom and royal absolutism to the reformed Junker state that was capable of hauling Germany into the capitalist world (Green, 1990; Landes, 1969).

France

Educational development in France, unlike in Prussia, owed less to absolutism and more to the process of post-revolutionary bourgeois reconstruction. National edu-cation in France was first conceived by the *philosophes* of the eighteenth century enlightenment. However, it was not actually constructed until the period of Empire and as part of Napoleon's project of using the exceptional form of the Bonapartist state to restore order to post-revolutionary France and to finalize the revolutionary task of unifying and fortifying the state according to the principles of the bourgeois revolution of 1789 (Artz, 1966; Prost, 1968).

The educational innovations of the Empire reflected the purposes and struc-tures of the Napoleonic state. The development of a centralized educational bur-eaucracy and the subordination of education to state control was designed to promote bourgeois interests and the collective goals of the nation state. The devel-opment of the public lycée embodied the secular rationalist philosophy of the revolutionary period and offered a limited form of meritocratic promotion for the middle orders (Anderson, 1975). The continuation and development of the voca-tional and special schools reflected the desire for efficient and well-trained recruits for the military and public authorities, providing a technical education that com-plemented the broad humanistic education of the lycée (Artz, 1966). Finally, the re-admission of the Church into education under state control was calculated to ensure that elementary education for the masses was still steeped in patriotic and moral values. Throughout, the accent was on the use of education to promote a uni-fied and cohesive national culture which would celebrate the glory of France and underwrite the hegemony of the Bonapartist state. 'To instruct is secondary,' said

Napoleon, 'the main thing is to train and to do so according to the pattern which suits the state' (Archer and Vaughan, 1971; Green, 1990).

Japan

The development of a national education system in Japan after the Meiji Restoration of 1868 can also be understood as part of a process of intensive state formation. As Herbert Passin (1965) has written, 'educational reform ranks as one of the key measures in the transformation of Japan from a feudal to a modern nation state. ... Through the use of uniform teaching materials and the diffusion of a national language . . . , the schools helped promote a common sense of nationhood and the displacement of regional by national loyalties' (p. 62).

During the pre-Meiji Tokugawa period, Japan had a thriving educational culture amongst the Samurai elite whose children were educated in the domain schools run by the feudal authorities, but less than 50 per cent of the population as a whole (by 1860) went to school and most of these in the privately-run Terakoya basic schools (Passin, 1965; Dore, 1984). Towards the end of the Shogunate, and after the arrival of Commodore Perry in 1853, Japanese culture began to be more open to western science, but the schools remained dominated by traditional Confucian values. It was the Samurai reformers after the Meiji Restoration who sought to modernize Japan and saw education as a means of mobilizing the entire population in this process of state formation.

As in Prussia half a century earlier, the impetus towards state formation in Japan was driven primarily by the fear of foreign domination. In this case, unlike in Prussia, the invasion was cultural and only putatively military, but it evoked no less a reaction for that, not least because it came after centuries of isolation such as no European state had experienced. The Meiji restoration of 1868 was the result of a social movement triggered in part by the opening up of Japan to western influences during the 1840s and 50s. It was the realization of the superiority and threat of western technology which prompted the formation of new social alliances dedicated to resisting foreign domination. This was to be achieved through the adoption of western technology and the reassertion of Japanese identity symbolized by the restoration of the Emperor.

Under the new Meiji regime it was the Samurai reformers and the enlightened bureaucracy who spearheaded an intensive programme of modernization which drew on and adapted western principles to the Japanese context. With the abolition of the feudal class system in 1871, the adoption of a new constitution, and the introduction of representative political institutions, a new order was established. Under the slogan of *slogen shokusan koguo* (develop industry and private enterprise), the reformers promoted a national banking system; built railways, harbours and telegraph networks; established and later sold-off plants in the cement, silk, copper and glass industries; and provided start-up loans and subsidies to the private sector (Marquand, 1988, pp. 102–3).

Education had a major part to play in all this. It was required to furnish the new bureaucratic elite so vital to the modernizing process; to inculcate new modernizing principles amongst the masses, whilst re-enforcing traditional Japanese traditions and identity; and it was critical for the administrative and linguistic integration of a nation formerly divided into over 300 separate feudal units (Cummings, 1980, p. 8). The Japanese authorities proved themselves to be particularly adept at all this, simultaneously emphasizing the importance of adapting western science and technology whilst stressing the uniqueness and historical continuity of Japanese culture and traditions. As Burkes has noted: 'In Japan certainly, experience has demonstrated that an education system can be a powerful instrument in the forging of national unity' (Burkes, 1985, p. 257).

With the establishment of a Ministry of Education in 1871, a new education system was developed which drew heavily on western influences, incorporating French principles of centralized administration and American modern curricula. A later conservative backlash against westernization led to a return to traditional Japanese values in education, epitomized in the revised Education Ordinance of 1880 and later in the ultra conservative Imperial Rescript, which stressed the role of education in promoting loyalty to the state and to the Emperor. After 1885, Japan's celebrated education minister, Mori Arinori, sought to reconcile modernity and tradition by promoting a westernized secondary education for the elite whilst preserving traditional values in popular education. Though later assassinated by nationalists, Arinori expressed his mission for eduction in classic nation-building terms: 'In the administration of all schools . . . what is to be done is not for the sake of the pupils, but for the sake of the country'. . . . 'Our country must move from its third class position to second class, and from second class to first, and ultimately to the leading position amongst countries in the world' (quoted in Passin, pp. 88 and 68).

Japan, though modernizing later than France and Germany, provides one of the clearest examples of a developmental state using education as a vehicle for state formation. Cummings' statement that: 'Japan, as a late developer, was one of the first societies to treat education as a tool of national development' (1980, p. 7), may not be strictly true in global terms, but it certainly captures several important ancillary truths. Japan under the Meiji regime was exceptionally clear sighted in its understanding of the role of education in modernization, and it provided the first example of this process in Asia, which several other countries were subsequently to follow. Cummings' statement also recognizes that late development required an especial attention to education — a point which is developed by Amsden in her work on South Korea (Amsden, 1992).

Canada

The construction of the 'educational state' in Ontario in the mid-nineteenth century provides another illustration of education as state formation but in rather a different sense from the other examples cited here since the formative period of educational development occurred during a period of as yet unresolved struggle over colonial rule. As Bruce Curtis (1988) clearly demonstrates, educational reform in the period

1830–1870 was inextricably tied up with struggles over the nature of the colonial state and different parties had different ideas about what kind of state they wished to promote through their educational reforms. What they had in common was a belief that education was essential for the creation of a new type of political subject whose own internalization of discipline and moral responsibility was seen as a precondition for political order in an emerging polity, which, whatever form it eventually took, would involve greater independence and more representative government. As elsewhere, the reforms were essentially constructed from above, and reflected the class aims of the dominant groups, but they cannot be construed as a crude process of imposition and unmediated social control. What Curtis demonstrates so well in his book is the process by which the reformers sought through education to 'anchor . . . the conditions of political governance in the selves of the governed' (p. 15). As described by Curtis, this amounted to a classic exercise in the construction of a cultural hegemony by dominant groups through education, whereby 'official knowledge presented the patriarchal, linguistic, ethical, political, economic and religious interests of the ruling class as the general interests of society' (Curtis, 1988, p. 371).

England

In England the development of education was no less a process of state formation than it was in these other countries. However, due to the particular nature of the state, and of its relationship to civil society, a national education system did not occur until relatively late compared at least with France and Prussia. Although the terminology can be deceptive, this can be seen as a question of early 'strengths' and later 'weaknesses'. Throughout the sixteenth, seventeenth and eighteenth centuries, the British state was characterized by relative unity of its kingdom and the relative stability and durability of its institutions and ruling groups. One of the first consolidated nation states in Europe (despite the protracted and bloody process of colonization in Ireland), the British state benefited from the early centralization of state power under the Tudors, and the advantages afforded by its geographical insularity and maritime strength, from which grew its colonial power. The early termination of absolutism through Cromwell's revolution, added to its other advantages, made possible the early development of capitalist relations in agriculture, commerce and later, industry. During the eighteenth century, the relative absence of military conflict, combined with the economic advantages of natural resources and colonial trade, allowed capitalist development to take advantage of the home markets provided by a relatively fluid society undergoing a demographic explosion. Early industrialization could thus occur organically, from the bottom up, without excessive intervention from the state (Perkin, 1985).

State formation, or 'nation-building' to use Walter Bagehot's nineteenth-century phrase, was thus a comparatively precocious affair in Britain, and though bloody and violent at times, to be sure, occurred more gradually than in many other countries considered here. It also occurred without the enlarged, 'forcing' apparatus of the absolutist state which was so central to modernization in other countries. With a history of long-standing and relatively stable institutions and ruling groups to draw on, national identity did not have to be invented as in other countries where nation-building required the elaboration of various nationalist ideologies which literally had to manufacture traditions. If nationalism in other countries meant creating what Benedict Anderson calls 'imagined communities' (1983), Britain had no need of it, since the nation was the past. Such a state also had less need for national education during the eighteen century, since there was not the great demand for bureaucrats and military recruits which existed in absolutist states and since the population scarcely had to be schooled in 'nationhood'.

The absence of a national education system in eighteenth century England was thus certainly not the product of a 'weak state', as some have construed the argument (Davey and Miller; 1993, p. 6). What can be argued, however, following Hobsbawm (1969), Gamble (1981) and Marquand (1988), is that the early 'strengths' of the British state and economy later became fetters on the development of a modern state and economy.

During the period 1815–1860 it would be quite inaccurate to talk of a 'weak state' in Britain for, as Polanyi (1957) famously argued, the creation of *a laissez-faire* system precisely required a strong — albeit streamlined — state to remove all the old barriers and restrictions to 'free enterprise'. The state properly described as 'liberal' or *'laissez-faire'* emerged after the end of Napoleonic Wars (although its principles derived, of course, from Adam Smith in the previous century), and then only developed gradually through deliberate state action. The liberal state was deliberately minimalist, or tried to be, but was not so much weak as limited in the extent of its apparatus and functions. This became a problem after 1860 and has remained so since, in the sense that after the so-called second Industrial Revolution, and in what later became known as the era of monopoly capitalism, successful economies came to require more effective state intervention in all spheres of life to ensure their conditions of existence. Corrigan and Sayer's account of British state formation, which consciously plays down its uniquely *'laissez-faire'* features, is unable to explain these later obstacles to modernization, and it is to explain this later course of development that emphasis has been placed on the so-called 'peculiarities' of the English (Gamble, 1981; Green, 1990). However, whilst that *'laissez-faire'* was certainly a defining characteristic of the British liberal state in the nineteenth century, 'weakness' was not. During the 'golden age' of Victorian capitalism, the British state certainly did not appear as 'weak', even though it may be said to have been storing up problems for the next generations.

Education was, however, in a sense, 'weak' or 'underdeveloped' in that provision was in various respects both less extensive and less appropriate than it might have been to the needs of the time, and compared with other comparable countries. Admittedly these 'needs' were often not generally recognized, except by the long-sighted, until later (say in the 1860s) and one may thus be accused of hindsight and anachronism in applying them to earlier periods like the 1840s and 1850s. However, there were clear social and political 'needs' for more education even at that time, as many did in fact recognize, and arguably also long-term economic needs, for even if the British economy developed rapidly in these years without improved education, the absence of that education would have consequences for the economy of the next generation.

This underdevelopment of education was the result of the failure to develop a national system until late in the day; this in turn was the result of the specific nature of state formation in Britain where *laissez-faire* liberalism continued to provide powerful arguments against the use of the state in education.

State Formation from the Age of Empire

Since the period when national systems of education were first consolidated, the process of state formation has gone through many changes and the role of education in it likewise. The function of education in economic development has become more important, whereas in the earlier period it was probably the political and social aspects of nation formation which most exercised educational reformers. The nature and role of the nation state — and the ideologies of nationalism which underscored it — have changed.

National education systems were first formed at a point when the modern, capitalist state was emerging through the twin revolutions in industry and society. Nationalism meant support for the liberal Mazzinian ideal of the viable nation-state as formed through the agglomeration of smaller territorial and ethnic units. Education was important to the formation of a cohesive citizenry out of these heterogeneous populations, particularly in immigrant nations such as the USA.

Since that time concepts of nationalism and nation-state have been through successive changes. The late nineteenth century saw the emergence of expansionist imperial states and the recrudescence of new forms of nationalism which, unlike the earlier nationalisms, stressed the ethnic and linguistic bases of national identity (Gellner, 1983; Hobsbawm, 1990). The First World War led to the break-up of the old empires and the emergence of a multitude of smaller nation-states under the Wilsonian doctrine of national sovereignty. The unstable political settlement reached at Versailles, combined with the economic catastrophes of the late 1920s, led to the ultra nationalist fascist regimes of the pre-war era. In the post-World War Two period we have seen the rise and fall of new super-powers, successful national independence movements and, with the demise of the former communist regimes, a resurgence of small state formation.

This and the other nationalisms associated with it, have occurred simultaneously, and possibly in reaction to, other apparently long-term tendencies which suggest the partial supersession of the nation-state. Economic and cultural globalization, facilitated by the information revolution, and the proliferation of supernational entities, like the EU, have fundamentally placed in question the role of the nation-state and its sovereign powers. Whilst Hobsbawm (1990) has suggested that nationalism and the nation-state can no longer be considered the 'primary vector' of historical development, current movements across the world suggest a major resurgence of nationalism.

Education has clearly played different roles at different times and in different national contexts in this changing process of state formation. Whilst the economic function of education may have become increasingly important, and whilst in the older nation-states increasing cultural pluralism and internationalism would seem to be weakening the roles of education in fostering national cohesion (as the post-moderns would have us believe), there are clearly still notable instances in this century where education has been closely associated with nationalist objectives, and this continues to be the case. This includes both the negative examples of the roles played by education in the fascist regimes of the 1930s and the more positive roles played by education in forging national identity in the emerging nations of East Asia. Arguably, education's role in fostering social cohesion and national solidarity in these countries is part and parcel of the process of accelerated economic development (Wielemans and Chan, 1994).

There are certainly examples in the post-war western world of countries going through intensive periods of state formation where education was also a major factor in development. Reconstruction in post-war France and West Germany was rapid and led to long periods of sustained economic growth, with both countries achieving average annual rates of growth of over 4.5 per cent in the post-war decades (Porter, 1990). In both cases the state played a major role in planning and directing development. Sweden provides another case of a relatively corporatist centralized state engineering simultaneous economic growth and substantial educational expansion during the three post-war decades. The first country to institute comprehensive secondary schooling in Europe (in the 1950s), and the first also to create a comprehensive upper secondary system (in the 1970s), Sweden has long been seen as a pace-setter in educational reform. One could also, of course, find examples of expansionary periods in education in states not committed to the state-developmental model, like Britain and the USA after the Sputnik shock and with the Keynesian welfare surges of the 1960s, although these were short lived. In what follows, however, the focus is on the East Asian states since they would seem to provide the clearest example of the developmental state using education in the pursuit of rapid state formation.

Education and State Formation in East Asia

In the last three decades East Asia has experienced a period of economic development which has been described as 'unprecedented' and 'miraculous' (World Bank, 1994). During the quarter century from 1960, the four 'little tigers' of East Asia — Hong Kong, Singapore, South Korea and the Taiwan (ROC) — grew by over 8 per cent a year (Wade, 1990, p. 34). This was faster than any other region in the world at the time and represents a level of sustained regional growth over three decades that has few, if any, historical precedents. It took Britain 58 years to double its real per capita income from 1780. The USA did it in 47 years from 1839 and Japan in 34 years from 1900. South Korea took 11 years from 1966 (Morris, 1995). At current rates of development Taiwan will probably have the same average rates of income as Italy and Britain by the end of the century, if not before (Wade, 1990, p. 38).

The same period has seen enormous expansion in education in the region. Each of the four countries had quite high levels of basic education prior to industrial take-off; primary schooling expanded fast during the early period of growth so that enrolment was more or less universal in each country by 1965. Secondary school expansion followed. In 1965 the enrolment rates in secondary schools were generally below 50 per cent in each country. By 1986 they had reached 92 per cent in Taiwan, 95 per cent in South Korea and 69 per cent in Hong Kong (Morris, 1995). Expansion in tertiary education in the recent period has been equally dramatic. Taiwan and South Korea now have amongst the highest rates of upper secondary completion in the world, and a large proportion of those who complete go on to higher education. South Korea has over 100 universities for a population of some 42 million and well over 30 per cent of its 18–22 year olds in higher education, significantly more than in the UK (Adams and Gottlieb, 1993; Porter, 1990, p. 465).

The coincidence in these countries of rapid economic advance with educational expansion clearly suggests a close relationship between the two; indeed, there have been few accounts of the 'economic miracle' in East Asia which have not stressed the contribution of education and human capital development to economic growth (Amsden, 1992; Porter, 1990; Wade, 1990; World Bank, 1994). It is not always an easy matter to separate cause and effect in this relationship, but few would doubt that the two are connected. My purpose here, however, is not so much to enter this debate but to consider more broadly the relationship between educational development, state formation and the developmental state in these countries and how it compares with the relationships described earlier for certain nineteenth century states.

One parallel is immediately obvious. The intensive process of state formation with which educational expansion has been associated in each of the four tigers has been about much more than economic development. As in the nineteenth century states experiencing this process, state formation in at least three of the East Asian states has involved an effort of nation-building prompted by nothing less than the need for national survival. Not only has each state experienced protracted and unresolved conflicts with other states in the region but the whole area, in the period before economic take-off, found itself at the front-line of Cold War tensions involving substantial financial and military investments by the then super powers.

At the time of independence in 1965 Singapore was experiencing multiple political, social and economic crises. Manuel Castells has described it as 'a devastated economy . . . forcibly cut off from its natural Malaysian hinterland, and abandoned as an entrepôt and military base by a retreating British Empire' (1992, p. 37). In addition to its ambivalent and contested regional status it was a multi-cultural society torn by violent internal ethnic and religious strife between the Chinese majority, and the Muslim Malay and Hindu Tamil minorities. South Korea in the late 1950s was economically depressed and still recovering from one of the bloodiest wars of the post-war era. Four decades of Japanese colonialism shortly followed by a civil war which became a primary global focus of the Cold War, had left South Korea, like Singapore, with an enormous task of reconstruction to repair its social fabric and re-establish its national identity. Taiwan in the 1950s, like South Korea, found itself at the centre of Cold War tensions and thus also the recipient of considerable US aid. Like South Korea, it was the product of a national territorial division which remained unresolved and which, arguably, provided an enormous impetus for national reconstruction.

Each of these countries had a lot to do and a great deal to prove. As Castells has written: 'if there is a fundamental common thread to the policies of (these) . . . countries it is that, at the origin of their development we find policies dictated by the politics of survival' (1992, pp. 522–23). In this they also had much in common with those nineteenth century states, like Prussia, France and Japan, whose accelerated state formation was also a form of reconstruction for national survival made necessary by the dislocations of revolution, military conquest or foreign cultural invasion.

The other obvious feature common to these diverse instances of state formation is the degree to which they were state-driven. There has been much debate about the common factors underlying the rapid simultaneous development of these East Asian states. Sociologists and political scientists have debated the effects of cultural and religious traditions and the common geopolitical context. Economists have stressed the fortuitous conjuncture of global growth and free trade with the existence of industrializing nations with the right characteristics and policies to take advantage of the situation: i.e. low labour costs, high rates of savings, and the ability to respond swiftly to changing export markets (Castells, 1992; Wade, 1990). However, the one common factor which seems to overarch all others — indeed which seems to set the other in motion — is the existence of a certain type of developmental state. As Castells has put it: 'behind the economic performance of the Asian tigers breathes the dragon of the developmental state' (1992, p. 56).

In economic terms the developmental state is a state which consistently intervenes to direct and regulate economic activity towards certain national goals. Whilst not directly owning or controlling the majority of production, the state exercises strategic influence through its policy levers. In the cases of Taiwan, South Korea and Singapore this has variously involved government subsidies for exports and new product developments; controls over banking and capital movements; the use of differential interest rates; measures to encourage domestic saving and foreign investment; imports and licensing controls to protect infant industries; and substantial support for education and research and development. In Wade's model such methods are seen not as contravention of market realities but as ways of governing markets (Wade, 1990). They are successful to the degree that state planners and policy makers understand global market trends and are able to encourage others in the economy to respond to them in ways which promote the best long-term interest of the national economy.

The role of the developmental state, however, goes beyond economic planning and regulation. It also involves the construction of national identity and the legitimation of state power. As Castells argues: 'ultimately for the developmental state, economic development is not a goal but a means. To become competitive in the world economy, for all Asian NICs, (is) first their way of surviving both as a state and as a society' (1992, p. 57). From these beginnings it becomes 'a nationalist project of self-affirmation of cultural/political identity in the world system' (p. 58).

The state has therefore intervened not only to promote economic development but also to improve social conditions. The emphases have, of course, varied between states. Governments in Singapore and Hong Kong have invested heavily in health care and housing but relatively less (as a proportion of their public spending) on social security and welfare. Taiwan has invested proportionally more on social security and welfare than health and housing. All, however, have invested heavily on education. Public spending on education as a proportion of total public spending in 1987 was 62.5 per cent in South Korea, 47.2 per cent in Taiwan, 49 per cent in Singapore and 34.4 per cent in Hong Kong (Deyo, 1992).

Another common feature of the developmental states has been their ability to plan strategically, and their authority, in most cases, to win consent or compliance to the policies chosen to promote the planning goals. Given the problems faced by many western democracies in implementing policies in the face of volatile electorates and strong interest groups this often seems remarkable. A number of factors have been associated with this facility. The developmental states in South Korea, Taiwan and Singapore have certainly faced crises and unrest at different periods. However, they appear to have achieved a certain degree of autonomy relative to the different social classes and interest groups in society and this has given them an added authority. As Ashton and Sung have commented in relation to Singapore: 'in order to achieve these political goals, the government has had to act independently of the immediate interests of capital and labour' (1994, p. 9).

The governments of the 60s and 70s had some advantages in this. Rural landowning classes, which have sometimes provided resistance to modernization in other states, were practically non-existent in Hong Kong and Singapore and partially destroyed by US-inspired land-reform in the 50s in South Korea and Taiwan. Trade Unions were also severely weakened in several of these countries in the more labour-repressive periods of early industrialization (Castells, 1992). Taiwan and South Korea also grant exceptional powers to the President and have been through substantial periods of presidential rule when elections have been largely suspended and the state had achieved a transcendence of the political process reminiscent of Bonapartism in France. The legitimacy of the state during these periods has depended very largely on its ability to deliver rapid economic growth and to make sure the benefits accrued to all sections of society.

Now, with the electoral process restored in all the countries, and democratic politics undergoing rapid revival, these developmental states face new challenges. However, they will continue to benefit from their expert bureaucracies which, working closely with the business and financial leaders, have an impressive record in economic and social planning. The commitment and relative success of these technocratic bureaucracies in long-term strategic planning would seem to be another common feature of the 'developmental state' (Wade, 1990).

Clearly education is of fundamental importance to this project. It not only provides the high level technical skills and knowledge which future industry will need and on which the state bureaucracies rely for effective strategic planning; it also develops the attitudes and motivations in individuals which will ensure continuing collective commitment to and active participation in the goals of national development. This means not only a commitment to work, discipline and individual achievement but also an understanding of the collective social meaning of the development goals. It involves cultivating productive employees and active citizens. Where, as in Singapore, the society is multi-cultural and multi-faith, it also means developing social solidarity and cultural cohesion, through the integration of different traditions.

Two characteristics, above all, distinguish educational developments in these states, and they both relate to the function of education in this process of state formation. The first is the degree to which educational development is planned and the role the central state and bureaucracy plays in this. The second is the emphasis placed on the moral and social dimensions of education. These would seem to be defining characteristics of the educational systems of not only Singapore, Taiwan and South Korea, but also of Japan.

Educational planning, at least in its more explicit and directive forms, is not currently so fashionable in many western countries. There has been growing scepticism amongst governments about the efficacy of central planning in general and particularly that which links educational development with future manpower needs. Many governments have preferred to limit their role to indicative planning and leave the rest to the workings of the market. However, in many East Asian states, government planning has remained absolutely central to development, and this has generally entailed an integrated approach to the planning of economic development and human capital formation. Medium-term (four and five year) plans have been a common feature of government strategy in South Korea, Taiwan and Singapore since the 1960s. Numerous planning authorities in each of these countries have been active in translating economic plans into education and training plans and in devising policies to meet the targets set in these plans. Actual developments do not, of course, always follow exactly the intentions of the planners. However, the existence of clear goals and targets has had clear effects in stimulating and focusing activity in a concerted national effort of educational development (Ashton and Sung, 1994).

The second defining feature — the emphasis on moral and social education — is particularly evident to observers from Britain, whose national curriculum, uniquely, omits social or civic education from its compulsory core. National curricula in most of the East Asian states reserve a central place for learning which encourages moral understanding and which promotes social cohesion through appreciation of national traditions and goals and the meaning of citizenship. This can take various forms but it is always in evidence. The reintroduction of moral education was one of the first reforms undertaken in Japan in the 1950s as the country began to reassess the educational changes instituted under American influence during the post-war occupation, and it has remained important since (Schoppa, 1991). In Taiwan, the national curriculum prescribes courses on Life and Ethics designed, in the official language, to develop 'traditional values', inspire 'patriotism' and 'cultivate good citizens' (Young, 1994). In South Korea, guidelines on middle school education explicitly refer to the importance of developing 'skills and attitudes essential for citizenship in a democratic society' and of instilling in students 'an awareness of the mission of the nation' (Adams and Gottlieb, 1993, p. 50).

These social goals often seem to be more fundamental to education in many Asian societies than are the more strictly economic goals of human capital development, despite the importance accorded to economic growth. It is notable for instance that the majority of education at the high school level in Japan and South Korea is general rather than vocational and that even the vocational education remains fairly general in character. This does not, however, seem to have undermined economic development and may, indeed, have been beneficial to it since employers seem to value recruits with broad, general skills and good work discipline, rather than those with specific job skills (Dore and Sako, 1989; Stephens, 1991). Indeed, as McGinn et al. have noted, 'what distinguishes the curriculum of Korean schools from that of countries whose attempts at development have failed is not the emphasis on science and technology . . . (but rather) the heavy stress on moral education and discipline' (Amsden, 1992, p. 219).

In each of these countries it would seem that the primary motivation behind educational development lies in the drive towards achieving national identity and cohesion. In South Korea in the 1960s the slogan was 'nation-building through education' and that sentiment still remains central to the educational mission of elementary schools which, according to Adams and Gottlieb, is to provide 'basic skills and general education in support of Korean culture and national integration' (1993, p. 50). National integration and social cohesion is likewise a primary objective of education in Taiwan, according to Young (1994). In both cases this motive has been intensified by the territorial divisions which continue to put national identity in question. As the authors of *Korean Education 2000* have put it: 'the repeated pounding of hammers steeled the will of the people to develop education as the driving force of national development' (KEDI, 1985, p. 33).

It is the importance of education to this wider project of state formation which has been the driving force behind educational development in all the countries mentioned. It is also the reason why the 'developmental states' have intervened and forced this educational development more deliberately and purposefully than in other states. Other reasons can be found for the rapid educational advances of East Asian states. Cultural traditions have no doubt played their part. Confucian values, like Protestant values in nineteenth-century Europe, have provided certain dispositions towards valuing education in certain countries where they are predominant. However, they provide no explanation for the educational advances of Asian states like Malaysia, where they are not part of the majority culture, nor do they explain the sudden surge of educational development in a particular historical conjuncture. Like Protestantism in Europe, they can be considered only a predisposing factor, but not a necessary or sufficient condition. The main spur for educational development, rather, has been the drive towards accelerated state development and the historical causes that have engendered that drive.

2 The Logic of Protection: Citizenship, Justice and Political Community

David Hogan

Introduction

'What effectively distinguishes the citizen proper from all others is his participation in giving judgements and in holding office,' Aristotle writes in *The Politics*. '[A]s soon as a man becomes entitled to participate in office, deliberative or judicial, we deem him to be a citizen of the state; and a number of such persons large enough to secure a self-sufficient life we may, by and large, call a state' (Aristotle, 1981, pp. 169, 171). He then goes on to suggest that 'The good citizen should know and have the capacity *both to rule and be ruled*, and this very thing is the virtue of a citizen' (Aristotle, 1981, pp. 362–3, emphasis added). Citizenship may vary according to the constitution, but for Aristotle, its core notion is membership of, and participation in, a self-governing political community. It is this above all that defines the 'liberty' characteristic of 'democratic constitutions' (Aristotle, 1981, pp. 362–3).

Although Aristotle himself was hardly a fan of democratic constitutions — he preferred a mixed constitution that blended elements of monarchy, oligarchy and democracy — he insisted that humans are by nature *zoon politikon*. Human beings are sociable beings whose development and flourishing depend on their membership of, and full participation in, the life of the polis: 'by nature man is a political animal . . . men have a desire for life together, even when they have no need to seek each other's help. Nevertheless, common interest too is a factor bringing them together, in so far as it contributes to the good life of each. The *good* life is indeed their chief end, both communally and individually; but they form and continue to maintain a political association for the sake of life itself' (Aristotle, 1981, p. 187). Where social contractarians from Hobbes to Rawls would later think of the state instrumentally, as a means to secure peace or promote commerce and justice, for Aristotle

> the state is not an association of people dwelling in the same place, established to prevent its members from committing injustice against each other, and to promote transactions. Certainly all these features must be present if there is to be a state; but even the presence of every one of them does not make a state ipso facto. The state is an association intended to enable its members, in their households and kinships, to live well; its purpose is a perfect and self sufficient life.' (Aristotle, 1981, pp. 197–98)

Aristotle's image of Athenian democracy has long captured the nostalgic, romantic, utopian and civic republican corners of the Western civic imagination — Cicero, Machiavelli, Harrington, Rousseau, Hegel, J.S. Mill, G.H.D. Cole, Hannah Arendt, contemporary participationists, deliberationists, communitarians and like-minded fellow travellers. It has also repeatedly inspired neoclassical civic revivals over the course of Western history, from republican Rome through Renaissance Florence and Venice and on to that last great paroxysm of classical civic virtue, the Jacobin phase of the French Revolution. The underlying civic logic of the classical model is plain: the purpose of politics is the full realization of human capacities; the liberty of the polis is necessary to human flourishing; civic virtue is necessary (although not entirely sufficient) to secure the liberty of the polis; and extensive participation in the civic life of the polis in the form of 'ruling and being ruled in turn' is necessary to the cultivation of civic virtue. But there is little doubt that the dominant discourse of Western citizenship from the early modern era has not been merely indifferent to the classical model, but hostile to it. From its first tentative jurisprudential intimations in Roman jurisprudence to its first formal statement in the sixteenth century by the French lawyer and political theorist, Jean Bodin, the 'modern' conception of citizenship explicitly eschews rulership or participation in governance as the *sine qua non* of citizenship (Pocock, 1993, 1975, 1985; Reisenberg, 1992; Skinner, 1978a). Instead, modern conceptions of citizenship revolve principally around what might be called 'the logic of protection' as part of a broader 'civic exchange' between citizens constituted as legal or judicial subjects and the sovereign state. The terms of the civic exchange and the forms and depth of protection have been highly variable and contingent, and principally dependent on the forms and levels of social and political conflict characteristic of particular processes of state formation rather than a hypothetical social contract between citizens, as in the contractarian theories of Hobbes, Locke, Rousseau, Kant or Rawls. But formally, at least, the civic exchange involves some combination of service, obedience, allegiance or obligation, on the one hand, for protection, rights, benefits and security, on the other hand. Early modern versions of the civic exchange, for example, focused on an exchange of benefit for service, or protection for allegiance; contemporary liberal democratic formulations centre more on an exchange of rights for obligations. But whether early modern or liberal democratic, protective models of citizenship reject Aristotle's teleological conception of human nature and his view that human beings fulfil their human potential in and through their participation in the public life of the community. Instead, 'protective' conceptions of citizenship tend to take human nature 'as it is' and to locate the good life in the mundane and prosaic affairs of civil society rather than in the public life of the polis. In addition, unlike classical models of citizenship, protective models, of citizenship and the civic exchange are essentially jurisprudential in character. That is, protective models of citizenship focus on the formal political relationship between citizens as legal subjects and a sovereign state. Consequently, although protective models of citizenship have assumed the existence of broader structures of social relations, power and modes of what Michel Foucault terms 'governmentality' in civic society, until the

last quarter of the nineteenth century, the discourse of protective citizenship paid little attention to them (Foucault, 1991, 1988).

This chapter briefly traces the historical development of protective models of citizenship from the late sixteenth century through to the present. It begins with a brief discussion of two absolutist models of protective citizenship formulated by Jean Bodin and Thomas Hobbes, proceeds to a discussion of the liberal model associated with John Locke, and then outlines two liberal democratic models formulated by Jeremy Bentham and James Mill in England, and James Madison in the United States. The chapter then examines four critics of the liberal democratic model: Jean Jacques Rousseau in the eighteenth century, J.S. Mill in the nineteenth century, and T.H. Marshall and John Rawls in the twentieth. The latter three essentially embrace liberal democratic citizenship but want to reform it; Rousseau would have preferred to replace it with a civic republican model.

Over the course of the chapter I develop five arguments. The first is that liberal democratic citizenship, derived from 'protective' models of citizenship, is preoccupied with what Benjamin Constant (1988) termed 'the liberty of the moderns' rather than 'the liberty of the ancients'. That is, liberal democratic citizenship is preoccupied with protecting the fundamental interests of citizens through a variety of constitutional and institutional devices, normative principles and the deployment of an array of decentralized 'disciplinary' mechanisms rather than through the practice of 'rulership'. Second, since the mid-sixteenth century, the logic of protection has been as much the parent of a discourse of justice as the source of liberal democratic conceptions of citizenship. The discourse of justice has been far from homogeneous or unitary. Instead, it is discourse of multiple and even conflicting grammars of justice: toleration (Castellion, Spinoza, Bayle, Locke), natural law (the Levellers, Locke), natural rights (Locke), utility (Hume, Bentham, James Mill, J.S. Mill), respect for persons (Kant), equal liberty (Rawls), and a vast array of local and popular dialects of justice. But from at least the mid-sixteenth century we cannot accurately or usefully isolate the discourse of citizenship, and I suspect its institutional development, from the discourse of justice. Third, while eighteenth and nineteenth century liberal democratic conceptions of citizenship focused on protecting the citizen from the rapacity of their fellow citizens or the ambitions of powerful states, twentieth century formulations have focused as much, if not more, on protecting citizens from the competitive logic of the marketplace — what Marx termed the 'dull compulsion of economic relations' — in the name of equality, social justice, and social democracy (Marx, 1967, p. 737). Fourth, liberal democratic theory has been far more preoccupied with extracting a discourse of justice from the logic of protection rather than generating a discourse of political community from the logic of participation. Finally, I suggest that a liberal democratic education is one committed to the development of a range of capacities that permit students to frame, pursue, revise and protect their higher order interests or good as interdependent members of a liberal democratic community rather than to 'active citizenship', 'civic virtue' or 'national identity'.

David Hogan

'Protective' Citizenship

In 1566, in *Method for the Easy Comprehension of History* and again in 1576, in *Six Books of the Commonwealth*, Jean Bodin, a prominent Parisian and Catholic lawyer appalled by the savagery of the Wars of the Religion, penned the first formal statement of modern, or as it is sometimes called, 'protective', citizenship (see Franklin, 1963, 1973, 1992; Skinner, 1978b, pp. 284–301; Plamenatz, 1961, Ch. 3; Allen, 1977, Pt. 3, Ch. 8; and Sabine, 1937, Ch. 20). Traces of this conception can be found in the later Roman Republic and the Empire, but it does not get a full hearing until Bodin. Bodin's argument has two interwoven strands: the first is a rigorously instrumental and secular defence of absolute sovereignty in the interests of peace and security, while the second is a conception of the citizen as a subject bound to obedience to the sovereign in exchange for the sovereign's protection. Indeed, part of Bodin's project is to reconstruct the Aristotelian notion of the citizenship-as-agent into a new notion — the citizen-as-subject — and to define citizenship as an exchange of protection for allegiance or obedience to a sovereign power rather than as active participation in deliberation, judgment and office holding. Consequently, Bodin defines citizenship in a way that makes absolutely no reference to eligibility for public office, ruling or participation in the affairs of the political community, although he far from ignores Aristotle's views. In fact, he explicitly rejects Aristotle's account of citizenship as active participation. 'It is a very grave error to suppose that no one is a citizen unless he is eligible for public office, and has a voice in the popular estates, either in a judicial or deliberative capacity', he wrote in *Six Books of the Commonwealth* (Bodin, 1962, pp. 19–20). Where Aristotle had defined citizenship in terms of full and active participation in self government, Bodin defines a citizen as a passive subject of a sovereign power granted rights and privileges by the sovereign power. A citizen, Bodin writes, 'may be defined as a *free subject* dependent on the authority of another'. The citizen is not an active civic agent sharing in the exercise of sovereign authority; he is instead a passive subject of the sovereign power. It 'is not the rights and privileges which he enjoys which makes a man a citizen, but the mutual obligation between subject and sovereign, by which, in return for the faith and obedience rendered to him, the sovereign must do justice and give counsel, assistance, encouragement, and protection to the subject' (Bodin, 1962, pp. 20–21). Furthermore, Bodin contends, the sovereign can only protect his subjects if his sovereignty is 'perpetual and absolute'.

Finally, Bodin insisted that a good life did not depend on participation in the work of the state. Instead, a good life, required the protection of an absolute sovereign power and the quiet 'contentments' of a secure family life protected from civil tumult and disorder (Bodin, 1962, p. 3). Bodin's identification of the good within the quiet enjoyments of family life was not in the least idiosyncratic; rather, it was very much an expression of a post-Reformation sensibility that we might describe as the sanctification of ordinary or private life. In the century or so after the Reformation, Europeans created for themselves a new image of the good life centred on family life and commerce rather than the life of the warrior citizen, as in civic republicanism,

or in celibate monasticism in preparation for the after-life, as in Catholicism. For this we are indebted principally to the development of civil society in the towns and cities of Renaissance and early modern Europe, the impoverishment and mono-polization of public life by aristocratic elites, the enrichment of private life during the early modern period, and, under the auspices of the Protestant reformation, the sanctification of ordinary life. The Puritan Divines of the Reformation, for example, mapped out a conception of a good life based on affirming the sublime moral dignity of ordinary everyday life — a life of domestic intimacy, of rising in the morning, of quiet and steady industry, of toiling in the vineyard, of the nurturing of children, of the systematic and periodic interrogation of their conduct and con-science, and of deliberate and wilful moral commitment in the discharge of one's calling. John Milton is the great poet of this view of the human condition, Johannes Vermeer its great artist, John Locke its great philosopher, J.S. Bach its great composer, and Max Weber its great sociologist (Taylor, 1989a; Habermas, 1991; Stone, 1977 and Pateman, 1988a).

Meanwhile, some sixty years after Bodin's formulation, Thomas Hobbes developed a similar, but far more innovative and influential, version of sovereignty and the civic exchange in the midst of the English Civil War. Like Bodin, Hobbes too was dismayed by religious conflict and civil war, and as equally committed to the principle of absolute sovereignty as a means of combating it and to protecting the fundamental interests of individuals defined in terms of self preservation. Among 'the Desires, and other Passions of men', Hobbes wrote in *De Cive* (1642), the pre-eminent and controlling desire was a universal 'Feare of Death' (Hobbes, 1962, p. 102; and 1978, Ch. 1, sect. 7). It is this fear that 'incline men to peace' and provides the motive to create a sovereign power to ensure it and to protect their fundamental interest in a peaceful life and all that it bestows (Hobbes, 1962, p. 102). From this Hobbes went on to argue that in a state of nature each man possesses an equal natural right to protect his life in any way possible; that the creation of political society is the product of a primal social contract between individuals designed to ensure self protection; that the social contract consists of the transfer of one's natural rights to an absolute sovereign power; that the sovereign power itself is not a party to the contract through which its power is established and constituted; that the absolute sovereignty of the state was the necessary and sufficient condition for the protection of the human estate; and that the citizen was a subject of the sovereign power. Consequently that by virtue of the transfer of their natural rights to the sovereign power in order to ensure their self preservation, men freely choose to constitute themselves as subject of the sovereign power (Hobbes, 1978, pp. 169, 170, 171). However, where natural law theorists (for example, Sir Edward Coke) had argued that the reciprocal obligations between sovereign and subject were grounded in an indissoluble natural bond of allegiance between a king and his subjects, Hobbes emphasized that the relationship between protection and obedience was contingent and contractual. Allegiance derived from a civic contract between an individual and a sovereign power, not from nature: 'The obligation of subjects to the sovereign, is understood to last as long, and no longer, than the power lasteth, by which he is able to protect them' (Hobbes, 1962, p. 167).

Like Bodin then, Hobbes constructed an account of citizenship that explicitly rejected classical conceptions of citizenship as active participation in rulership. For Bodin and Hobbes citizenship was a form of 'civic exchange' based on an exchange of obedience for protection that constituted the citizen as a subject of the sovereign power. But before the ink was dry on the pages of *De Cive*, the absolutist model of sovereignty and the civic exchange were directly challenged by the champions of Parliamentary and popular sovereignty — Henry Parker, George Lawson, and the Levellers in the 1640s, and later, in the 1670s and 1680s, by John Locke. The theorists of popular sovereignty repudiated the extreme asymmetry of the absolutist model of the civic exchange and insisted that sovereignty resided in Parliament, and through Parliament, the people themselves, rather than the monarch. Indeed, the Levellers went so far as to argue that the authority of the people was prior to, and independent of, Parliament. Thus Richard Overton: 'Every man by nature being a king priest, prophet, in his own natural circuit and compass, whereof no second may partake but by deputation, commission, and free consent from him whose right it is' (Woodhouse, 1938, p. 69). A little later, as the lingering conflict between Parliament and the Stuart monarchy was about to come to its second denouncement, John Locke drew upon notions of popular sovereignty and the natural rights tradition of Althusius (1557–1638), Pufendorf (1632–1694) and Grotius (1583–1645) to redefine the terms of the civic exchange and to develop an argument for limited constitutional government (Tuck, 1979, 1993; Phillipson and Skinner, 1993; Franklin, 1978; McNally, 1989; and Ashcraft, 1986). Like Hobbes, Locke thought that the fundamental purpose of the state was to protect the fundamental interests of the citizen. Unlike Hobbes, however, he defined these interests in terms of 'natural rights' or what he called the 'mutual *Preservation* of their Lives, Liberties and Estates, which I call by the general Name, *Property*. The great and *chief* end therefore, of Mens uniting into Commonwealths, and putting themselves under Government, *is the Preservation of their Property*' (Locke, 1963, pp. 395–95). The moral legitimacy of political society depended entirely on consent to the social contract and the obligations that citizens voluntary assume when they agree to it. 'Men being, as has been said, by Nature, all free, equal and independent, no one can be put out this Estate, and subjected to the Political Power of another, without his own *Consent*,' Locke wrote (1963, 374–75). (And it was 'men' who were the parties to the social contract, since only men were free and equal in nature, and therefore capable of contracting with each other to form political society. Women were subordinate to men not because of the political power exercised by men but by and in nature. Eve's subordination to Adam, Locke insisted, was an expression of 'Conjugal Power, not Political' [1963, p. 210; see also Pateman, 1988a, 1989].) In exchange for the protection extended to his life, liberty and property, the citizen is expected to honour the obligations he voluntary assumes to his fellow citizens in consenting to the social contract. These include the obligation to obey the law and the security of life, liberty and property. In fulfilling his obligations the citizen 'protects the protection' of his fellow citizens; likewise, to the extent that they honour their obligations, they 'protect his protection' (Walzer, 1970, p. 206). But where Hobbes had argued that the protection of individual interests depended on the creation of an absolute sovereign power, Locke insisted that the defence of individual interests and a 'peaceful and commodious' life depended, in the first instance, on a limited, constitutional state honouring the natural rights of individuals. Leviathan would not so much protect as devour its subjects. To think otherwise was 'to think that Men are so foolish that they take care to avoid what Mischiefs may be done them by *Pole Cats*, or *Foxes*, but are content, nay think it Safety, to be devoured by *Lions*' (Locke, 1963, p. 372).

Apart from a limited constitutional government, Locke also identified two additional but inter-connected mechanisms to support the civic exchange and 'protect protection': the 'Law of Opinion and Reputation', and 'self government'. Locke's account of the 'Law of Opinion and Reputation' arises in his discussion on moral order in Chapter 18 of *An Essay Concerning Human Understanding*. Locke begins his account of moral order by claiming that notions of good and evil are a matter of the 'conformity or disagreement' of individual actions to one of three kinds of law: Divine, Civil, and the 'Law of Opinion and Reputation'. He then goes on to argue that human conduct is deeply responsive to sentiments of approbation and disapproval that circulate as a normal part of social life and that these form the social foundation of notions of virtue and vice. 'But no Man scapes the Punishment of their Censure and Dislike, who offends against the Fashion and Opinion of the Company he keeps, and would recommend himself to', Locke writes. Consequently, although men transferred the right to execute the laws of nature to the government in consenting to the social contract, they 'retain still the power of Thinking well or ill; approval or disapproving of the actions of those whom they live amongst, and converse with' (Locke, 1964a, pp. 222, 224, 225). Indeed, in Locke's view, the ability of 'opinion and reputation' to secure morality was generally greater than either Divine or Civil Law and formed the basis of that 'secret and tacite consent' necessary to a stable social order (Locke, 1964a, p. 224).

The third mechanism necessary to help protect protection Locke called 'self government'. By this he meant the development and use of reason to govern the desires and to will only what reason authorizes. Individuals are born, Locke notes, 'ignorant and without the use of Reason'. The responsibility of parents is 'to inform the Mind, and govern the Actions of their yet ignorant Nonage, till Reason shall take its place . . .' (Locke, 1963, p. 348). Elsewhere Locke writes that 'the principle of all virtue and excellency lies in a power of denying ourselves the satisfaction of our own desires, where reason does not authorise them' (1964b, pp. 28, 32). And this could be most effectively accomplished, Locke suggested, not by a stern and hard discipline but by a strategic combination of love and authority seeking to develop autonomous and 'rational creatures' able to subordinate their desires to their reason. 'If therefore a strict hand be kept over children from the beginning, they will in that age be tractable, and quietly submit to it, as never having known any other: and if, as they grow up to the use of reason, the rigour of government be, as they deserve it, gently relaxed, the father's brow more smoothed to them, and the distance by degrees abated: his former restraints will increase their love, when they find it was only a kindness for them, and a care to make them capable to deserve the favour of their parents, and the esteem of every body else' (Locke,

David Hogan

1964b, pp. 29–30). Rational autonomy required, Locke argued, a careful cultivation of reason and virtue.

> Every man must time or other be trusted to himself, and his own conduct; and he that is good, a virtuous, and able man, must be made so within. And therefore, what he is to receive from education, what is to sway and influence his life, must be something put into him betimes; habits woven into the very principles of his nature; and not a counterfeit carriage, and dissembled outside, put on by fear, only to avoid the present anger of a father, who may perhaps disinherit him. (Locke, 1964b, p. 31; see also 1964b, p. 29)

At the same time, however, Locke was very careful to insist that 'self-government' promoted rather than undermined the 'law of Opinion and Reputation'. For Locke, 'the great secret of education

> depended on cultivating in children an understanding that 'those that are commended and in esteem for doing well, will necessarily be loved and cherished by every body, and have all other good things as a consequence of it; and, on the other side, when any one by miscarriage falls into dis-esteem, and cares not to preserve his credit, he will unavoidably fall under neglect and contempt; and, in that state, the want of whatever might satisfy or delight him, will follow. (Locke, 1964b, p. 37)

Indeed, he concluded, 'esteem and disgrace are, of all the others, the most powerful incentives to the mind, when once it is brought to relish them. If you can once get into children a love of credit, and an apprehension of shame and disgrace, you have put into them the true principle, which will constantly work, and incline them to the right' (Locke, 1964b, p. 36).

Locke's educational regime then assumes a patriarchal family and a fraternal social contract and combines two pedagogical prescriptions — a system of 'affectionate authority' to promote a child's reason or 'internal governor' in the interests of self government, and a system of rewards and punishments that cultivated the desire for esteem and approbation to underpin 'the law of opinion and reputation'. In 1960 Sheldon Wolin observed that Locke, like a long line of liberal theorists from Adam Smith to Talcott Parsons after him, emphasized the importance of developing a 'socialized conscience' through the internalization of social norms in order to secure social order in a centrifugal commercial society with limited constitutional government (Wolin, 1960, pp. 343–51). More generally, Locke's pedagogy represents an effort to specify a particular 'art of government' to complement and support liberal constitutionalism and the civic exchange. Finally still, Locke's pedagogy was an expression of a broader movement dating back to the sixteenth century to promote 'governmentality' or the 'conduct of conduct' in the new nation states (Foucault, 1991). For Locke then, the government of the self was necessary to underwrite the new system of liberal government: the viability of liberal autonomy depended on the exercise of affectionate authority, the cultivation of self-government and responsiveness to the 'law of opinion and reputation'. In a word,

Locke suggested that the conduct of conduct was necessary, although not sufficient, to protect protection. Before long, Locke's view of pedagogical authority would provide not merely a prop but a model for political authority on a revolutionary scale in the New World (see Fliegelman, 1982, Ch. 1; and Hogan, 1990).

While Locke was very much a liberal, he was not particularly democratic in his political sympathies or committed to the enlargement of the political community beyond men with substantial property holdings. But in repudiating the absolutism of Hobbes and formalizing the idea of a liberal polity based on a limited constitutional government and the consent of citizens, he laid down key principles of liberal democratic theory. But not all of Locke's formulations made it through the eighteenth century unscathed. Locke's keenest critic and one of the key figures in the transition from Locke's liberalism to utilitarian theories of justice and liberal democracy was David Hume. Writing some half century after Locke, Hume expressed considerable sympathy, for example, for Locke's efforts to ground political obligation in considerations of interest (or, in Locke's terms, life, liberty and property) and consent rather than the compulsions of duty, but could find no reason at all why he should accept Locke's theory of the natural rights, social contract, consent, or obligation. Like Locke, Hume had little doubt that human behaviour is driven by the principle of interest, although he was far more forthright about it than Locke and refused to dress it up in the transcendental language of natural law and natural rights. 'Nothing is more certain, than that man are, in a great measure, govern'd by interest, and that even when they extend their concern beyond themselves, 'tis not to any great distance; nor is usual for them, in common life, to look farther than their nearest friends and acquaintance' (Hume, 1978, p. 534). And interests, unlike 'natural rights', could not be transferred, exchanged or surrendered (see Burchell, 1991). Moreover, the formation of political society — what he called the 'origin of government' — along with our conceptions of justice, right and obligation, are based entirely on our desire to protect our interests. Furthermore, Hume argued, the stability of government — 'the easiness with which the many are governed by the few' — depended solely on 'opinion' — (Hume, 1948a, p. 307). He thus dismissed Locke's 'state of nature' explanation of the origins of property and political society 'as mere fictions, not unlike that of the golden age which poets have invented' (Hume, 1978, p. 493). Instead, our notions of justice and 'the origin of government' should be traced to the inconveniences and insecurities of life without justice and government. Our preference for justice is an 'artificial' rather than 'natural' virtue, born of our natural desire to protect our interests (Hume, 1978, pp. 477, 536–37). 'Here then is a proposition,' he wrote, 'which I think, may be regarded as certain, that 'tis only from the selfishness and confin'd generosity of men, along the scanty provision of nature has made for his wants, that justice derives its origins' (Hume, 1978, pp. 495; see also 488, 494, 519–20). Similarly, government can be traced to the principal 'advantages' of justice by 'civil magistrates' with a strong and immediate interest in the prevention of injustice and the preservation of justice. 'By means of these two advantages, in the execution and decision of justice,' Hume wrote, 'men acquire a security against each other's weakness and passion, as well as against their own, and under the shelter of their governors, begin to taste at ease the sweets of society and mutual assistance' (Hume, 1978, pp. 536–38; see also Hume, 1948b, pp. 366–67).

Given their respective views about human nature, interest and justice, the intellectual distance between David Hume and Jeremy Bentham was not great. But Bentham went considerably beyond Hume in formulating a general utilitarian principle of justice — namely, that an act, activity or policy promotes justice if it promotes the greatest good of the greatest number — and in arguing that justice required equal protection of interests. From the principle that all human beings are governed by a desire to satisfy their desires (or maximize their 'utilities' — the term is Bentham's own invention) and the assumption derived from the principle of justice that the end of politics was the maximization of aggregate individual utility, Bentham deduced that a representative democracy was the form of government most likely to maximize aggregate utility by permitting individuals to define, pursue and protect their own interests relatively unhindered by the rapacious activities of an oppressive government. Democracy protected the governed from the governors by holding the governors accountable to the governed: 'A democracy then, has for its characteristic object and effect, the securing of its members against oppression and depredation at the hand of those functionaries which it employs for its defence . . .' (Bentham, 1843, p. 47). Similarly, Bentham's collaborator, James Mill, argued in his *Essay on Government* (1825) that the one form of government capable of protecting the interests of persons individually and in the aggregate is a representative democracy: 'We have . . . seen that the interest of the community . . . is, that each individual should receive protection, and that the powers which are constituted for that purpose should be employed exclusively for that purpose' (J. Mill, 1967, p. 15). Indeed, the system of representation was 'the grand discovery of modern times' (J. Mill, 1967, p. 16).

Meanwhile, across the Atlantic, the founders of the American republic devised a constitutional order that married principles of popular sovereignty and representation to federalism. The Federalists were scornful of 'theoretic politicians' (to wit, Rousseau) who lauded the virtues of 'pure democracies' and the civic virtue of democratic citizens. 'Pure democracies', Madison admonished, were notoriously indifferent to individual liberties and the rights of property, even as they celebrated the principle of popular sovereignty. Furthermore, if men were virtuous, government itself would be unnecessary; since men were not, a democracy would be unwise to rely on civic virtue to protect the rights and liberties of its citizens. Instead, a democracy must rely on constitutional and institutional devices. Unlike Bentham, however, the Federalists were deeply suspicious of majoritarian democracies, and looked to the separation of powers and federalism to protect the interests of all citizens from the grasping ambition of democratic majorities (Stourzh, 1970, p. 77). Madison argued that the key to a stable republic of self-interested and property-minded individuals was a carefully calibrated constitution that regulated the effects of interest and faction in the polity by multiplying the number of interests and factions in an expanding commercial republic and divided political power between the separate branches of government in a representative democracy. The good citizen of a federalist republic was far from a paragon of civic republican virtue and rarely involved in 'rulership', but he would be able to pursue his own interest in his own way in a self-governing democratic community.

Liberal Democracy and Its Discontents

The liberal democratic model of 'protective' citizenship did not sit well with everyone. Some were friendly critics, others hostile. Some come from within the liberal tradition, others from within civic republicanism; others had primary intellectual allegiances elsewhere. The critics range from Rousseau, Thomas Paine, Mary Wollstonecraft, Edmund Burke and Immanuel Kant in the eighteenth century, through Frederick Hegel, Benjamin Constant, Alexis de Tocqueville, Karl Marx, J.S. Mill and T.H. Green in the nineteenth century, to John Dewey, Joseph Schumpeter, Robert Dahl, John Rawls, Carole Pateman, Bernard Barber and sundry pluralists, civic republicans, feminists, participationists, deliberationists and communitarians over the past couple of decades. Since I cannot hope to discuss all of these here, I will focus instead on four critics of liberal democratic protective citizenship — Rousseau in the eighteenth century, J.S. Mill in the nineteenth, and Marshall and Rawls in the twentieth. I do so not necessarily because they are the most important or representative theorists, or even the theorists with the best solutions to the challenges confronting contemporary liberal democratic citizenship, but because they raise questions about liberal democratic citizenship and the civic exchange that bear directly on the nature and role of civic education in liberal democratic societies.

J.J. Rousseau

Rousseau, J.G.A. Pocock once suggested, is the Machiavelli of the eighteenth century (Pocock, 1975, p. 504, quoted in Held, 1987, p. 73). More accurately, we might see him as the last of the great classical civic republicans preoccupied with the importance of civic virtue and citizen participation in creating a political community and the first of the modern democrats committed to the principle of popular sovereignty. Specifically, Rousseau was dismayed by what he saw as a deep imbalance in liberal conceptions of citizenship between rights and obligations and by its abject failure to derive a logic of participation from the logic of protection.

Like Hobbes, Rousseau begins his political speculations with a theory of the human condition in a state of nature. Like Hobbes, Rousseau assumed, as he wrote in *The Social Contract* (1762), that the first law of nature is the desire of each man [sic] 'to attend to his own preservation' and that his 'first cares are those which he owes himself' (Rousseau, 1967, p. 8). In a state of nature each man is free and equal, but his self preservation is dependent on the forbearance and support of others. In political terms, the fundamental problem of social organization is 'how to find a form of association which will defend and protect with the whole force of the community the person and property of each associate, and by means of which each, coalescing with all, may nevertheless obey only himself, and remain as free as before' (Rousseau, 1967, pp. 17–18). In effect, how might citizens be both free and equal in a political community and thereby 'defend and protect their person and property'?

For Rousseau, like Locke and Hobbes, the solution was a social contract between men based on the consent of all. But where Hobbes had argued that sovereignty should be undivided, absolute, self perpetuating, and alienated to the sovereign power, Rousseau claimed that sovereignty was 'inalienable', 'indivisible', and the property of the people and the people alone (Rousseau, 1967, pp. 27–28). And where Locke had insisted the social contract involved only a very limited transfer of natural right (namely, an 'executive power' to discharge the law of nature in a state of nature) to the sovereign power in order to protect the life, liberty and property of citizens, Rousseau argued that the social contract involved 'the total alienation to the whole community of each associate with all his rights; for, in the first place, since each gives himself up entirely, the conditions are equal for all; and, the conditions being equal for all, no one has any interest in making them burdensome to others' (Rousseau, 1967, p. 18). The total alienation of all rights to the community, including property rights, establishes and secures the moral and political equality of all citizens. Unlike Hobbes, therefore, the alienation of all rights to the community did not involve the alienation of sovereignty. Moreover, in alienating their rights but not their sovereignty, the citizens did not renounce liberty, for the alienation of rights is not to other citizens but to the political community of which the citizen is a member. Each citizen gives himself to all and in so doing gives himself to no one but the law; in this way all citizens are equal and equally free. 'Each of us puts in common his person and his whole power under the supreme direction of the general will; and in return we receive every member as an indivisible part of the whole'. For Rousseau, then, the social contract creates a polity — 'a city' or 'a republic or body politic' — which acts according to its 'general will'. Individual members of the republic are simultaneously 'citizens' by virtue of 'participating in the sovereign power' and 'subjects' of 'the laws of the State' created by the sovereign people (Rousseau, 1967, pp. 18–19, 27). A democratic polity of this kind is the only legitimate form of government because all citizens are involved in establishing it, all citizens consent to it, and all citizens exercise authority in it by virtue of their role in generating the general will.

Like Bodin, Hobbes, Locke, Bentham and James Mill then, Rousseau's conception of political society and citizenship is fundamentally protectionist in its underlying presuppositions and commitments. Where he differs from them — and differs from them profoundly — is that he sought to derive a logic of participation from the logic of protection. In effect, Rousseau wished to reassert the civic republican view of the moral importance of public life, not condone the post-Reformation sanctification of ordinary life in civil society. But it is important to note that while Rousseau celebrates the participation of citizens in identifying 'the general will' and the passage of laws, he is very careful to limit their participation to these formal acts of sovereignty, apart from the formation of the original social contract. Generally speaking, citizens do not participate either in the framing of legislation or the administration of laws as they did in classical Athens. The first is the exclusive function of 'a superior intelligence' or 'Legislator' while the second is the exclusive province of the Prince (i.e., the Magistrates, the king, or 'government') (Rousseau, 1967, Bk. 2, Ch. 7; Bk. 3, Ch. 1–4, 11–14, 18).

Rousseau differs from liberal democratic theorists in a second respect as well. For Rousseau, the people had exclusive authority to identify the general will and determine the law. Indeed, Rousseau insisted that the people, as the 'sovereign power' have 'an absolute power over all its members' (Rousseau, 1967, 32). Unlike Locke, then, Rousseau recognized no distinction between the state and civil society. In fact, Rousseau recognized no limit to the power that the 'body politic' might exercise over individuals and minorities. Rousseau might have celebrated the 'sovereignty of the people', and he might have insisted that the social contract involved no loss of equality or liberty, but generations of liberals since have not been convinced. Isaiah Berlin, for example, wonders what happens to 'the sovereignty of individuals' in Rousseau's theory of democracy (Berlin, 1969, p. 163). Moreover, his defence of citizen participation is very much framed in protectionist rather than developmental terms: the point of citizen participation is not so much to develop individual capacities as to identify the common good or 'the general will'. As a consequence, Rousseau's reputation as a theorist of participatory and developmental democracy is not quite deserved (see Pateman, 1970; Held, 1987).

If Rousseau was no liberal and no classical democrat, neither was he enamoured with modern or representative democracy. In *The Social Contract*, he insists indignantly that contrary to the claims of those who would substitute representation for direct participation in the exercise of sovereign power, sovereignty is inalienable and indivisible and cannot be represented. 'I say, then, that sovereignty, being nothing but the general will, can never be alienated, and that the sovereign power, which is only a collective being, can be represented by itself alone . . .' (Rousseau, 1967, p. 27). Representation, he argues, destroys the possibility of citizenship and the affirmation and development of moral personality in and through civic action. How is it possible for the individual to be a citizen in a political community and to grow in civic virtue, Rousseau demands, if he is not able to participate in public deliberation? Indeed, as 'soon as the service of the State ceases to be the principal business of the citizens, and they prefer to render aid with their purses rather than their persons, the State is already on the brink of ruin' (Rousseau, 1967, p. 98). Citizens can only become masters of their needs, and not slaves to their desires, when they are actively engaged in the exercise of sovereign power — of simultaneously ruling and being ruled — and when they subject themselves to the rule of law that they themselves consent to in a social contract.

Rousseau's celebration of civic virtue went hand in hand with his repudiation of representative democracy and his indifference to issues of individual autonomy. If a democracy required the continuous involvement of citizens in the deliberation and passage of legislation in order to identify 'the general will', and 'the general will' protected the common good, then the common good required 'virtuous' and 'patriotic' citizens. And he was not in the least doubtful about the nature of the preconditions that nurtured and protected the 'virtue' of its citizens. Beyond a highly limited commercial culture and market system, virtue also depended on a small polity, economic independence, social equality, active participation in the affairs of the polity, simplicity of manners, the absence of luxury, a love of duty and patriotism and a robust program of republican education to develop the 'virtue' and 'patriotism' of the citizenry (Rousseau, 1967, p. 70–71). Indeed, for Rousseau, the cultivation of civic virtue is the chief business of the state. 'There can be no patriotism without liberty, no liberty without virtue, no virtue without citizens,' he wrote in *A Discourse on Political Economy* (1755). 'Create citizens, and you have everything you need'. However, 'to form citizens is not the work of a day; and in order to have men it is necessary to educate them when they are children . . . From the first moment of life, men ought to begin learning to deserve to live; and, as at the instant of birth we partake of the rights of citizenship, that instant ought to be the beginning of the exercise of our duty'. The education of the citizen was 'the most important business of the State' and should be under the direct control of the state. The task was simply too important to be left to the 'prejudices of fathers' (Rousseau, 1913, pp. 268–69). Almost two decades later, in *Considerations on the Government of Poland* (1772), Rousseau took up the issue again:

> It is education that must give souls a national formation, and direct their opinions and tastes in such a way that they will be patriotic by inclination, by passion, by necessity. When he first opens his eyes, an infant ought to see the fatherland, and up to the day of his death he ought never to see anything else. Every true republican has drunk in love of country, that is to say love of law and liberty, along with his mother's milk. This love is whole existence; he sees nothing but the fatherland, he lives for it alone; when he is solitary, he is nothing; when he has ceased to have a fatherland, he no longer exists; and if he is not dead, he is worse than dead. (Rousseau, 1953, p. 176)

Rousseau's preachings on the importance of civic identity and civic virtue — indeed, their fusion — was not without immediate effect and long term consequence. In a recent essay, Michael Walzer describes the Jacobin phase of the French Revolution in the following terms:

> In its Jacobin phase, the revolution is best understood as an effort to establish citizenship as the dominant identity of every Frenchman — against the alternative identities of religion, estate, family and region. The replacement of the still honorific title Monsieur with the fully universal citizen . . . symbolises that effort. Citizenship was to replace religious faith and familial loyalty as the central motive of virtuous conduct. Indeed, citizenship, virtue, and public spirit were closely connected ideas, suggesting a rigorous commitment to political (and military) activity on behalf of the community — *patria*, not yet nation. Activity (meetings, speeches, public service) was crucial; this was an emphatically positive conception of the citizen's role. A distinction between active and inactive citizens, drawn on economic rather than political lines, was introduced in 1791 but suppressed a year later . . . In Jacobin ideology, citizenship was a universal office; everyone was to serve the community. Thus the *levee en masse* (1793), which goes well beyond all subsequent conscription laws; it literally conscripts everybody, setting tasks for men and women of all ages. (Walzer, 1989, pp. 211–12; see also Taylor, 1994, p. 51)

What Walzer is hinting at here is that the spectre that haunts contemporary forms of classical revivalism and civic republicanism is the spectre of Jacobin virtue and principled Terror. For Walzer and for liberal democrats generally, Jacobinism is the offspring of a quest for civic virtue and civic identity untempered by a concern for pluralism, individual liberty and mutual respect. Not the least of the objectives of a line of liberal democratic theorists from Kant to Rawls has been to contain the presumptions of civic republican citizenship within the prerogatives of justice.

J.S. Mill

Unlike Rousseau, but very much like his father, James Mill, John Stuart Mill agreed that a representative democracy was the most practicable and desirable form of government. Certainly, a direct democracy was no longer possible or desirable. 'Since all cannot, in a community exceeding a singly small town, participate personally in any but some very minor portions of the public business, it follows that the ideal type of government must be representative,' he wrote in *Considerations on Representative Government* (1861) (J.S. Mill, 1958, p. 55). He also agreed that the primary value of a system of representative democracy was the protection it provided citizens against the rapacious activities of governments. The superiority of representative government rested on a principle 'of as universal truth and applicability as any general propositions which can be laid down respecting human affairs'. The principle is

> that the rights and interests of every or any person are only secure from being disregarded when the person is himself able, and habitually disposed, to stand up for them ... Human beings are only secure from evil at the hands of others in proportion as they have the power of being, and are, *self protecting* ... (each person) is the only safe guardian of his rights and interests ... (J.S. Mill, 1958, pp. 43, 44, 55)

On other matters, J.S. Mill did not quite see eye to eye with his father or Bentham, and so set about reconstructing liberal democratic theory. For example, J.S. Mill developed an argument he derived from de Tocqueville that ordinary citizens should be actively involved in the governance of local public institutions and voluntary associations. Participation was more than just a means to protect the interests of the governed from the arbitrary exercise of power by the government. It was also a mechanism of moral education and a means of promoting the public good. Indeed, towards the end of *On Liberty*, Mill argues that although popular participation and decision making may not always be efficient, it promoted 'mental education' (J.S. Mill, 1989, pp. 109–10). A few years later, Mill returned to this argument at greater length in *Considerations on Representative Government*. For Mill, democratic governments were the 'ideally best polity' because a democratic polity, and a democratic polity alone, 'promotes the good management of the affairs of society by means of the existing faculties, moral, intellectual and active, of all its members

. . .' Participation, he argued, advances individuals 'in intellect, virtue, and in practical activity and efficiency' (1958, pp. 25, 43, 53, 54–55, 216–17).

In addition, while John Stuart shared his father's enthusiasm for Bentham's 'principle of utility', he nonetheless feared that Bentham's doctrine lacked moral depth. Thus, for Mill, the principle of 'utility' remained the 'ultimate appeal on all ethical questions'. But he also insisted that 'it must be utility in the largest sense, grounded on the permanent interests of man as a progressive being'. He then went on to draw a distinction between different kinds of pleasures and utilities and to develop a richer account of human flourishing and individual liberty than offered by his father or Bentham (J.S. Mill, 1989, p. 14). For John Stuart, the principle of 'utility' should not assume a narrow, pinched conception of interests, but a broad notion 'grounded on the permanent interests of man as a progressive being'. For Mill, these centred on 'the region of liberty' defined as 'all that portion of a person's life and conduct which affects only himself, or if affects others, only with their free, voluntary and undeceived consent and participation'. That is, liberty consists *'of framing the plan of our life to suit our own character;* of doing as we like, subject to such consequences as may follow: without impediment from fellow creatures, *so long as what we do does not harm them,* even though they should think our conduct foolish, perverse or wrong'. He goes on to conclude that '[n]o society in which these liberties are not, on the whole, respected, is free, whatever may be its form of government; and none is completely free in which they do not exist absolute and unqualified. The only freedom which deserves the name, is that of *pursuing our own good in our own way,* so long as we do not attempt to deprive others of theirs, or impede their efforts to obtain it' (J.S. Mill, 1989, pp. 14–16, emphasis added).

Mill's defence of the principle of autonomy, along with the very different account offered by Immanuel Kant, helped establish the notion of autonomy at the very heart of modern liberal notions of justice. The principle difficulty with Mill's account, at least from the perspective of contemporary liberal democratic theory, is that Mill's account of autonomy and citizenship is compromised on at least three counts. One is Mill's objections to the democratic principle of one person, one vote, and his support for a plural system of voting that gave multiple voting rights to 'the highly educated and public spirited persons' (J.S. Mill, 1958, Ch. 8). In addition, despite his powerful plea for individual liberty, Mill's progressive version of utilitarianism is no more capable of protecting the autonomy of all citizens equally than Bentham's original version of requiring politics to bend its knee to justice (Rawls, 1991, Ch. 1, 2, 4). Finally, Mill failed to develop an adequate account of the social pre-conditions of equal protection or to anticipate the effects of capitalism on liberal democratic citizenship. For much of his life he defended the principle of *laissez-faire* and assumed that citizens needed only to be protected from state power. In his later years (principally in the third edition of the *Principles of Political Economy* of 1853) he admitted that government intervention was necessary to resolve 'coordination problems' and to promote the establishment of various public goods, including education. It was only a small crack in the *laissez-faire* defence of the free market, but before long it had developed into something much more.

T.H. Marshall

In the 1840s, Karl Marx levelled a withering indictment of the inability of 'bourgeois rights' to protect individuals from the rapacity and greed of the capitalist class and 'the dull compulsion' of the competitive marketplace. While not prepared to dismiss the value of political rights out of hand, Marx emphasized that citizenship was fundamentally a political category and unable to address the social and economic inequalities generated by the social relations of capitalism (Marx, 1975, p. 219). By the time of Marx's death in 1883, however, English social reformers, Liberal Party intellectuals, trade union officials, Fabian socialists, philanthropists, settlement house workers, and a number of leading philosophers (T.H. Green especially) were determined to prove Marx wrong by reconciling the demands of social justice and capitalism. And they determined to do so by creating a new family of rights in education, health and housing and the passage of legislation to protect women, children, the aged, the sick, the poor and even the working class generally from the cold, impersonal logic of the capitalist marketplace.

Half way across the world in Australia a similar if more radical movement got up a head of steam in the 1890s. Dismayed by the hardening of class relations in the 1890s, suddenly aware of the vulnerability of the Australian economy to international economic pressures, and convinced that political community could no more grow out of the barrel of a gun than it could out of the competitive relations of the marketplace, New Protectionist politicians, liberal reformers and the fledgling labour movement pursued a series of initiatives that they hoped would secure social justice and create a viable democratic political community in Australia. 'Instead of the State being regarded any longer as an object of hostility to the labourer,' Alfred Deakin wrote in 1890, 'it should now become identified with an interest in his works, and in all workers, extending to them its sympathy and protection, and watching over their welfare and prosperity' (quoted in Macintyre, 1985, p. 40).

The first major initiative of the Australian reformers centred on the regulation of factory conditions for women workers. This was shortly followed by even more dramatic intrusions into the marketplace — factory acts, industrial arbitration, public works, old age and mothers' pensions, and above all, the judicial determination of minimum wage rates for working men (Macintyre, 1985, Ch. 3, 4, 5; and 1991). Together these initiatives have come to be considered part of the 'Federation settlement' adopted during the period leading up to and immediately after Australian federation in 1901. It is important to emphasize that Australia's adoption of a 'protective' state was not so much a repudiation of the conventional logic of protective citizenship as a novel extension of it. Nor did it involve a radical break with nineteenth century views of the state. Despite its first incarnation as a military dictatorship, over the course of the nineteenth century the state had become less a power to be feared, as it was in Lockean liberalism and Madisonian federalism, than an instrument to be used to advance the interest and happiness of the majority. In the nineteenth century, this had principally involved opening up the land to the people as a 'haven from wage labour' and combating the tyrannies of distance, isolation and loneliness with a vast public utilities program financed with British capital (Macintyre, 1985, p. 140). What was different — and pioneering — about the 'Federation settlement' was a commitment to protecting the interests of citizens, promoting social justice and ensuring social order and political stability by providing (male) citizens with a measure of protection from the capitalist marketplace through the semi-judicial determination of wage rates. 'Permanent prosperity can only be based upon institutions which are cemented by social justice,' Alfred Deakin wrote. 'Under the influence of a sense of injustice, of inequality, of fairness and helplessness, the working population cannot be expected to submit to their lot' (quoted in Macintyre, 1985, p. 141).

At the same time, state governments committed themselves to the provision of free, secular and compulsory schooling in the interests of social efficiency, equal opportunity, good order and nation building. But these were secondary; essentially, Australia remained what Frank Castles has termed a 'wage earners' welfare state' (Castles, 1985). Later, at the end of World War Two, the Commonwealth Government augmented this novel construction of protective citizenship by committing itself to the maintenance of full employment as the basis of social protection in Australia supported by non-contributory social assistance for the aged, the poor, the disabled and ex-servicemen. None of this involved a repudiation of capitalism or market relations. At a very general level, the Federation settlement institutionalized a distinctive Australian combination of market citizenship (based on centralized wage fixation rather than universal or contributory forms of social insurance), the patriarchal family (women were excluded from the benefits of market citizenship for many years), bourgeois individualism (centred on home ownership and social mobility), and a non-socialist, highly instrumentalist state collectivism. 'To the Australian,' W.K. Hancock wrote in 1930, 'the State means collective power at the service of individualistic "rights." Therefore he sees no opposition between his individualism and his reliance upon Government . . . [for] he has come to look upon the State as a vast public utility, whose duty is to provide the greatest happiness for the greatest number' (Hancock, 1930, p. 55). He went on to conclude that 'this then is the prevailing ideology of Australian democracy — the sentiment of justice, the claim of right, the conception of equality, and the appeal to Government as the instrument of self realization' (Hancock, 1930, p. 57).

Of course, Australia was far from alone in extending social rights or developing a welfare state. Other countries followed suit, each in their own fashion, and each of them pushed along by the Depression of the 1930s and World War Two. By the end of the Second World War, in the UK, western Europe and North America liberal democratic citizenship had acquired a wholly new set of meanings. If liberal democratic citizenship in 1850 had generally been defined by the possession of a set of civil and political rights intended to protect male citizens from the power of the state, by 1950 it had also come to mean (at least for the disciples of the welfare state) the use of state power to offer those with limited resources modest levels of protection from the market. In effect, the reformers had not so much repudiated the logic of protection as given it a radically new and expansive meaning that implied a far more porous boundary between civil society and the state. Although bitterly contested then and now by those appalled by the breach of the boundary between the state and civil society, the violation of the 'free market', and the expanded meaning of citizenship, the early twentieth century discourse of social rights and the welfare state proved to be but a prologue to later assaults upon other institutions and social relations in civil society that exercised or protected arbitrary and unaccountable power (corporate, patriarchal, paternal, heterosexual, disciplinary) that violated the principles of justice, whether in the workplace, in the labour market, in the family, in the bedroom, or even in schools.

Among the first to recognize and formally announce the new civic dispensa-tion was T.H. Marshall, a professor of sociology at the University of London. In a series of lectures delivered at Cambridge University in 1949, Marshall concep-tualized citizenship as a particular kind of legal status of 'official identity' attached to 'full membership' of a sovereign of self-governing community. In so doing, he refused to limit the meaning of citizenship to a narrowly political relationship between the individual and the state. As a legal status, citizenship confers a right to have rights. Moreover, those who possess this status are generally equal with respect to the rights and responsibilities associated with it. Analytically, therefore, Marshall's conception of citizenship links two separate notions: the idea of member-ship of a particular political community, and the idea of individual entitlement or justice. 'Citizenship is a status bestowed on those who are full members of a community,' Marshall writes. 'All who possess the status are equal with respect to the rights and duties with which the status is endowed. There is no universal principle that determines what those rights and duties shall be but societies in which citizenship is a developing institution create an image of an ideal citizenship against which achievement can be measured and towards which aspiration can be directed' (Marshall, 1964, p. 92). The desire for citizenship, he argued,

> is an urge towards a fuller measure of equality, an enrichment of the stuff of which the status is made and an increase in the number of those on whom the status is bestowed. . . . Citizenship requires a . . . direct sense of community membership based on loyalty to a civilisation which is a common possession. It is a loyalty of free men endowed with rights and protected by a common law. Its growth is stimulated both by the struggle to win those rights and their enjoyment when won. (Marshall, 1964, p. 92)

Having defined citizenship in these broad terms, Marshall went on to identify cit-izenship as an evolving, institutionally grounded array of civil, political and social rights:

> I propose to divide citizenship into three parts . . . I shall call these three parts or elements, civil, political, and social . . . The civil element is composed of the rights necessary for individual freedom — liberty of person, freedom of speech, thought and faith, the right to own property and to conclude valid contracts, and the right to justice. By the political element I mean the right to participate in the exercise of political power, as a member of a body vested with political authority or as an elector of the members of such a body . . . By the social element I mean the whole range from the right to a modicum of economic welfare and security to the right

to share to the full in the social heritage and to live the life of a civilised being according to the standards prevailing in the society. (Marshall, 1964, p. 78)

Marshall suggested that the specification and elaboration of each of these bundles of citizen rights was a contingent function of the differentiation and development of distinctive institutions — the law courts, parliamentary democracy, and the welfare state — at different moments in the history of citizenship. Marshall's argument here departs significantly from the normative discourse of rights: instead of deriving citizenship rights from the moral status that individuals possess as persons (Kant), or from a hypothetical social contract (Hobbes, Locke, Rousseau, Rawls), or from their property rights grounded in natural law (Locke), he argued that rights are attached to, and derived from, particular institutions, and are only explicable in terms of the contingent histories of these institutions and of conflicting 'institutional principles'. In his account of the development of social rights, for example, Marshall explains their evolution in terms of a 'war' between the imperial logic of the 'capitalist class system' and the normative logic of equality associated with liberal democratic citizenship (Marshall, 1964, p. 93). In the new system of social rights, the right of children to an education was the first and, in some ways, the least controversial social right granted. In part this was because education promised direct benefits to the state (the development of civic virtue, enhanced labour market participation), and in part it was because the right of children to be educated could be 'regarded, not as the right of the child to go to school, but as the right of the adult citizen to have been educated' (Marshall, 1964, pp. 89–90). More broadly, for Marshall social rights have transformed the relationship between the individual, the state, and the class system by imposing limits on the power of market relations of 'contract' to determine the living standards of citizens. In creating 'a universal right to a real income which is not proportionate to the market value of the claimant', welfare states subordinated market price to social justice. In this way, 'the components of a civilised and cultured life, formerly the monopoly of the few, were brought progressively within the reach of the many . . .' (Marshall, 1964, p. 106). Marshall did not believe that such forms of 'class abatement', even those that seek to modify 'the whole pattern of social inequality', necessarily entailed or portended strict equalitarianism, let alone a socialist utopia (Marshall, 1964, pp. 106, 128). Certainly no one could claim — Marshall for one didn't — that a social right to a public education, for example, has eliminated social inequality. Rather, the development of a formally meritocratic educational system has simply altered the relationship between education and market-based social inequalities, both in terms of how pre-existing inequalities shape educational outcomes, and in terms of the effect of differential educational outcomes on the pattern of social inequality through their relationship to the labour market (Marshall, 1964, pp. 117–22).

The historical adequacy of Marshall's account of the development of citizenship rights has been challenged on any number of grounds. Not the least of them, feminist critics point out, is that Marshall's historical account is for men only, since the history of women's rights is dramatically different from the history of male citizenship. Women in Britain, for example, did not achieve comparable civil and political rights to men until as late as 1928, many civil rights were not granted until *after* the achievement of political rights, and social rights continue to be structured by public and private forms of patriarchy. More broadly, feminist scholars have argued that the history of citizenship is as much about an on-going 'war' between patriarchy and citizenship — including the use of citizenship rights to undermine public and private forms of patriarchy — as it is about a 'war' between class and citizenship. But despite these differences, Marshall and his feminist critics share some common moral ground. Marshall, for example, recognized that the desire for citizenship represented 'an urge towards a fuller measure of equality' and that citizenship was a developing institution that had created 'an image of an ideal citizenship against which achievement can be measured and towards which aspiration can be directed'. And that is no less true now as it was in 1949. For the social democratic tradition particularly, citizenship is not merely a political or judicial category that delimits the relationship between the individual and the state and limits the power of the state over civil society. Rather, citizenship is a morally privileged category — a secular moral imperative — that draws its moral authority from expansive notions of equality and liberty and authorizes the use of state power to reform the institutions, social relations and modes of governmentality within civil society in order to promote substantive, as opposed to merely formal, membership of the political community and social justice. It is this standard that progressive liberals, socialists, social democrats, feminists and others have appealed to in their various efforts to make civil society conform to the demands of justice and full and effective citizenship. While these efforts by no means necessarily involve eliminating the boundary between civil society and the state, they certainly involve generalizing the moral presuppositions of liberal democratic citizenship to civil society. And they certainly reflect the social democratic conviction that social rights, no less than constitutionalism and the institutions of representative democracy, are necessary to protect protection and to ensure full membership of the political community.

From the beginning of the twentieth century, social rights and the welfare state have been embroiled in controversy. Contemporary New Right critics, for example, claim that social rights are a bogus invention and assert that the welfare state incites dependency, decouples rights and obligations, deforms individual character, destroys self respect, inhibits participation in civil society — particularly in the labour market — bankrupts the public purse, overtaxes hardworking, disciplined, prudent and industrious citizens, and politicizes the distribution of the 'social product' and social inequality (see Nozick, 1974; Novack, 1987; Murray, 1984; Mead, 1986; and Roche, 1992, Pt. 1, 2). Supported by public choice theorists, New Right apologists go on to argue variously for a contraction of social rights and the welfare state and for an expansion of consumer choice (via vouchers and lower taxes, for example) in the selection of public services from private providers. For the New Right, it is imperative that the market replace the state as the primary locus of citizenship, the preferred medium of civic exchange, and the *deux ex machina* of social inequality.

Critics on the left have also excoriated the welfare state, although for very different reasons. They criticize the failure of the welfare state to eliminate poverty and egregious racial and class inequalities, despite its success in reducing some forms of social inequality. They criticize the decoupling of the modern democratic project and welfare through the persistent indifference of the welfare state to the effective representation of citizens in the institutions of the welfare state and the more general development of the civic capacities of citizens (Ignatieff, 1987, p. 415). They criticize the embedded patriarchalism of welfare state presuppositions, programs and policies and the partial and incomplete constitution of women and minorities as full and equal members of the political and social community. They are concerned about the deeply vexed relationship between employment and welfare: should social citizenship be linked to participation in the labour market or should social rights be independent of labour market status (Pixley, 1992, p. 217 and 1993; Cappo and Cass, 1994; Watts, 1995a, pp. 95–102 and 1995b; Moon, 1988; and Pateman, 1988b)? Currently, the debate centres on the tension between market-based and non-market-based models of citizenship and whether we view social rights simply as a necessary means to the effective *exercise* of civic and political rights, or whether we view them as *constitutive* of the very meaning of social justice and citizenship (King and Waldron, 1988, pp. 424, 436; see also Barbalet, 1988, pp. 67, 68). Marshall seems to suggest both answers, although his historical sociology of citizenship, for all its liberal democratic sympathies, fails to explore the normative (as opposed to the institutional) foundations of individual rights and liberal democratic citizenship (see Roche, 1987, pp. 363–99; King and Waldron, 1988; Plant, 1992, Ch. 7; Weale, 1983). Others have been much less reticent in this regard (see Nussbaum, 1990; Walzer, 1983; Dworkin, 1981; Plant, 1992, 1988; Moon, 1988, pp. 32–5). Of these efforts, the work of John Rawls has been especially important.

John Rawls

Like J.S. Mill and T.H. Marshall before him, the contemporary American political philosopher, John Rawls, shares with Bentham and James Mill the assumption that liberal democratic citizenship is intended to protect the fundamental interests of citizens from the untoward acts of their fellow citizens and the state. Like Mill and Kant, Rawls is convinced that the protection of individual interests requires developed notions of autonomy and self-determination, although in his early writings he leans far more to Kant's view of autonomy than Mill's. Like Marshall, Rawls is convinced that self-determination requires a significant measure of social justice that, among other things, ensures that all citizens have adequate access to what he terms 'primary social goods'. Finally, Rawls is convinced that utilitarianism — either as a theory of distributive justice, or as a defence of majoritarian democracy — is incapable of generating defensible principles of social justice and democracy.

The starting point of Rawls's argument is that 'the primary subject of justice is the basic structure of society, or more exactly, the way in which the major social institutions distribute fundamental rights and duties and determine the division of advantages from social cooperation'. On this account, institutions include 'the political constitution and the principal economic and social arrangements' (Rawls, 1991, p. 7). Justice therefore is an 'artificial' virtue (to use David Hume's term), and it is an artificial virtue created by an agreement between citizens to a set of fundamental principles or rules of social co-operation that protects — and protects equally — the highest-order interest that each person has in framing and living a life of their own choosing. The principles of justice, Rawls writes at the very beginning of *A Theory of Justice*, are those

> principles that free and rational persons concerned to further their own *interests* would accept in an initial position of equality as defining the fundamental terms of their association. These principles are to regulate all further agreements: they specify the kinds of social cooperation that can be entered into and the forms of government that can be established. This way of regarding the principles of justice I shall call justice as fairness. (Rawls, 1991, p. 11)

Rawls argues that ideally individuals should come to an agreement about the principles of justice — those 'principles which are to assign basic rights and duties and to determine the division of social benefits — in a condition of initial equality with all other individuals' (Rawls, 1991, p. 11).

Of these, the first and most important is the principle of 'equal liberty'. Equal liberty is the equal right of each individual to the most extensive basic liberties compatible with the same liberties of others: the right to freedom of conscience, the right of free association, the right of access to information, the right to participate in public life, and so on. Equal liberty, however, imposes a fundamental obligation on all citizens, namely, the requirement that we each respect the moral autonomy and agency of all persons and their right to develop — and change if they will — their conceptions of their good and to fashion a life that allows them to pursue it. The right to pursue our own good, in other words, is constrained by the principles of reciprocal equality and mutual respect or by what Rawls calls the priority of the right over the good. It is this priority of the right over the good that establishes Rawls's theory, at least in *A Theory of Justice*, as an expression of Kantian or 'deontological' liberalism and sets it apart and in opposition to utilitarianism. Where utilitarianism justifies the use of majoritarian power if it secures the greatest good of the greatest number, Rawls insists that majoritarian power is not justified if it infringes the principle of equal liberty or the right of each individual to lead a life of their own choosing. Finally, Rawls goes on to argue that the 'stability' of a constitutional democracy depends, first, on the creation of an 'overlapping consensus' about the basic principles of justice in a society, and second, on the development of two individual moral capacities or powers — the capacity to form an effective 'sense of justice', and the capacity to imagine, revise and pursue a life based on a rationally-formed conception of the good (Rawls, 1993).

Rawls's critics — and there are many of them — have either questioned or repudiated many of Rawls's core arguments. Feminist critics, for example, have argued that Rawls failed to apply the principles of justice as fairness to the patriarchal family (see Okin, 1988, Ch. 6). His communitarian critics argue, on the other hand, that protective models of citizenship generally lack an adequate understanding of the preconditions of political community. Justice, the priority of liberty, or the logic of protection, they argue, is much too thin a reed on which to establish or sustain a viable political community and ignores the fundamental importance of identity — including our identities as citizens — in constructing a life that is good. A viable political community requires various kinds of 'common social goods' — a substantive and comprehensive notion of the common good, a particular ensemble of civic virtues, strong forms of civic identity, extensive participation in the civic life of the political community — that develop attachments, form identities, confer dignity, create disciplines of self-government, motivate social action, and inform conceptions of the good, interests and the self. A viable political community thus requires a conception of citizenship that is different, or at least far broader, than a conception based on a rational calculus of the costs and benefits of social cooperation. Instead, it requires a conception of citizenship that emphasizes a sense of attachment to, and identity with, an historically specific political community with its particular traditions and values. In addition, it requires a willingness to promote a kind of politics in which active citizens and duly constituted democratic majorities develop and pursue a particular substantive conception of the common good that is prior and superordinate to individual desires and interests. Communitarians differ in how they conceive a civic republican politics of this kind — Bernard Barber suggests a 'strong democracy', Michael Sandel recommends a democratic 'politics of the common good', Alisdair Macintyre wants a rehabilitation of an Aristotelian politics of 'civic virtue', Charles Taylor thinks the answer lies in 'patriotic identification' or a 'politics of recognition' — but they all have in common the idea that citizenship programs ought to focus not so much on the protection of individual interests as on social integration and the common good (Sandel, 1982, 1984a, pp. 81–96, 1984b, pp. 15–17; Macintyre, A. 1981; Taylor, 1989b, Ch. 9, 1985, 1994; Barber, 1984).

In short, where the liberal democratic model of citizenship focuses on the instrumental logic of the civic exchange, communitarians focus on the constitutive qualities of social life and civic identity; where the liberal democratic model seeks to protect the autonomy of individuals by limiting the power of the state through a combination of constitutional and normative constraints, communitarians prefer mechanisms that enhance the attachment of citizens to the political community.

The communitarian critique of Rawls deserves serious respect. On some key arguments, communitarians win hands down; plainly, liberalism, including the 'political liberalism' of Rawls and others, has ignored the constitutive qualities of social action and identity and what we might term the ontological (as opposed to the moral) priority of community. While justice might very well require the capacity to frame, revise and pursue one's own good, it also requires a form of political community that permits citizens to do so. Furthermore, it also requires the development of those civic capacities that permits citizens to protect their interests and sustain the political community that makes the protection of their interests possible. Justice, in other words, requires the capacity to protect protection. Consequently, I'm sympathetic to civic republican assertions that a viable liberal democratic community requires something more than a common legal status, liberal democratic institutions, the cultivation of self-government, or an overlapping consensus on the principles of justice, to sustain it. At the same time, however, there is little doubt that civic republican theorists are best blasé, and at worst, indifferent, to the claims of individual autonomy, justice and pluralism. Partly this is because they have yet to develop anything like an adequate empirical account of the state, civil society or the organization and deployment of social (including 'disciplinary') power generally. Partly it is because they have failed to develop a principled account of community that recognizes the demands of justice and pluralism. Community might very well be a precondition of justice, but justice requires that community not come at the expense of pluralism. Communitarians have been far too preoccupied with the preconditions of political community and defined political community in pre-modern terms (as a form of *Gemeinschaft*) rather than developing an account of political community that assumes the priority of protecting protection and ensuring pluralism (Mouffe, 1992, 1993). From this perspective then, communitarians have highlighted the thinness and incompleteness rather than the incoherence of liberal democratic conceptions of political community and education, and challenged defenders of the liberal democratic credo to offer a more adequate account of a viable liberal democratic community and education.

Conclusion: Towards a Liberal Democratic Education

The nature of citizenship, Aristotle declared in *The Politics*, is a question about which 'there is no unanimity, no agreement'. Ever the good political anthropologist, Aristotle noted that the nature of citizenship varies 'according to the constitution in each case' (Aristotle, 1981, pp. 168, 170). And well he might: as early as 1576 Jean Bodin complained in exasperation that he could identify some 500 definitions of citizenship (Reisenberg, 1992, p. 222). But Aristotle also had no doubt that 'of all the safeguards that we hear spoken of as helping to maintain constitutional stability, the most important, but today most universally neglected, is education for the way of living that belongs to the constitution in each case'. He went on: 'It is useless to have the most beneficial laws, fully agreed upon by all who are members of the constitution, if they are not going to be trained and have their habits formed in the spirit of that constitution . . .' (Aristotle, 1981, p. 331).

I have suggested in this paper that the moral appeal of liberal democratic citizenship lies in its commitment to the logic of protection and the discourse of justice, and that its principal weakness resides in its failure to generate an adequate theory of political community that identifies the conditions that protect protection without violating principles of justice. Consequently, a liberal democratic education is an education shaped not so much by the right to pursue one's own interests irrespective of the rights of others or the requirements of liberal democratic political community, on the one hand, or by the demand for 'active citizenship', 'political community', 'civic virtue', or 'national identity' irrespective of the claims of justice, on the other, but an education shaped principally by the logic of protection and political community within the limits of justice. Granted this argument, we might conclude that a liberal democratic education is one that seeks to serve two objectives simultaneously and without contradiction: protecting the highest order interests of individual citizens, and promoting a form of political community that protects protection. It is important to emphasize that this view by no means precludes supporting an education that promotes the development of a range of civic capacities that promote political community or facilitates what Amy Gutmann terms 'conscious social reproduction' (Gutmann, 1987). Rather, it simply means that we can and should support an education that develops a range of capacities consistent with the requirements of justice, including those capacities necessary to protect protection in a liberal democratic community. In more formal terms, we might define a liberal democratic education as one committed to *the development of those capacities that permit individuals to frame, pursue, revise and protect their own conception of the good as interdependent members of a liberal democratic community*. Specifically, a liberal democratic education is one that develops the following capacities of student-citizens: the capacity to *frame* and *revise* a conception of a good life within the limits of justice as interdependent members of a liberal democratic community; the capacity to *pursue* and *protect* their conception of the good — i.e., the capacity to exercise effective forms of civil and civic agency; the capacity to form a modulated *civic identity* as a full member of pluralistic political community, and the capacity to develop a range of liberal democratic virtues, including a sense of obligation, a 'sense of justice', civility, self government, and so on appropriate to a liberal democratic community committed to protecting protection (see Hogan, 1996b).

Let me make three observations about this conception of liberal democratic education.

First, this account of liberal democratic education draws heavily on a long tradition of liberal democratic political theory. It particularly relies on a line of argument that runs roughly as follows: individuals, other things being equal, are the best judges of their own interests; the highest order interest of individuals is to live a life of their own choosing; the value of liberty or autonomy is dependent on the ability of individuals to frame, revise, pursue and protect their own conceptions of the good; individual interests are interdependent with the interests of others and embedded in, and constituted by, patterns of sociability and community life; the moral legitimacy of conceptions of the good or individual interests depends on their compatibility with the principles of justice, defined in terms of equal liberty and mutual respect; the framing of interests should be embedded in deliberative processes wherever possible and appropriate; and the principle of autonomy authorizes the state to pursue a limited variety of policies designed to protect and expand a public culture of autonomy and pluralism (see Hogan, 1996a).

Second, this view of liberal democratic education does not preclude the development of those civic capacities that protect liberal democratic institution and promote political community. Indeed, it presupposes that a necessary precondition of protective citizenship is the existence of an array of liberal democratic constitutional and institutional arrangements and social norms — a political community

— that protects protection. This does not imply, however, that the promotion of political community has priority over, or should come at the expense of, the protection of citizen interests. Rather, it simply means that we can and should support an education that develops a range of capacities consistent with the requirements of justice and pluralism, including those capacities necessary to protect protection in a liberal democratic community. In a word, political community is, therefore, a necessary precondition for a liberal democratic citizenship and education rather than an end in itself. Or, to put it another way, a liberal democracy values political community because it values justice rather than because it values 'civic virtue' or 'civic identity' *per se*. Consequently, it is perfectly appropriate — indeed, incumbent — upon a liberal democratic education to promote the reproduction of liberal democratic institutions, norms and virtues necessary to cultivate a liberal democratic political community and protect protection. It simply cannot do so, however, at the expense of developing those capacities that promote the capacity of citizens to frame, pursue, revise and protect their conception of the good as interdependent members of a liberal democratic community.

3 Feminist Theory and the Construction of Citizenship Education

Victoria Foster

Citizenship Education in the Modern Patriarchal State

It is taken to be a truism that education is, or should be, in part a preparation for citizenship, directed towards active and successful participation by all students in a modern democratic society. Since the mid-1980s, there has been a revival of interest in participatory democratic theory and in particular, a renewed focus on the concept of citizenship as a new organizing principle for democratic politics (Pateman, 1992, p. 30). This revival is reflected in the current interest in citizenship education and in the contemporary goals of education which are concerned broadly with the preparation of students to participate actively and successfully in social life.

However, despite the clear evidence of widely disparate outcomes from women's and men's education across western industrialized nations (OECD, 1996), and in Australia (New South Wales Government, 1994, p. 1), the gendered nature of citizenship as both a philosophical and social educational goal has received little attention from educational theorists. Furthermore, little is known of girls' and women's lived experiences of the gendered curriculum of schooling.

This chapter addresses the question of whether citizenship for women is possible in the modern state which is predicated on a division between public and private life. Using examples from Australia, Holland and Scandinavia, it explores some of the ways in which curriculum mirrors the modern state's valorization of public life and devaluing of the private. The citizen-as-male has his counterpart in the learner-as-male. Curriculum development in citizenship education has not adequately addressed the public–private dialectic in social life. Consequently, it has not succeeded in incorporating private life into the curriculum. Thus, despite the current revival of interest in Australia and other countries in citizenship education, education continues to perpetuate women's and girls' lack of citizenship status.

The Critical Literature on the Gendered Nature of Citizenship in the Modern State

Running parallel to the revival of interest citizenship education is a vast literature (for example, Benhabib, 1992; Cass, 1994; Leech, 1994; Pateman, 1988, 1989,

1992; Shanley and Pateman, 1991; Young, 1987) on the gendered nature of citizenship, and 'the problem of women's standing in a political order in which citizenship has been made in the male image' (Pateman, 1989, p. 14). Much of this literature focuses on women's exclusion from the ideal of the civic public realm of citizenship which is both normatively masculine, and relies on an opposition between the public and private dimensions of human life. This broad-ranging literature has demonstrated that women are in fact outside the frame of patriarchal citizenship and that there is an enormous gulf between the apparent guarantee of full citizenship for women and women's actual lived experience of that guarantee (Leech, 1994, p. 81); and that women's status as citizens is underwritten by a sexual contract (Pateman, 1988) denying them free and equal status with men. Feminist legal theory in particular (for example, Charlesworth, 1992; Gavison, 1992; Graycar, 1992, 1993) shows that the burden of women's responsibility for work associated with the private sphere has implications for their legal status as citizens.

The consensus is that equality for women is not, and will not be delivered merely by attempting to include women in the normative conception of man as citizen by 'laundering some of its ideals' (Young, 1987, p. 58). Furthermore, Pateman (1989, p. 14) argues convincingly that women, as *women*, cannot meet the criteria for citizenship. Elaborating this point she observes that

> democratic theorists have not yet confronted the implications of the patriarchal construction of citizenship and so they provide little or no help in elucidating or solving the complex dilemma facing women ... within the contemporary patriarchal order, and within the confines of the ostensibly universal categories of democratic theory; it is taken for granted that for women to be active, full citizens they must become (like) men ... although women have demanded for two centuries that their distinctive qualities and tasks should become part of citizenship — that is, that they should be citizens as women — their demand cannot be met when it is precisely these marks of womanhood that place women in opposition to, or, at best, in a paradoxical and contradictory relation to, citizenship. Women are expected to don the lion's skin, mane and all, ... there is no set of clothes available for a citizen who is a woman.

The substance of the feminist critique of citizenship, then, is firstly that women are not only outside the realm of citizenship but secondly, that the notion of including women and women's work within conceptions of democratic citizenship is contradictory since citizenship is itself defined in opposition to women and the sphere of work which is relegated to them. This contradiction is encapsulated in very practical terms by Michel Hansenne (1992, p. 5) the Director-General of the International Labor Organization;

> Family responsibilities are at the heart of much discrimination against women. Women are expected to stay at home and look after children and are then treated as second-class workers because of this.

It is this contradiction which poses the dilemma for inserting women into conceptions of citizenship. Although this contradiction is addressed in depth by the feminist critique, it is largely ignored in curriculum development in the field of citizenship education. Further, the conclusion of the feminist critique is that nothing less than an entire reconceptualization of citizenship is required if its present inadequacies in relation to women, and women's diversity and differences, are to be addressed.

Cass (1994) has pointed out that the 'mainstream resurgence of writings on the components of "citizenship" pays almost no attention to the gendered nature of citizenship'. Similarly, one is left with the disappointing impression that curriculum development in the field of citizenship education has failed to come to grips with the critical literature on the relationship of women with the state and within civil society, briefly surveyed above, and the implications of that relationship for citizenship education.

Despite the challenges which feminist political theory and philosophy have posed to understandings of women's place in participatory democracy, there has not been a great deal of critical analysis of the importance of women's relationship with education in determining their status as citizens. Notable exceptions are the work of Martin (1981; 1985; 1991) in educational philosophy, and Foster (1989; 1992; 1996b) and Yates (1991a, b; 1993) in critiques of inclusive curriculum, which are discussed later in this article in the context of citizenship education. Similarly, Martin (1981; 1985) has shown that the philosophical ideal of the educated person still does not include women and girls. This fundamental philosophical point remains inadequately operationalized in terms of the curriculum and pedagogy of schooling, and consequent student experience. Elsewhere (Foster, 1994a; 1996b), I argue that girls are not only in a contradictory relationship with schooling as a preparation for citizenship, but that girls and boys experience the curriculum itself in quite different ways.

In Australia, attempts to achieve greater educational equality for girls have centred on positioning girls within a deficit framework, as lacking in relation to male norms of the educated person, and encouraging them to measure up to those norms (Foster, 1992). However, since 1993 it has become apparent that the gains girls might make as a result of this approach to sexual equality are being vigorously contested on an international scale (Elgqvist-Saltzmann, 1995; Foster, 1994b; 1995; 1996a). Less apparent are the implications for girls' place within conceptions of citizenship as an educational objective. This chapter attempts to clarify some of them.

The Public–private Dialectic in Citizenship Education

In her 1996 John Dewey lecture delivered to the American Educational Research Association, Jane Roland Martin described society's 'great unmooring' (p. 3). This she defined as 'the revolution in gender roles and relations that has occurred in the last decades of the twentieth century (which) has profoundly affected the basic institutions of society, thereby impinging on the lives of every last one of us'. Martin, however, argues forcefully that education systems have been 'unresponsive in rising to the challenge presented by this world historic event'.

A vexed relationship exists between schooling and society, in relation to a productive working-out of society's great unmoorings. Martin (1996) argues that both society and education are divided into two separate public and private worlds. It is taken for granted that the function of education is 'to transform children who have theretofore lived their lives in the one world into members of the other' (p. 10).

Martin (p. 10) elaborates education's relation with the public–private division in society as follows:

> Assuming that the private house or home is a natural institution and that, accordingly, membership in it is a given rather than something that one must achieve, we see no reason to prepare people to carry out the tasks and activities associated with it. Perceiving the so-called public world as a human creation and membership in it as something at which one can succeed or fail and therefore as problematic, we make the 'real' business of education preparation for carrying out the tasks and activities associated with it.

Martin notes further that each of these two worlds is 'gender-coded' respectively as a male or female domain, but that education concerns itself only with the public world. Thus, educational ideals reflected in curriculum and student participation and outcomes, for instance, are predicated on a division between public and private. Most particularly, this division has resulted in a separation between so-called 'work' and 'care' in curriculum development in a number of countries, referred to hereafter as a 'work-care dialectic'. The most valued school subjects are linked increasingly to the world of 'work', and the educated person is one who has mastered those skills and knowledge. Both these aspects of education, the curriculum and the nature of the true learner citizens, are strongly gender-differentiated.

Perhaps not surprisingly, then, recent Australian research (Wolcott and Glezer, 1995, p. 95) shows that household tasks continue to be strictly divided along gender lines. Analysing time allocation of unpaid work between 1974 and 1992, Bittman (1995) concluded that there has been little change and that there are no 'new men'.

Addressing the Public–private Dialectic in Citizenship Education: Some International Comparisons

The next section presents an overview of recent curriculum developments related to citizenship education in Australia. It is interesting to compare these developments with those in other countries, for example, the Dutch 'care' curriculum (ten Dam and Volman, 1995) and in Sweden (Eveline, 1995) and Norway (Ve, 1989). In all of these cases, the most contested issue has been the curriculum status of knowledge and skills related to the private, domestic sphere of life, embodied in subjects such as Household Management and Family Studies.

Curriculum Development in Australia

In 1992, Australian curriculum development took a decisive step in the direction of placing 'work' as the centrepiece of the curriculum, with the establishment of 'work-related Key Competencies' as newly defined areas of skills and knowledge. These included mathematical, technological and communication skills and knowledge, and so on (Mayer Report, 1992).

After a great deal of debate, however, the Mayer Committee decided not to include the proposed 'Family and Household Management' subject as a work-related Key Competency, claiming that it did not constitute a generic area of skills. This is a decision which put Australia somewhat out of step with curriculum developments addressing the gendered nature of work in other countries, for example, the Scandinavian countries and Holland.

In 1994, the Civics Expert Group released a national report on citizenship education, with directions for curriculum change, entitled *Whereas the People . . . Civics and Citizenship Education*. This report provides a practical illustration of the theoretical problems inherent in women's relationship with citizenship outlined in this chapter.

Problems in the Australian Report's Conception of Citizenship: Women, a 'Group with Special Needs'

Of the Report's thirty-five recommendations, only one (No. 26) deals with women (p. 112). It recommends that the community citizenship education program should 'make explicit provision for specific groups', listing women as one of a number of groups.

The Report itself dispenses with women in two pages, pp. 99–101, as a 'group with special needs', in a chapter entitled 'Citizenship Education and the wider community'. These two pages do make the important historical point that earlier, more liberal-progressive notions of citizenship inspired by first-wave feminism were crowded out by the idea of the citizen as a male worker. It is noted that women as a group are 'less equipped' than men to make their voices heard in the public arena. Rather than critically evaluate the public arena itself, and the ways in which the development of the citizen-as-male has depended on public–private divisions in society forged along gender lines, the report favours a 'feminization' of citizenship. This entails the 'translation of private values into the public sphere' which 'must result in the recognition of alternative forms of citizenship'. An example is given of women's active community work which should be 'acknowledged and valued alongside more traditional, public forms of citizenship'.

Bacchi and Eveline (1996) describe how setting women apart as a political category has the effect of creating a range of 'women's issues', resulting in the strategic isolation of 'women' from a broader political agenda. In a politics of incorporation, 'women' can then be added without disturbing the agenda, and leaving men situated as the unquestioned norm. Women can be added to established national images, such as those associated with citizenship, without considering that these may be inadequate.

The report states that the Civics Expert Group believes that education has a vital role to play in both increasing the participation of women in national affairs and 'enabling them to introduce new ways of conceiving citizenship into the public sphere'. Surprisingly, however, neither of these objectives is then taken up and developed within the curriculum chapters of the report. The basis of the civics competence curriculum is to be the Mayer Committee Key Competencies (p. 77) with a third added, cultural understandings. The report comments (p. 70) that 'it is not surprising that the Key Competencies are so attuned to civic competence since they were intended to apply generically to emerging patterns of work and the demands of adult life'.

The report thus effectively endorses a conception of effective citizenship as residing in the public arena of paid work and civic responsibility and involvement. Women may take part in the public world and may attempt to create alternative ways of being citizens, but these remain external and marginal to the actual locus of citizenship, which is public life. Women may attempt to introduce private virtues into the public sphere but these are merely alternatives to public sphere virtues. Although 'in recent years people have again begun to urge the feminization of citizenship' (p. 100), this goal is in no way reflected in the proposed citizenship curriculum. The next section discusses some of the problems inherent in the report's conception of citizenship.

I discussed above the report's failure to embody in its curriculum proposals any new valuing of private sphere values and activities, despite its statement of the need to do this, and its acknowledgment of community support for equal participation by women and men in public decision-making processes (p. 100). Perhaps the most serious flaw is thus the lack of any challenge, in the framing of citizenship, to the public–private division in social life which ensures that men and women still have a different and unequal relationship with citizenship. This omission is carried through to the curriculum proposals which endorse a very narrow and traditional view of citizenship, which is normatively masculine. There are several important aspects to the report's retention of a normatively masculine framework of citizenship.

The report acknowledges, albeit cursorily, women's secondary status as citizens as a result of the under-valuing of private sphere work and life. Its strategy, however, is to transfer women's secondary status to the public arena, by failing to address men's and women's different and asymmetrical relations with private life. It takes what is fundamentally a liberal position, in which differences of race, nationality, sex, class and religion are assumed not to preclude equal participation in civil society (Manning, 1976, p. 24). Differences which result from being a member of a 'group with special needs' can be overcome by an inclusive approach which helps the individual or group become part of the mainstream citizenry. So as is the case with women, Aboriginal and Torres Strait Islander people are allocated two pages. Similarly, however, these differences present no challenge to mainstream curricular assumptions and content, a point to which I will return.

A number of writers (for example, Benhabib, 1993; Luke, 1992; Tapper, 1986) have pointed out that reforms directed towards women's equality in the public sphere, which fail to take account of the sexual structuring of the public–private division and the maleness of the supposedly abstract, gender-neutral individual, will not overcome women's secondary status, but simply relocate it within the public sphere. The report exemplifies the tendency in liberal theory to conceptually relocate the feminine, which is tied to the private nexus of nuclear family and mothering, into the public sphere, leaving intact the dichotomous gendered political structure of the public–private division. Pateman (1989, p. 135) notes a double separation, of domestic life from civil society, and of the private from the public within civil society itself.

As Pateman (1989, p. 14) points out, 'women have always been incorporated into the civil order as "women", as subordinates or lesser men', a tradition of liberal, democratic theory which is continued in *Whereas the People*. However, Lloyd (1984, p. 104) articulates very clearly the contradiction inherent in the notion of extending the liberal conception of the individual to women, and thus the imposs-ibility of success via this strategy:

> Women cannot easily be accommodated into a cultural ideal which has defined itself in opposition to the feminine. To affirm women's equal possession of rational traits, and their rights of access to the public spaces within which they are cultivated and manifested, is politically important. But it does not get to the heart of the conceptual complexities of gender difference . . . For it seems implicitly to accept the downgrading of the excluded character traits traditionally associated with femininity, and to endorse the assumption that the only human excellences and virtues which deserve to be taken seriously are those exemplified in the range of activities and concerns that have been associated with maleness.

Some General Curriculum Issues

Just as Pateman urges a radical transformation in democratic theory, so a transforma-tion in curriculum theory and formulation is needed, beyond 'inclusive' approaches which merely seek to incorporate marginalized groups within a mainstream cur-riculum which fundamentally represents hegemonic world views (Connell, 1987; Foster, 1989; Schuster and Van Dyne, 1984; Yates, 1991a, b).

Connell (1987, p. 3) points out that although feminist theory has produced an analysis of a large domain of social life through concepts such as sexual politics, patriarchy and the sexual division of labour, the implications of this 'conceptual revolution are still to be felt across much of the curriculum'. Elsewhere (Foster, 1989, p. 27), I note firstly, that philosophically and pedagogically, 'inclusive cur-riculum' is in fact a valuable, long-term educational objective, rather than being a strategy for affirmative action on behalf of those students whose needs it claims to address, and secondly, that 'inclusive curriculum' has never been adequately dis-tinguished from the 'common' curriculum, which we know is utilized by boys and girls in quite different ways. Yates (1991a) in particular has offered a forceful critique of the theoretically acritical nature of 'inclusive' curriculum:

> The Australian policy discourse concerning 'inclusive' curriculum largely implies that ethnic, race and gender differences can be drawn on and integrated, as if

no challenge, no questioning of power, no anti-racism, no competing notions of rationality were at issue.

In addition to its philosophically not challenging dominant notions of rationality, Yates (1991b) points to the method of inclusive curriculum as

> incorporating add-on bits and pieces about girls' educational needs, such as how best to give girls more attention, how to cater for girls' different learning styles and preferences, how to be sensitive to cultural and racial differences and how to create school and learning environments that are more supportive of girls as learners, with no clear commitment to what mainstream learnings we will introduce to the next generation.

Further, just as a radical transformation of democratic theory concerning women and citizenship is needed if 'democracy' and democratic participation are not to remain the preserve of men (Pateman, 1989, pp. 14–15), so a radical transformation in curriculum philosophy and content is needed if citizenship education in Australia is to move beyond the 'add-women-and-stir' approach of inclusive curriculum. Unfortunately, *Whereas the People* fails on both counts, lacking a sound theoretical framework for conceptualizing women's relations with citizenship, as well as a vision of a curriculum which would address the issues identified in this article. These inadequacies are surprising since, as pointed out earlier, these issues have had a good airing in the theoretical literature as well as in the literature on inclusive curriculum.

In the following section, I will briefly set out several reasons why add-on approaches to including women in a normative framework of the citizen-as-male are incoherent. I will then relate this discussion to the different ways in which boys and girls experience contemporary school settings.

Adding Women to the Citizen-as-male: Some Curriculum Issues

I have already discussed the ways in which citizenship education as conceptualized in *Whereas the People* obfuscates the gendered nature of citizenship itself. First, it relies on a notion of the free, autonomous citizen/individual who is in fact male. Second, it fails to deal adequately with the civil distinction between public sphere, 'productive' work and private sphere, domestic/care work. Women's private sphere status is briefly alluded to (p. 100), but is ultimately deemed separate from, and alternative to, citizenship itself. That these two spheres are at once separate and inseparable (Pateman, 1988, p. 4), having implications for both men and women as citizens, is glossed over. Consequently, the work/care dichotomy remains embedded in the report's curriculum framework. As I have suggested, this is a flaw which has far-reaching and serious implications for future curriculum development in Australia, at least.

However, the report also glosses over other important dimensions of men's and women's different relations with citizenship. Most important perhaps as Pateman

(1988, p. x) insightfully observes, the social contract of citizenship and democratic civil freedom is actually underwritten by a 'sexual contract' within modern patriarchy. This sexual–social pact not only concerns the identification of women's activities with the private sphere, as is the case in *Whereas the People*, it also concerns the fact of patriarchal domination of both spheres, and while women's movement between the two spheres is constrained within a patriarchal society, men may pass freely between them.

Discussing the 'deep and fundamental differences in the ways in which men and women arrive at citizenship', Leech (1994, p. 86) and Cass (1994) pinpoint the role of women as primary caregivers as the major factor limiting their participation as citizens. Cass notes that women's caring responsibilities are antithetical to the idea of the 'citizen' as an 'independent actor, participating as an individual in the labour market, participating democratically as an individual citizen in political processes, receiving social benefit entitlement as a right based on individual citizenship'. In addition, allied to the notion of patriarchal sex-right is the material advantage which men gain from women's domestic and care work (Eveline, 1994, p. 141). Connell (1994, p. 4) refers to this as the 'patriarchal dividend' which, he comments, is increasing rather than decreasing, and whose significance and size is constantly underestimated in discussions of the gender order and of masculinity. As I have stressed throughout this chapter, it is important to begin to relate the patriarchal dividend in society with patriarchal norms embedded in the curriculum.

Eveline (1994, p. 141) suggests that this 'indirect approach to male privilege' is actually, at least in part, the result of a fear of retaliation for the 'recalling' through redistributive equal opportunity policies, of the benefits and privileges of men. Further, Shanley (1991, p. 170) points out that radical critiques of theories of sexual equality dating from Mill's *The Subjection of Women (1869)*, have emphasized not only men's reluctance to give up their position of material advantage, but also their 'fear of living with an equal' in both domestic and civil life. Male resistance to female equality is a very real factor in women's continuing underrepresentation in public life (Cockburn, 1991) and their right to participate as citizens as men's equals. It has its counterpart in education which is discussed below.

I have discussed above some of the complexities and nuances in men's and women's different relations with citizenship, which are obscured in *Whereas the People*. The final section of this article briefly discusses some contemporary manifestations of sexual inequality in schooling, which bear directly on questions of women's relationship with citizenship.

Schooling and Citizenship

That men's and women's lived experiences of citizenship are quite different has parallels in school life, and in the 'lived curriculum' of Australian schooling (Foster, 1994a; 1996a). I have already referred to the ways in which a work–care dichotomy is perpetuated by the formal curriculum framework of *Whereas the People*, with respect to its view of work-related competencies. However, just as important are the differences in the ways in which girls and boys experience and live the curriculum day-to-day. For instance, women's caretaking functions have their counterpart in coeducational classroom life where girls are expected to be caretakers of the learning environment. For example, girls are routinely expected to moderate the behaviour of boys, soften the classroom atmosphere, be 'good girls', and not to exhibit the kinds of undisciplined behaviours which are taken to be 'natural' for boys and which often gain sympathetic attention for them. This expectation can be seen on one level to be a transfer of the practices of the private, domestic sphere into the public setting of the school's learning situation, the classroom. Specifically, 'private' imperatives relating to women's perceived primary functions in the areas of sexuality, motherhood and caretaking are brought into the micro-public domain of the school. On another level, however, this expectation can also be seen to be a particular feature of educational settings.

At this second level, there is a profound sense in which despite the Australian policy discourse of educational equality, educational practices reflect an assumption that boys' interests and their learning are of prior importance to girls'. There are many examples of the greater importance placed on boys' learning and associated problems, such as the greater amount of teacher time devoted to boys, the attention given to boys' learning difficulties and discipline problems, the greater amount of physical space and school sporting facilities used by boys, and boys' domination of technical and computer equipment. In New South Wales, for instance, up to 90 per cent of specialist education resources currently go to boys. These barriers to girls' equal status in education have been repeatedly documented in Australia since the 1975 Report, *Girls, School and Society.*

Girls' Status as Learner Citizens

Nevertheless, since 1993 Australian equal education policies and programs have increasingly been contested as girls began to be erroneously constructed as beating boys in the prestigious male-dominated curriculum terrain of mathematics, science and technology. The hostility on the part of some to equality in schooling for girls has taken the form of a refrain around *What about the boys!* in an attempt to reassert male educational interests as prior (Foster, 1994b; 1995). This refrain is echoing internationally (Elgqvist-Saltzman, Prentice and Mackinnon, in press). For example, Elgqvist-Saltzman (1995, p. 1) reports that an international conference on gender and education held in June, 1995 at the University of Umea, Sweden

> resulted in a strong feeling of unease around the topic. Why did we feel that gains made were insufficient, were painfully slow, and furthermore were vigorously contested? Common themes emerged which highlighted continuing tensions between girls and boys, men and women, in a range of educational settings. When females approach male performance levels and access, a discourse of male disadvantage reverberates through the research literature and the popular press. 'What shall we do about the boys?' trumpet the headlines in Australia, Great Britain, Canada and Scandinavia.

The largely unexpressed subtext of this refrain is that notions of educational equality for girls entail taking something very crucial away from boys, their supremacy as learners, as well as the caretaking resources of women and girls, to which boys are assumed to be entitled. An unspoken question is, what would happen to boys if girls were to become their equals in schooling and its outcomes, and stop being their caretakers?

At the same time that priority is given to boys' learning problems, there has been a failure to date to address comprehensively within the curriculum, the problem of sex-based harassment of girls as an endemic feature of schools, and its effects on girls' learning (Australian Education Council, 1992; NSW Department of School Education, 1994). This is an issue which has been strenuously avoided in recent discussions of boys and their education.

In effect, it seems that girls and boys are engaged in rather different projects at school — that they live ostensibly the same curriculum in somewhat differing ways. Many boys see school primarily as the avenue to paid work, whatever that may be. The present overwhelming instrumental emphasis on work-related competencies (where the nature of 'work' is not interrogated) is not helping to broaden that view. Girls, on the other hand, see a range of present and future priorities. They seem to see participation in school life and its responsibilities, including learning, as more relevant and important than boys do. Boys, on the other hand it seems, want to distinguish their masculinity from girls' diligence, to dissociate themselves from the 'good girls'. On this point, the NSW Evaluation (1994, p. 61) observes that in some schools 'there is a pervading culture of anti-intellectualism fuelled by significant numbers of boys, resulting in severe disruption of learning and denigration of the academic achievements of both boys and girls'. Further, girls said they would not answer questions in class, or appear to try to succeed, as they were inhibited by the likely reaction of boys.

In the discussion above, I have highlighted some of the real issues of continuing sexual difference and inequality in curriculum participation and its outcomes, which bear directly on men's and women's participation as citizens. I have argued, as Leech (1994, p. 87) does, that 'in order for citizenship to assume its full meaning for women, theory development is needed at such a deep and fundamental level, that an "add women and stir" response would be of no value'. In terms of citizenship education, for real progress to be made in women's assuming full citizenship, both educational philosophy and curriculum theory and practice need to be radically reinvestigated.

4 Issues for Citizenship in a Postmodern World

Rob Gilbert

The English speaking democracies have in recent times seen a remarkable resurgence of interest in education for citizenship, at least in terms of their simultaneous production of inquiries, reports and curriculum recommendations. From the United Kingdom come parliamentary inquiries and national curriculum statements (Commission on Citizenship, 1990; National Curriculum Council, 1990); in the United States agencies have produced guidelines and statements of national standards for education for citizenship (Bahmueller, 1991; Center for Civic Education, 1994); the Canadian Senate has reported on the issue (Standing Senate Committee on Social Affairs, Science and Technology, 1993); and in Australia, the source of this chapter, the Senate has conducted two important inquiries (Senate Standing Committee on Employment, Education and Training, 1989, 1991), and the Government commissioned a third (Civics Expert Group, 1994).

No doubt local questions have contributed to these developments — in the United Kingdom, European citizenship; in Canada, Quebec; in Australia, the republican debate. However, it is also true that the recent past has seen economic, social, cultural and political trends which have potentially powerful effects on all these nations. If the simultaneity of the interest in citizenship is the question, then these common experiences are part of the answer.

Much recent discussion of these trends has been couched in terms of a concept of postmodernity, though enthusiasm for the concept seems recently to have moderated, especially as an analytical tool for understanding contemporary culture and its political significance (Kellner, 1992; Goldman and Papson, 1994). The hyperbole surrounding the proclaimed changes associated with postmodernity has been balanced with a greater recognition of continuity and diversity within the modern/postmodern relation (Lash, 1990). Also, it is now clear that postmodernism as a cultural movement was dominated by Western middle class perspectives, to the neglect of its significance for the rest of the world (Morley and Robins, 1995). Equally, postmodernism proved difficult to define, especially when attempts were made to essentialize and periodize it as postmodernity.

Despite these caveats, any attempt to characterize contemporary society and culture must acknowledge the speed of change in traditional patterns of social and cultural formations and their significance for politics and citizenship. The information age and its superhighway, changes in the production and dissemination of knowledge, and changing political cultures are important aspects of these changes (Gilbert, 1992). In economic terms, globalization, deregulation, privatization and post-Fordist production interfere with the contractual relations of state and corporation which have underpinned the economic significance of nationhood. The consequences for employment, regional economies and labour/management relations are in the direction of less stability over time, greater movement over space, and a general threatening of the old certainties of the economic system. The precariousness of the cults of the market and individual enterprise can be seen as a threat to any historic compromise or social contract between citizens and the economy.

Postmodernism at the very least serves as a convenient label for these changes, and it is in this periodizing sense that the term is used here, that is, to refer to a series of related and apparently accelerating trends, each facilitating and feeding into changes in the others. This approach is intended to avoid some of the essentializing definitional debates about whether postmodernism should be seen as an exclusively cultural phenomenon, whether it is better seen as 'high modernism' or a totally new social formation, and the rather pointless arguments about when postmodernism might be said to have begun.

Whether or not these changes account for the interest in education for citizenship mentioned above, they do provide a context and a set of criteria which might be used to evaluate the various policies and prescriptions which the reports and curricula have produced. What follows is a review of certain aspects of these changes, key dimensions of the postmodern world, and their implications for education for citizenship.

Disorganized Capitalism and Post-industrial Production

Perhaps the most basic of changes associated with the postmodern world is the move from modern forms of industrial production to postindustrial or post-Fordist modes of production, and disorganized capitalism. In their summary of this disorganization, Crook, Pakulski and Waters (1992, p. 29), drawing on Lash and Urry (1987), include a range of elements with important implications for the idea and experience of citizenship.

First, disorganized capitalism involves the geographical dispersal of production and distribution through the globalization of markets and industrial deconcentration. One indicator of this is the trebling of international direct investment during the decade of the 1970s (Massey, 1994). The growth of the transnational company and the disaggregation of national economic power threatens national economic organization based on corporate arrangements between the state and the national private sector. The risk that this poses for the power and authority of national governments is obvious. Along with this spatially mobile industrial organization comes flexible work organization and the decline of old industrial cities. This produces new differentiations of classes and labour markets with the emergence of a service class of managers and professionals, a reduced manufacturing working class, and decentralized industrial relations. One effect of these changes is to reorient traditional political allegiances of industrial societies, and to break down the corporate relationships among industry, labour and the state.

This change in corporate capitalism erodes the concept of citizenship which developed in conjunction with its earlier forms. For instance, the decline in class voting raises the question of what will replace it. Low voter turnouts, an increasing cause of concern in those countries with voluntary voting (Heater, 1990, p. 289), threaten the legitimacy of the state as the embodiment and guarantee of citizenship, and reduce the role of the electoral system as a form of citizen participation and action. Equally, decentralized industrial relations weaken the form of political involvement organized around labour unions.

In addition, disorganized capitalism with its reduced national-political control over economic enterprises contributes to the weakening of the resources of the state, with challenges to the services and especially welfare provisions it is able to sustain. With this threat to the welfare state, the Western democracies risk losing a key element of the modern concept of citizenship as outlined by T.H. Marshall (Marshall, 1964). This view has seen citizenship as 'a status bestowed upon those who are full members of a community. All who possess the status are equal with respect to the rights and duties with which the status is endowed' (p. 92). A key element of this status of citizenship, along with the civil and the political, is the social element, ranging from 'the modicum of economic welfare and security to the right to share to the full in the social heritage and to live the life of a civilised being according to the standards prevailing in the society' (p. 78).

The decline in state provision of welfare is most evident in privatization of public enterprises in such areas as education and public housing, reductions in state controlled health care, and various cost-recovery schemes. If welfare rights are not guaranteed by the state, who will guarantee them? Will the status of citizen lose its connection with the entitlement to welfare rights if the state loses its ability or desire to protect them?

These threats may of course be balanced by other developments in the postmodern world. The growth of social movements could lead to a greater and more direct form of citizen participation than that previously found in the more centralized bureaucratic states. This could restore the legitimacy of the state if electoral systems became more sensitive to minority interests than the currently dominant two party systems. Similarly, decentralized industrial relations could increase workers' involvement in decisions about their working conditions, if they can be supported by legislated power to ensure fair bargaining arrangements. Nonetheless, these trends in postindustrial production have clear implications for the viability of the concept of citizen in the modern nation state. Consequently, they raise important questions about desirable directions for education for citizenship if it is to respond to this changing context.

Key questions here are whether the concept of citizenship includes the relation of citizen to economy, and whether it recognizes the importance of social and economic entitlements at global, national and local levels.

Rob Gilbert

Consumption

While post-Fordist production reduces the stability of productive relations around which much of modern industrial life has been organized, at the same time, post-modern lifestyles are seen increasingly to focus on consumption as people's most direct and conspicuous connection with the economy. Miller (1995, p. 31) argues that people seek to establish identities as consumers in the face of the large-scale and anonymous rationalization of modern industry, trade and bureaucracy:

> This means that people increasingly come to face the world in a secondary relation, in which they do not themselves identify with the institutions that produce and distribute goods and services. To that extent they increasingly see themselves as consumers as opposed to producers . . . this establishes one of the main imperatives behind much modern consumption, which is an attempt by people to extract their own humanity through the use of consumption as the creation of a specificity, which is held to negate the generality and alienatory scale of the institutions from which they receive goods and services.

Most commentators see the role of consumption in this postmodern world to be damaging to the sociality on which a sense of community must be based. Also, while it may be true, as Miller claims, that past politics has relied on a formal public rationality which has alienated the citizenry, few observers see the move to consumption as an improvement, as 'the new consumerism on the other hand is all about floating visual images, pleasures and impossible dreams' (Mort, 1989, p. 169), emphasizing a private sphere in which people find solace and satisfaction in getting and spending.

The growth of consumption as central to people's experience of the economic, and of the mass media and informationalism as the dominant mode of the cultural, are increasingly closely related:

> From spiralling prices on the international art market to the legitimation of consumer culture even in the Eastern bloc and the role of PR and image in hyping everything from global brands to green issues and government policies, all the evidence points to the collapse of any firm line between 'culture' and 'commerce'. (Hebdige, 1990, p. 19)

For Wexler (1990), this kind of consumerism, and the role of advertising and the media, especially television, constitute consumer objects as a system of signs, in which people find meaning and an illusory sense of self-determination in the act of consumption. In this process of commodification and communication, goods are valued for what they mean as much as for what they 'are' or for what they are 'used'. Advertising and product image themselves become goods consumed for their own sake and are no longer simply representations of 'real' products. Signs and codes become part of the fundamental dynamic of society, with the result that 'Citizenship is like being a fan, who votes favorably for media products by purchasing them, extolling their virtues, or wearing their iconic packaging on one's bill cap or tee shirt' (Wexler quoting Luke (1986–7, p. 72)).

Miller (1995) puts a different interpretation on the changing practices of consumption, arguing that much of the doomsaying from the right and the left is based on a series of myths which exaggerate the homogeneity, superficiality, novelty and asociality of consumerism. In fact, Miller sees consumerism as 'the vanguard of history', in which the rhetoric of consumer choice can be a progressive force if people are empowered to use it to arbitrate the moralities of institutions that provide goods and services. Consumption in his view is 'a relatively autonomous and plural process of cultural self construction' which, unlike the constraints of state-imposed controls and reforms, acknowledges 'the potential and creative power of diverse human groups to make of their resources what they will' (Miller, 1995, p. 41). It 'allows room for a morality of egalitarianism that posits equality at a more appropriate place within societal self-construction than that postulated by socialism' (p. 42).

Citizenship as entitlement becomes central to this issue, since in the consumer society where even basic services are being privatized and 'user pays' principles applied, rights of welfare entitlement in a market context take on new and important meanings, becoming more difficult to guarantee as universally available. This also heightens the importance of social and economic rights. Where previously civil and political rights have dominated rights debates, social welfare rights increasingly take centre stage, and principles of equality which drive civil and political citizenship raise challenging questions when applied to the economic sphere.

As Miller (1995, p. 44) points out, the literature on citizenship seems preoccupied with political discussion about the proper relationship of the citizen to the state, neglecting the relation of the citizen to the market: 'The neglect of this issue has left the field wide open for a quite different position, which equates consumer interest solely with the market' — and an idealized form of the market at that. Miller argues the need for a pluralism in which the rights of consumerism are more fully articulated with the responsibilities which those rights entail, responsibilities which can be found expressed by many green and cooperative consumer movements. This task will be assisted by an understanding of 'the massive influence of consumption upon the political economy, while acknowledging the political economy inscribed in the historical projects given to people as consumers' (Miller, 1995, p. 55).

Education for citizenship in a postmodern consumer society needs to acknowledge the role of consumption as a key dimension of life whereby people find pleasure, identity and forms of expression as well as utility. Consumption becomes a link with the (increasingly global) economy, and a means of showing how economic processes affect people's daily lives. It demonstrates in very palpable and salient ways an important dimension of citizenship rights, a dimension which is particularly relevant to people of school age. Acknowledging consumption is therefore an important need but also a clear opportunity for education for citizenship.

The Information Society

The information revolution is among the most pervasive forms of social change experienced by the present generation. In the advanced capitalist economies, information workers (including computer manufacturing, telecommunications, mass media, advertising, publishing, accounting) comprise more than half the workforce. Central among these is the growth of the culture industries, especially in the English speaking world, where the international market for film, television, music, sport, and the promotional trappings that go with them, are leading to a standardization of the everyday cultural experiences of millions across the globe. The implications of these developments for identity and attachments to the nation are still rather speculative, but they cannot be passed off as insignificant.

In the Western democracies, the mass media and its images, especially television, now construct the network for social relations, but this makes these relations much less stable than before. Baudrillard sees in this effect a metaphor of society as 'a random gravitational field, magnetised by the constant circulations and the thousands of tactical combinations which electrify them', with the result that 'the rational sociality of the contract . . . gives way to the sociality of contact' (Baudrillard, 1983, p. 83). Kroker and Cook elaborate this style of analysis in the following way:

> Our general theorization is, therefore, that TV is the real world of postmodern culture which has *entertainment* as its ideology, the *spectacle* as the emblematic sign of the commodity-form, *life-style advertising* as its popular psychology, pure, empty *seriality* as the bond which unites the simulacrum of the audience, *electronic images* as its most dynamic, and only, form of social cohesion, *elite politics* as its ideological formula, the buying and selling of *abstracted attention* as the locus of its marketplace rationale, *cynicism* as its dominant cultural sign, and the diffusion of a *network of relational power* as its real product. (Kroker and Cook, 1986, p. 270)

Living through television fragments and displaces the real; experience is diffused by the seriality and lack of differentiation in the representation of the world as images. One result is that it is more difficult to envisage far reaching social change and reform, and political activism, always an uncertain commitment to the long haul, becomes a doubtful investment.

> With the development of mass consumption and mass systems of information, social styles and cultural practices become mixed into an indefinite medley of tastes and outlooks. With this fragmentation of culture there also goes a fragmentation of sensibilities, a mixing of lifestyles and the erosion of any sense of a cogent political project or coherent political programme, as the lives of individuals become increasingly merely a collection of discontinuous happenings. (Turner, 1989, p. 212)

Telepolitics and network news, mass audience soaps, the production of demand through the manipulation and consumption of images — these are conspicuous features of the information society. Wexler (1990) takes up the implications of this 'semiotic society' for individual identity, since 'identity dynamics, like knowledge, are different in the semiotic society', and if citizenship is to survive as a meaningful term, 'it will have to be recreated within this new social, class, and psychological reality' (p. 171). Wexler is pessimistic about how this trend can be reversed, what possible alternatives can arrest the power of the semiotic society, where individual moral autonomy is lost in the face of the media's fragmented rendition of the world.

The tendency, in this view, is for people to see consumption, and especially consumption of the products of the culture industries which seem most compatible with this lifestyle, as the mark of social success and the good society:

> a world full of 'designer cultures' created for the needs of groups, presented by media persons, film and pop stars, advertisers, sportsmen, evangelists and million-aires, to fill the cultural void left by the collapse of cultural traditions. Political culture in a postmodern world may become more like a script and less an inherited narrative for life. (Gibbins, 1989, p. 24)

An alternative view is that, far from being a threat to citizenship, television coverage of politics, world events and investigative journalism has shown a different set of possibilities, which are potentially critical, as demonstrated in the democratic revolutions of Eastern Europe. Even the much maligned talkback shows can give voice to those who would otherwise be silenced. The difficulty lies in the tension between the profit motive and commercial interests which dominate the media and the need for a public morality in the production of news and information. As Brune points out (1993, p. 157, quoted in Morley and Robins, 1995), 'You cannot, at the same time, be treated as a marketing target and be respected as an active political subject'.

If the electronic media have undermined the sociality on which a communal public opinion and political tradition might be based; if politics has been reduced to a television spectacle, and debate to talkback shows; how will people work together to consider and resolve issues which affect them all? What new roles and practices must people enter into if they are to participate in a politics for these new circumstances? An education for citizenship which addressed these issues would give attention to the need for students to be empowered in their dealings with the information society, not only in their capacity to understand and critique it, but also in the ability to use the media of the information society to promote ideas and action.

Globalization, the Media and National Identity

The process of globalization in production, consumption and information exchange is far from complete, but it shows no signs of abating. In the present context the most important implication is for the role of the nation state as the essential base on which citizenship and democracy are founded. Globalization, and its associated processes of localization, are in many respects reducing the power and importance of national governments. The legitimacy of national governments is put in question when their decisions can be challenged in international forums, and their authority over their citizens is similarly weakened. This, along with the significance of immigrant minorities in much of the world, must raise questions about the nation as a source of identity and a base for community.

Political globalization is evident in the growing importance of political blocs such as the European Union and others, where what were once trade alignments are being broadened into cultural and political responsibilities. International organizations like the United Nations are also taking more active roles with respect to national governments, not least through the range of important treaties and agreements based on the UN Declaration of Human Rights. Membership of these global political entities places the notion of national citizenship in a new light, sometimes challenging the authority of national government, at other times providing national governments with powers and arguments on which their own internal decisions can be argued and implemented.

The quintessential site of globalization is found in the media industries, for not only do they demonstrate the transnational ownership structures and production and distribution features of economic globalization, but they are able, through their ideological power, to promote it as a desirable form of world progress. Transnational media companies, with strong vertical integration across hardware and various forms of production and distribution, have overtaken the earlier nationally based media of newspapers and public broadcasters.

Morley and Robins (1995) provide telling evidence of the strength of the commitment to globalization in the media industries. They quote the ex-head of Time Warner, Steven Ross that 'the new reality of international media is driven more by market opportunity than by national identity' (Ross, 1990, quoted in Morley and Robins, p. 11). Ross sees a new world order 'on the path to a truly free and open competition that will be dictated by consumers' tastes and desires', where 'The competitive market place of ideas and experience can only bring the world closer together'. 'It is up to us', says Ross, 'the producers and distributors of ideas, to facilitate this movement and to participate in it with an acute awareness of our responsibility as citizens of one world. We can help to see to it that all peoples of all races, religions, and nationalities have equality and respect' (Ross, 1990, quoted in Morley and Robins, p. 12). Whether the kind of equality and respect desired by the peoples of the world coincides with Ross's version is the obvious question here.

To such proponents of media globalization, nations are becoming obsolete, a hindrance to the free flow of commerce and ideas. Morley and Robins quote an IBM spokesperson as saying:

> For business purposes the boundaries that separate one nation from another are no more real than the equator. They are merely convenient demarcations of ethnic, linguistic and cultural entities. They do not define business requirements or consumer trends. (Morley and Robins, 1995, p. 10)

The Americanization of the media, while a more complex process than the simpler forms of the cultural imperialist model might have it, nonetheless operates powerfully to differentiate the cultural experiences of people around the world (Lash, 1990). Morley and Robins (1995, p. 18) report that the American share of the European cinema market is 75 per cent, whereas the non-US share of American box-office takings is only 2 per cent.) In such a context the commonalities and differences on which national identities rely are under threat. If Morley and Robins are correct in the following prescription for sustaining national identity, then the transnational media are less likely to provide it than the national ownership, production and distribution structures they replaced:

> The cohesion of collective identity must be sustained *through time*, through a collective memory, through lived and shared traditions, through the sense of a common past and heritage. It must also be maintained *across space*, through a complex mapping of territories and frontiers, principles of inclusion and exclusion that define 'us' against 'them'. (Morley and Robins 1995, p. 72)

The history of citizenship is intimately bound up with the nation state as the site of civil and political power. The history of citizenship education has been equally national in character. Lyotard, consistent with the postmodern suspicion of grand narratives, sees this as symptomatic of the constraining nature of citizenship based on nationhood. In his view, 'The State resorts to the narrative of freedom every time it assumes direct control over the training of the "people", under the name of the "nation", in order to point them down the path of progress' (Lyotard, 1984, p. 32). There is little doubt that national histories have seen the development of nations and hence national identity (or, at least, their own) as a logical step in the path to progress.

The challenge for the proponents of national identity is to find a moral basis for selecting the traditions which will be promoted as the collective memory, and for distinguishing the 'us' from the 'them' without engendering ethnocentrism or xenophobia. Their dilemma is that any genuine search for national traditions which will promote the welfare of all their people can be satisfied only by universal humanitarian principles; but these must then undermine any attempt to distinguish the welfare of the nation from the welfare of those outside it. National identity may be an important basis for explaining the attempts by a certain collectivity to promote human welfare (if that has been its aim), but in a time of increasing globalization, the moral high ground, and ultimately the most fertile for universal citizenship, will more and more be the territory of the internationalists.

This must be one of the greatest questions by which to test the theories and practices of education for citizenship. Promoted as they are by nation states, and historically grounded in such a strong tradition of grand narratives of progress through the story of the nation, programs in education for citizenship will surely find the concept of world citizenship difficult to accept and even more difficult to reconcile with the nationalist agenda.

Environment, Place and the Sense of Nation

Discussions of citizenship involving political philosophies of the relation of individual and state are inevitably abstract. Educators have long struggled to make this abstraction concrete in their attempts to explain the significance of national identity and citizens' rights and responsibilities. This difficulty has been complicated in recent times by the recognition of the world as a single system in which changes in one part have important and very concrete effects on others. Environmental problems extend beyond states, and again distract from the national focus which has so dominated education for citizenship.

Modern industrial production has bequeathed to the postmodern world an inheritance of environmental degradation which has strengthened the globalization of political decision making and again shown the limitations of a world order based on the nation state. The energy crisis, pollution, the ozone layer, nuclear power, the use of deep sea resources, the question of Antarctica are among a range of environmental changes external to the nation state, and requiring a multilateral approach and new forms of international political power. Beck (1992) argues that the range of hazards has produced a social framework built on the need to contain risks. The significance of this 'risk society' is that the hazards and risks know no national boundaries, and that their effects are not distributed on class lines. Nuclear, chemical and genetic technology developed on a global scale in supra-national corporations is not controllable in traditional national terms. It also produces dissensus on the value of progress. However, citizen concern is stimulated by media reports of international disasters like Chernobyl, threats to the ecosphere from depleted ozone and the greenhouse effect, and images of 'skeletal trees or dying seals' (Beck, 1992, p. 119).

An important outcome of these concerns is the flourishing environmental movements, and organizations like Greenpeace and green political parties parallel the movements of identity politics. Lash and Urry (1994, p. 297) argue that environmental concern has led people increasingly to view humans as part of nature, and become less committed to conquering or dominating it. People are thought to have special responsibilities *for* nature, partly because of their unprecedented powers of global destruction. They also have such responsibility because of the particular human capacity to act reflexively, to project environmental degradation and see the need for behavioural change.

Further, environmental concern leads to a view of nature as global or holistic, a perception promoted by the media which has generated an imagined community of all societies inhabiting one earth. Finally, the notion of the rights of future generations to a sustainable future and a life in a quality environment is an important addition to the rights debate.

The significance of environmentalism is that environmental concerns, movements and politics raise new considerations for citizenship. They give material substance to the notion of global citizenship, offer important forms of political expression, introduce new concepts of rights, and, as illustrated by the Brundtland Report's title *Our Common Future* (World Commission on Environment and Development, 1987), are the basis of shared values and experiences in the material contexts of daily life. As a result, environmentalism raises the prospect of a citizenship firmly based in experience, and one which is more communal than individualism, and more material than communitarianism. The potential for motivation in environmental citizenship is therefore very strong (Gilbert, in press).

Further evidence of globalization is the increased migration of the late twentieth century, and other movements of people as refugees, migrant workers and the representatives of international government and corporations. The democratic rights of such minorities groups and individuals are important issues at the turn of the century, and are clearly a matter of global concern where the concept of citizenship is a crucial factor. In addition, footloose industry, the mobility of populations, the hybridization of cultures and the cultural effects of media globalization are breaking down the integration of political, linguistic and cultural power on which the traditional nation state was based.

National identity, not to mention loyalty, becomes problematic in a world of increasingly transient populations. The massive increase in the refugee populations of the world is the most spectacular and damaging indication of this, but members of immigrant middle classes in the first world are also affected in less conspicuous ways, but with important consequences for the notion of identity. Some insight into their situation is offered by Madan Sarup, who was taken from India to England at the age of 9, his mother having died earlier, Sarup's father returned to India for the war, and died during the partition of 1947. In his reflections on his move and its effects on his sense of home and the politics of place, Sarup (1994, p. 93) asks:

> Am I British? Yes, I have, as a friend pointed out, a 'white man's' house, and I've forgotten my mother tongue, but I do not feel British. I think of myself as an exile and it's painful here, *and* there in India when I return for short visits. I don't have the confidence to become, as some have suggested, cosmopolitan. But like so many others, I am preoccupied by ideas of home, displacement, memory and loss.

Massey (1994) discusses the sense of place as a foundation for identity, and the view that this foundation is threatened by the pace of postmodern change and time-space compression, leading to the vulnerability and displacement described by Sarup. Massey reviews attempts to search for the 'real' meaning of places, such as the unearthing of heritages, in the desire for fixity and security of identity in the midst of movement and change. The belief is that 'A "sense of place", of rootedness, can provide a stability and a source of unproblematical identity' (Massey, 1994, p. 151). However, this runs the risk of being a romantic evasion of the reality of change with potentially reactionary effects. (For instance, the search for security in a traditional territorial identity is a key element of the idea of ethnic cleansing.)

Massey acknowledges people's need for a sense of geographical difference, of uniqueness and rootedness, but says this need not lead to the idea that places have single, essential identities. Describing the special character of her local area of Kilburn, its diverse cultures and connections with the world, and her affections for it, she concludes:

> Kilburn certainly has 'a character of its own'. But it is possible to feel all this without subscribing to any of the static and defensive — and in that sense reactionary — notions of 'place'. It is absolutely not a seamless, coherent identity, a single sense of place which everyone shares. It could hardly be less so. People's routes through the place, their favourite haunts within it, the connections

they make (physically, or by phone or post, or in memory and imagination) between here and the rest of the world vary enormously. If it is now recognized that people have multiple identities then the same point can be made in relation to places. Moreover, such multiple identities can either be a source of richness or a source of conflict, or both. (Massey, 1994, p. 153)

A sense of place appropriate for the times would recognize in our world 'not just all the physical movement, nor even all the often invisible communications, but also and especially all the social relations, all the links between people', for the geography of social relations is changing: 'Economic, political and cultural social relations, each full of power and with internal structures of domination and subordination, stretched out over the planet at every different level, from the household to the local area to the international' (p. 154). This perspective gives rise to an alternative interpretation of place. In this interpretation:

what gives a place its specificity is not some long internalized history but the fact that it is constructed out of a particular constellation of social relations, meeting and weaving together at a particular locus. If one moves in from the satellite to the globe, holding all those networks of social relations and movements and communications in one's head, then each 'place' can be seen as a particular, unique, point of their intersection. It is, indeed, a *meeting* place. Instead, then, of thinking of places as areas with boundaries around, they can be imagined as articulated moments in networks of social relations and understandings, . . . And this in turn allows a sense of place which is extroverted, which includes a consciousness of its links with the wider world, which integrates in a positive way the global and the local. (Massey, 1994, p. 154)

One result of this understanding is that places need not be conceptualized only in terms of boundaries and counterposition to the outside, but can be defined also through 'the particularity of linkage *to* that "outside" which is therefore itself part of what constitutes the place' (Massey, 1994, p. 155).

If these networks of relations are increasing in number and importance in the postmodern experience, as the evidence suggests, then such an approach to place and identity will become even more necessary. What hope then for a notion of citizenship which relies on the construction of an identity based on an inward looking national territorial tradition whose existence is premised on its difference from and independence of all others? If connectedness rather than separation becomes the key to the character of places, then there will be an increasing tension between identity based on territorial exclusion and that produced by the experience of globalization. Education for citizenship will need to acknowledge this tension, seeing it as an opportunity to connect citizenship with the reality of the global village rather than something to be feared by the nation state.

Identity, Democracy and the New Politics

Some commentators see these developments in the globalization of economy and culture as major threats to democracy itself. Participation in the political project of citizenship requires some recognition of common interests and values derived from shared past experience, as well as a desirable future sufficiently general as to have a broad appeal. If life in the West is increasingly characterized by precarious economic relations, the instantaneous seriality of electronic information, and by views of knowledge which dissolve history's grand narratives, how can a common base for such a general vision be found? This problem constructs itself around the notion of identity. Harvey (1989, p. 53) sees the validity of the concept of post-modernism as depending on 'a particular way of experiencing, interpreting, and being in the world'. From this perspective, the importance of postmodernity lies not in the objective forms of media, technology, or information, but in how they are appro-priated into new modes of experience and expression — how they shape identity.

Jameson points out that if personal identity is found in the 'unification of the past and future with the present before me', and if this unification requires a consensual narrative and stability of meaning, then it is impossible in a postmodern world: like the schizophrenic, we are 'reduced to an experience of pure material Signifiers, or in other words of a series of pure and unrelated presents in time' (Jameson, 1984, p. 72). Harvey (1989, p. 54) concludes 'The immediacy of events, the sensationalism of the spectacle (political, scientific, military, as well as those of entertainment), become the stuff of which consciousness is forged'.

Wexler (1990) argues that the postmodern decline of independent universal standards of judgment deprives the individual of autonomy by dissolving the ground for a unified self. Lacking an autonomous moral discourse comparable to religious or cultural tradition, individuals can no longer centre their actions in a stable morality. Since societies and individual identity are so fragmented, the base for the individual–society contractual relation (on which citizenship has been said to depend), no longer exists.

> In the absence of collective memory of traditions, in conditions of simultaneous demand for orderly, serial practice — the administered world of modern corpor-atism — and flexible response to destabilizing sign circulation, the burden of identity labor falls toward the personal, narrative construction of a fictitious self order. Socialization is desocialized, deregulated, and like the more visible institu-tional apparatuses of the phase of industrial welfarism in decline, self-constructive practices are reprivatized. (Wexler, 1990, p. 172)

The problem here is not the loss of history *per se*, for there is no single history whose loss necessarily threatens democratic citizenship. In fact, some histories are themselves a threat, especially those which present the idea of progress as some natural working out of an inevitable historical force, or which see state or capital as the source of wisdom and order. What can be lost with history is the understand-ing that the present has been made by people, whether or not in conditions of their own choosing. History can demonstrate both the power and the frailty of people's attempts to improve their condition, and it is history as the record of the struggle for various versions of democratic citizenship that is so important, both in the successes that can be demonstrated, and the battles which have yet to be won.

However, the view that postmodernism poses a threat to longstanding features of Western democratic life is countered by a different assessment. Some see positive possibilities in the differentiation and proliferation of contacts and experiences flowing from the diversification of social worlds which constitute the postmodern experience. Hall (1989, p. 129) notes that each of these worlds has

> its own codes of behaviour, its 'scenes' and 'economies', and . . . 'pleasures', and for those who have access to them they do provide space in which to assert some choice and control over everyday life . . . to 'play' with its more expressive dimensions. This 'pluralisation' of social life expands the positionalities and identities available to ordinary people (at least in the industrialized world) in their everyday working, social, familial and sexual lives.

The new social movements and the identity politics they have generated can be seen as outcomes of these developments. A new politics has arisen in which political divisions and processes are decoupled from socio-economic structure and the market relations of production and exchange (Crook et al., 1992, p. 39). With the decline of class voting and major party membership, political constituencies are increasingly generated around general values and lifestyles, involving status, generational and special interest group categories rather than socio-economic groups.

This is associated with a new political culture which creates new forms and issues for political activity. Gibbins (1989) lists the characteristics of what he calls the postmodern political culture:

- an affluent 'postmaterialist' middle class has created new alliances around environmental, peace and feminist issues, and new forms of political expression in symbolic and life style politics;
- political order and legitimacy are threatened as objectivity, commensurability, unity and the integrated self are deconstructed, and replaced by relativity, pluralism, fragmentation and polyculturalism;
- postmodernism signifies discontinuity among economy, society and polity; an information and consumer economy coincides with heightened conflict between public and private spheres, growing distrust of government, and realignments of party and class allegiances;
- an eclectic and amorphous culture of plurality and mixed lifestyles is combined with an emphasis on leisure and consumption, and freedom, spontaneity and gratification take precedence over discipline, authority and predictability;
- the emerging character of contemporary political culture is pluralistic, anarchic, disorganized, rhetorical, stylized, and ironic.

Paralleling and encouraging this change is the sense that the state is no longer the key to basic civil and political rights. For instance, Crook et al. claim:

> The key rights associated with citizenship, especially civil and political rights, are gradually becoming detached from state guardianship. Many are being redefined

as 'universal rights', 'human rights' or 'individual rights', and their guardianship is increasingly located above and beyond the state, either in supra-state agencies (for example, the UN Commission for Human Rights) or in the general notion of 'human status' incorporated into international laws and conventions. Moreover, the publicity given to violations of these rights by the states changes public perceptions of the relationship between civil rights and the state. (Crook et al., 1992, p. 103)

These developments are strengthened by the political tenets of new social movements, whose activists often eschew the established political system, preferring media politics, self-organization and direct action to 'the established elites and centralized state apparatuses, whose effectiveness, rationality, and ability to represent collective good are all doubted' (Crook et al., 1992, p. 148). Groups such as Greenpeace, with their non- or even anti-nation state *modus operandi*, provide an interesting parallel with the transnational corporations with whom they are often in conflict.

Combined with this is the focus of new social movements on a symbolic language quite different from the language of ideology, interests and programs by which the state has identified politics as a separate social arena. This focus on the symbolic draws the new politics more closely into the cultural sphere, and 'merges well with such other symbolic elements as mode of dress, behaviour, aesthetic taste and dietary habits into a recognisable and distinctive counter-cultural lifestyle' (Crook et al., 1992, p. 155).

An important aspect of this identity politics is its challenge to the traditional restriction of the concept of citizen to the public sphere. The arena of citizenship has been the formal institutions of politics and law, and the definition of citizen rights have been located in these institutional relationships. It has therefore been difficult to include within this traditional concept a range of interpersonal and intrapersonal concerns. It has also meant that where these issues have been acknowledged, their solution has been conceived in formal legal terms which have often proven inadequate to the task at hand. The consequence is that, for instance, recognizing rights and obligations in the workplace or the home are not seen as part of being a citizen, and the ethics on which relationships are to be based are sought in established legal principle rather than the development of human values. Given the importance of these aspects of life, this is a limited concept of citizenship.

A key example of this problem is in the area of gender. Young (1987) argues that modern political theory has entrenched the dichotomy between reason and desire in the distinction between the universal, public realm of sovereignty and the state on the one hand, and the particular private realm of needs and desires on the other. The state has attained its generality by excluding particularity, desire, feeling and those aspects of life associated with the body. As a result, domestic violence, the sexual division of labour, and sexual preference have struggled to be recognized as issues worthy of consideration as part of the rights of citizenship. Similar difficulties have faced ethnic minorities in extending the fight against racism beyond the formal equalities of political and legal process.

Young's response is to reiterate the meaning of public as what is open and accessible, and to argue that no social institutions or practices should be excluded a priori as being the proper subject for public discussion and expression. In the case of education for citizenship, citizens' rights need to include consideration of the personal needs of people in areas of human experience related to differences such as gender and race. Both the formal and the informal curriculum in citizenship need to combine this concern for rights of the personal as well as the public spheres. For while participation in the public sphere through the rules that govern it is a key part of citizenship, unless people can see that the rules enshrined there can help them claim their rights in important aspects of their lives, including the private, they will sense a hypocrisy and futility in the claims of the public sphere itself. Citizenship in the age of identity politics needs to break down these barriers.

The implications of the new politics for citizenship education are rather clear. They offer models of citizen commitment and action which are much more tangible than the abstraction of idealist democratic theories. Their concerns are often close to the everyday experiences of citizens and therefore powerfully motivating. Their work is a clear demonstration of the importance of political knowledge and skills and the value of democratic process. In short, social movements and identity politics have brought citizenship to life in ways that offer great educational potential.

Conclusion

The future of citizenship in postmodern conditions depends on how people respond to the changes of postmodernity, how they see their desires and their options, whether they are able to coopt the diverse opportunities of fragmentation and change to their own benefit and to the democratic project. This is very much a matter of the power they have to deal with change, precariousness and uncertainty. It also depends on whether they see themselves not as members of an exclusive national community, but as constituted by the relations with other people and the world. Such a view might find solidarity in the acceptance of difference, stability in the commonality and constancy of change, and security in the collaborative response to precariousness. Such a possibility will require a major reorientation of past notions of citizenship and identity. While these possibilities are at present largely speculative, the fundamental challenge is to recast the relation of identity and nation so that these new notions of democratic citizenship can be addressed.

The solution does not lie in a return to the past in either national political histories or abstract concepts of idealist philosophy. These are too exclusive and monolithic to accommodate the diversity and change of the contemporary world. For instance, the concept of citizenship must give greater attention to an economic dimension to address the realities of post-Fordist production and the significance of consumption. The convergence of individual rights and social entitlements implies an integration of the political and the economic which past notions of citizenship have not acknowledged. Equally, recognizing rather than denigrating the importance of consumption would allow a new focus on how people make decisions about their preferred forms of life. Seeing consumption decisions as a form of citizen action, rather than merely a meaningless material activity, may provide connections with responsibilities to the poor, the environment, and similar issues.

Citizen identity must be seen to lie in the richness of diversity rather than the purity of uniqueness. Education needs to show how connecting with others allows us to share and multiply this richness. This will require a change from the separatist ethos of national formation to a more open regard for other cultures and people. Seeing the earth as the home of humankind is probably the most tangible basis for this acceptance of shared destiny and common purpose, and environmental education and citizenship education become a single project. Similarly, the creation of a world culture through the electronic media can construct a sense of shared experience connecting diverse groups across vast distances. The need to counter cultural imperialism and economic exploitation in this development does not deny the positive possibilities for communication and understanding among peoples. What is necessary is that the information society be one in which citizens are skilled in critically assessing and producing the messages of the new media, so that they are not reduced to being passive consumers of programs created only to produce profit.

Identifying these needs in general terms runs the risk of replacing the old grand narratives with a new set of sweeping claims about contemporary social change. However, in each case, the social diagnoses connect with quite specific elements of educational policy and practice. In this case, curriculum development in education for citizenship can be assessed in terms of the preceding arguments.

Do citizenship education programs integrate the social and economic with the political and civil elements? Is the practice of consumption seen as an arena for citizen action? How will citizen education empower people in their dealings with the media, and does it develop competence in using media forms to express and promote the practice of citizenship? Do programs recognize the importance of a sense of place in the construction of identity, and is this connected with concern for our common future on earth and for the quality of its environment? Does the consideration of the rights and obligations of citizens include their personal welfare in the private sphere as well as their formal status in the public sphere? Does citizenship education promote a view of political action which will empower students to participate in the new as well as the old politics? These are the new issues for citizenship education in a postmodern age.

Part 2:

Country Case Studies in Citizenship Education

5   Citizenship Education in England

Ken Fogelman

Introduction: Before the National Curriculum

Citizenship education has never had a formal place in the school curriculum in England. Of course, this reflects the fact that, prior to the 1988 Education Reform Act, there was no national curriculum and therefore no school subject that was compulsory (with the exception of Religious Education which was specified in the 1944 Education Act). That there was some uniformity in what schools taught was the result partly of tradition and partly of the influence of public examinations taken at the age of 16.

Citizenship education was not a traditional subject. Therefore, whether it was taught at all was entirely dependent on the interest and enthusiasm of individual teachers or schools. Such enthusiasm did exist. Batho (1990) has identified and reviewed the teaching of civics and citizenship in English schools since the Victorian era. The late 1920s and the 1930s were a period when discussion of the topic was particularly intense, and was accompanied by some activity in schools, largely in response to fears about the spread of totalitarianism.

A major contributor to the debate at that time was the Association for Citizenship Education, and it was in one of their publications that Lord Simon of Wythenshawe wrote what many of us would still accept as describing the fundamental purposes of citizenship education:

'. . . the good citizen of a democracy must possess four qualities:

* A sense of social responsibility,

* A love of truth and freedom,

* The power of clear thinking in everyday affairs and

* A knowledge of the broad political and economic facts of the modern world.' (Hubback and Simon, 1934)

The immediate post-war period did see some increased attention to the ideas of world citizenship, but there did not develop any general acceptance of the importance of democratic education for all pupils. If addressed at all, this was generally within subject areas such as social studies, largely for less able students, or within examination syllabuses for British Constitution or Sociology. These did become more common during the 1960s and 1970s, but still very much as minority subjects for grammar schools or the more academic streams of comprehensive schools.

Citizenship education as generally conceived in England does include voluntary and community service. The value of these was emphasized in the Newsom Report (DES, 1963), following which they became more common, both as extra-curricular activities and as time-tabled programmes — but again frequently restricted to less able pupils (for more detail, see Groves (1983) and Edwards and Fogelman (1991)).

In official documents such as those emanating from the Department of Education and Science (DES) and Her Majesty's Inspectorate (HMI), any mention of more general issues relating to citizenship education was rare and limited. One HMI publication, on the curriculum for 11–16-year-olds, did express concern that 'The 1980s may well be years of even greater political and economic tension than the present day . . . the greater will be the need for a basic political and economic education for all' (HMI, 1977). Similarly, in a DES (1980) discussion of a suggested curriculum framework, there was reference to the desirability of teaching leading to 'preparation for a participatory role in adult society', but this was not elaborated on at all.

The 1988 Act and the Whole Curriculum

The period of Conservative government throughout the 1980s and, so far, the 1990s has been one of dramatic changes for the education system in this country, many of them embodied in the 1988 Education Reform Act. Perhaps the most significant of all has been the introduction of a national curriculum. Defined in terms of ten core and foundation subjects, the detail of the national curriculum was developed, separately for each subject, by specialist committees. Neither citizenship education nor any of the other subject areas with which it might be linked, such as Politics or Social Studies, are among the compulsory subjects of the national curriculum.

However, the 1988 Act does place a statutory responsibility upon schools to provide a broad and balanced curriculum which 'promotes the spiritual, moral, cultural, mental and physical development of pupils at the school and of society' and 'prepares pupils for the opportunities and experiences of adult life'. It was in this context that the National Curriculum Council, (NCC), the body which had been established to oversee the national curriculum, began to issue a series of guidance documents on what it termed the 'whole curriculum'. In particular, they referred to supplementing the national curriculum through various cross-curricular. elements.

These first appeared in Circular Number 6 (NCC, 1989), which described three aspects of cross-curricular elements: dimensions, skills and themes. This was subsequently elaborated in Curriculum Guidance 3, on the 'whole curriculum' (NCC, 1990a), which identified:

- dimensions
    - a commitment to providing equal opportunities for all pupils
    - preparation for life in a multicultural society

- skills

    — communication
    — numeracy
    — study
    — problem solving
    — personal and social
    — information technology

- themes

    — economic and industrial understanding
    — careers education and guidance
    — health education
    — environmental education
    — education for citizenship

As indicated above, the themes were not part of the statutory national curriculum. Although Guidance 3 does contain the statement 'It is reasonable to assume at this stage that [the themes] are essential parts of the whole curriculum', elsewhere it is stated that they are 'by no means a conclusive list'. In several places it is emphasized that it is for schools to decide how the themes might be tackled.

Guidance 3 was followed by five further guidance documents, one on each of the themes, the final one of which, Number 8, was on education for citizenship (NCC, 1990b). Although once again there was much emphasis on the content being a 'framework for debate' and not a 'blueprint or set of lesson plans', the guidance offered was quite detailed and consisted of three elements: objectives, content and activities.

Objectives were further subdivided into:

- knowledge (of the nature of community, roles and relationships in a democratic society, the nature and basis of duties, and responsibilities and rights);

- cross-curricular skills (essentially as listed above from Guidance 3);

- attitudes;

- moral codes and values.

For the content, eight 'essential components' were outlined, each accompanied by areas of study and some suggested activities:

- the nature of community;

- roles and relationships in a pluralist society;

- the duties, rights and responsibilities of being a citizen;

- the family;

- democracy in action;
- the citizen and the law;
- work, employment and leisure;
- public services.

There is much which can be debated about this framework — its completeness, the clarity of some of the terms, the lack of an international perspective, and the underlying concept of citizenship which it appears to assume (see, for example, Bottery, 1992). Nevertheless, it remains the clearest and fullest description of a possible curriculum for citizenship education in England which has been offered to date.

Other Influential Reports

During the same period as the guidance documents were in preparation within the National Curriculum Council, the Speaker's Commission on Citizenship was deliberating, and produced its report in 1990. Although it did not have the formal status of the NCC, the political origins of the Commission and the patronage of the Speaker of the House of Commons ensured publicity for its report and recommendations. It is also possible that its influence was more direct, as it did submit evidence to the NCC at the time when Guidance 8 was in preparation.

The Commission was concerned with what it termed 'active citizenship' throughout the community, but a substantial proportion of its recommendations addressed educational issues and implications. In some respects its approach was distinctive from that of the NCC. For example, it did accept the challenge of attempting a definition of citizenship, drawing mainly upon the approach of Marshall (1950) and his distinction among the civil, political and social elements of citizenship. Secondly, the Commission did adopt a more international perspective, specifically by recommending that the study of citizenship should take account of the main international charters and conventions to which the UK is a signatory.

In other respects the Commission's approach was not dissimilar to that of the NCC. It recommended that citizenship should be part of every young person's education, and it offered a description of citizenship education as including: understanding the rules; the acquisition of a body of knowledge; the development and exercise of skills; and learning democratic behaviour through experiences of the school as a community.

A further important document which has appeared since the publication of the NCC guidance is the 1993 report of the National Commission on Education. Despite its title, this is an independent body which undertook a comprehensive review of education in England and Wales. Among its recommendations was that citizenship education should be part of the compulsory core curriculum from the age of seven. The report states that

We consider the teaching of citizenship of great importance. We define the subject in a broad way to concern the relationship between individuals and the world they live in. It relates not only to this country but to the European Community and the world as a whole. It concerns the institutions of democracy and the rights and responsibilities of individuals in a democratic society; the creation of wealth; the role of public and private employers and voluntary organizations; and the opportunities which people have to shape or play a creative part in the life of the community.

The essential point about all these documents, including those from the NCC, is that, unlike the regulations relating to the national curriculum, they have no statutory force. They can be seen as a stimulus to schools, and as providing suggested frameworks for content and approaches to citizenship education and the other cross-curricular themes, but it has been open to schools to decide whether to adopt them in their entirety or in part, to adapt them to their own purposes, or to ignore them completely.

Curriculum Models

The Speaker's Commission's evidence to the NCC included a brief discussion of the place of citizenship within the curriculum, noting the potential links with subjects such as English, History and Personal and Social Education (PSE). Similarly, Duncan Graham, in the foreword to NCC Guidance 8 wrote that 'Elements of [citizenship education] can and must be taught through the subjects of the National Curriculum and other timetabled provision, enriched and reinforced by being woven into the wider work of the school in the community'.

Guidance 3 had in fact suggested a number of ways in which the cross-curricular themes could be approached. These included teaching through other subjects (or 'permeation'), but also separate timetabling, teaching through Personal and Social Education, and long-block timetabling (e.g. activity weeks).

Subsequent publications have developed such ideas further and offered more detailed models. Several chapters in Edwards and Fogelman (1993) discuss the links between citizenship education and the core and foundation subjects of the national curriculum. Indeed the case is made that every subject provides opportunities for citizenship education. Fuller consideration of more general approaches to cross-curricular planning can be found in Morrison (1994).

In the context of an overcrowded curriculum, at least prior to the Dearing review (see below), the permeation model was probably the most realistic approach for schools to adopt, if they chose to address the cross-curricular themes at all. However, it does present a formidable challenge for planning and ensuring coherence and progression in the experiences of an individual student. Morrison (1994) and Edwards and Pathan (1993) do describe some techniques for auditing and monitoring the provision of the themes.

Ken Fogelman

Beyond the Formal Curriculum

It will be apparent from the various versions of citizenship education described above that they have implications which go beyond the content of the formal curriculum and how it is organized. The emphasis on skills, values and attitudes leads to more general questions about the nature of a young person's experience in school. A concept which is frequently mentioned in this context is that of participation. Stradling (1987) has elaborated on this, writing of citizenship education as being *about* participation, *for* participation and *in* participation. Education about participation entails content and knowledge. Education for participation provides skills such as powers of analysis and criticism, but also attitudes and values such as commitment to the community and integrity. Education in participation is based in action and experience. A central concept is that of empowerment.

Many would argue that citizenship education also has implications for teaching methods and styles. This is not a matter of stark alternatives in teaching methods, but many of the objectives of citizenship education do seem to imply, for example: a greater emphasis on group teaching as against whole class teaching; more collaborative and co-operative approaches; greater use of student projects and other student-led activities; more use of resources outside the classroom (see, for example, Kitson, 1993, and Newspapers in Education, 1995).

The broader concept of citizenship education also raises a number of issues about the nature of our schools and the atmosphere or ethos within them. If citizenship education is in part about promoting such values as tolerance and understanding, what models of our schools provide in this respect? What example is given by the relationships within the school — among students, among teachers, and between teachers and students? Do they consistently encourage respect for other points of view? Are systems of discipline and rules based on recognition of rights and responsibilities, or can they sometimes appear arbitrary and irrational?

Also, what opportunities do schools provide for young people to develop and practise the skills of participative citizenship? Are there, for example, school councils, or other structures, through which students can influence important decisions in a meaningful way?

Similarly, do schools foster links with and understanding of the local community? Are there opportunities for students to work with the community, for example with the elderly or with younger children? If so, are they supported by adequate preparation and follow-up so that they are integrated with other parts of the curriculum?

Such issues can be considered in terms of the experience of the student as a citizen of the community of the school, the implications of which are well summarized by Best (1994):

> What are the rights of the citizen? To what is the citizen of a community entitled? . . .
>
> • opportunities to participate in corporate activities, including decision-making;

- opportunities to feel a sense of belonging, pride and a common destiny;

- the right to be treated with respect and valued for oneself;

- the right to have one's liberty protected from the excessive behaviour of others (this will entail a set of rules and a system of sanctions);

- the right to be treated impartially and justly within the rules of the community.

The Schools' Response

The publication of the NCC guidance and other reports described above did at least alert schools that citizenship education was on the agenda for discussion. Furthermore, a number of educational organizations with interests in the area were quick to see the potential for promoting these interests under the banner of citizenship education, and to produce a range of excellent materials for classroom use. For example, the Citizenship Foundation, which had its origins in the promotion of teaching in schools about the law, has published materials for both primary and secondary schools (e.g. Rowe and Thorpe, 1993). Other materials have been produced by several charitable organizations (e.g. Children's Society, 1991; UNICEF — Save the Children, 1990). Funding from industry made possible the establishing of the Centre for Citizenship Studies in Education, at Leicester University, with a wider remit for research and development to support citizenship education in schools.

Thus, there has been no shortage of encouragement, advice and support for schools to respond to the ideas of citizenship education. However, as has been emphasized, citizenship education remained optional, and in a context where schools were having to assimilate and implement the national curriculum, its associated assessment, and many other reforms. Some schools certainly did respond enthusiastically, seeing citizenship education as justifying purposes and activities which they valued, but which were not to be found in the national curriculum. However, given the other pressures and changes which they could not ignore, it is not surprising that many put citizenship education to one side, with a sigh of relief that it was not compulsory.

Research enabling us to go beyond anecdotal impressions of how schools have responded has been rare, but what evidence there is suggests that their response has been surprisingly positive.

A survey of secondary schools conducted for the Speakers' Commission was carried out in 1989 (see Fogelman, 1990 and 1991), at a point where teachers (or at least those who read documents circulated by the National Curriculum Council) would have been aware of the early discussion of citizenship education as part of the whole curriculum, but before more detailed guidance had been issued. This study found a high level of reported activity, though with substantial variation both among schools and across different age ranges within schools. For example, about half of secondary schools reported that their 12–13-year-olds were engaged in community-related activities, rising to 85 per cent for 15–16-year-olds (these figures exclude the very common activity of fund-raising). Similarly, almost all schools indicated that some time was spent in the classroom on citizenship and community studies, although for only a minority was this in the form of regular lessons.

Fieldwork for the study of secondary schools by Whitty et al. (1994) was carried out in 1991–2. They found widespread support among teachers for the cross-curricular themes, including citizenship education, but again actual practice was much more variable, and their representation in school policy documents relatively rare (see also Rowe and Whitty, 1993).

The National Curriculum Review

As the national curriculum worked its way through the school system in the early years of this decade, it quickly became apparent to teachers, and eventually to politicians, that it was unmanageable. As described above, its detail was laid down by committees, whose members were experts in, and enthusiasts for, their particular subject. It was perhaps predictable that the result was a curriculum which was over-specified, and which did not fit into the time available. In addition there were problems with the associated system of regular assessment, which had come to be seen as overly bureaucratic and demanding of teachers' time.

For these reasons, in 1993 the government asked Sir Ron Dearing to chair a review of the national curriculum and its assessment, with a remit to reduce and simplify (Dearing, 1994). During the period of consultation, many of those committed to citizenship education (and the other cross-curricular themes) made representations that the opportunity should be taken to reinforce their importance. However, given the context and atmosphere within which the review was taking place, it was not surprising that this did not happen. Apart from the transporting of some aspects of environmental and health education into the Science curriculum, there was no mention of the themes, either of their content or of the cross-curricular concept. For the time being at least, these had become unmentionable, as they were seen as a complication and an additional burden.

Of course Dearing was aware of wider issues. As he wrote in his report:

> Education is not concerned only with equipping students with the knowledge and skills they need to earn a living. It must help our young people to: use leisure time creatively; have respect for other people, other cultures and other beliefs; become good citizens; think things out for themselves; pursue a healthy life-style; and, not least, value themselves and their achievements.

It was no doubt the compelling need to tackle and reduce the existing national curriculum that prevented further elaboration of these ideas.

Through its detailed recommendations for the reduction of the content of the national curriculum subjects, a major outcome of the Dearing review was the recommendation that the total national curriculum should be more flexible and reduced to account for only 80 per cent of the time available, the use of the remaining 20 per cent to be decided by individual schools. As these, and all other recommendations of the review, have been accepted and are being implemented by the government, it might be hoped that citizenship education would be one option considered favourably by schools for their discretionary part of the curriculum. However, it is early days yet, and many teachers have still to be convinced that the new curriculum will fill only the amount of time intended. Furthermore, there continue to be other pressures on schools, not least from the continuing, even though reduced, national assessment. Results are published for individual schools, often in the form of league tables, and can have a major impact on the reputation and popularity of a school. They are also an important factor in the judgments of school inspections. Schools may well feel that it is in their best interests to devote any discretionary time to further teaching of basic skills and other assessed subjects.

Research carried out a year after the Dearing review confirms that we should not be over-optimistic (Saunders et al., 1995). This survey, which obtained information on all five themes and included both primary and secondary schools, again found relatively positive attitudes to citizenship education: 43 per cent of primary schools and 62 per cent of secondary said that it is an essential or very important part of the curriculum. Few schools, 27 per cent of primaries and only 4 per cent of secondary, reported that they were not addressing it at all. On the other hand, it was still the case for almost all schools that there was no mention, or only a very brief one, of citizenship education in the school development plan. About two-thirds of schools (both phases) stated that pressures on the timetable had been a major constraint on their ability to provide citizenship education; lack of funding for resources and lack of staff expertise were also mentioned by significant numbers.

Schools were also asked about their intended use of the discretionary time made available by the Dearing review. This elicited several rather pointed comments on whether the discretionary time really existed; but the majority of both primary and secondary schools anticipated using it for either basic skills or national curriculum subjects. Nineteen per cent of primary schools and 25 per cent of secondary schools said that they intended to use the time for developing skills for adult life.

The Current Situation

Thus, the overall impression, from the research and from personal experience, is that most teachers are positive in their attitudes to citizenship education. Nevertheless, many feel unable to risk putting it into practice, mainly because of the pressures to meet national curriculum requirements and of league tables of assessment and public examination results.

If that were the end of the story, it would be a rather gloomy conclusion. However, there are two reasons for being a little more optimistic about the future of citizenship education. The first is to be found in the debates and consultations now being initiated by the Schools Curriculum and Assessment Authority (SCAA) (the successor body to the National Curriculum Council). At the time when the Dearing recommendations were accepted, it was announced that there would be a five-year moratorium on any further changes to the curriculum. In recent months it has become apparent that SCAA intends to use this period to conduct a debate on wider curricular issues. Conferences have already been held on, for example, spiritual, moral, social and cultural development, and on the link between education and national identity. Invited papers have been given, and those interested in citizenship education have been strongly represented. It appears likely that there will be a further review of the curriculum towards the end of the five year period; that, unlike when the national curriculum was first introduced, this will be preceded by some consideration of the fundamental purposes of education and the school curriculum; and that citizenship education may be seen as relevant to these.

The second reason for cautious optimism, though many teachers would be surprised to hear it so described, is school inspection. Another significant change brought about by the current government has been the translation of Her Majesty's Inspectorate into OFSTED (Office for Standards in Education). OFSTED's main responsibility is to manage the new, privatized system for inspecting schools. Whereas, in the days of HMI, the majority of teachers would have completed their professional lives without having experienced a full school inspection, the requirement now is that every maintained school will be inspected once in every four years.

School inspectors operate according to handbooks of guidance, revised versions of which were issued by OFSTED in 1995, which specify in detail what aspects of school life are to be inspected, and how. Reflecting the phrase from the 1988 Act which was quoted earlier in this chapter, the handbook contains a section on 'pupils' spiritual, moral, social and cultural development'. This identifies four areas on which inspectors' judgment should be made. The first two are concerned with spiritual awareness and teaching principles which distinguish right from wrong. The remaining two are even more redolent of citizenship education, and are worth quoting in full:

Judgments should be based on the extent to which the school:

- encourages pupils to relate positively to others, take responsibility, participate fully in the community, and develop an understanding of citizenship;

- teaches pupils to understand their own cultural traditions and the richness and diversity of other cultures.

It is well known that OFSTED have had particular difficulty in drafting this section of the handbook, and the revised version reveals a laudable move away from concentrating on pupil outcomes towards inspecting provision and processes. However, it has been in use for only a few months, and, once again, it is too early to know exactly what kinds of evidence inspectors are seeking in these areas, or what evidence schools will choose to present, or what will be the general impact on schools of this aspect of inspection.

In conclusion, citizenship education in England appears to be at a point of transition. Approaches to it in schools continue to be highly variable, but it has survived, at least in some schools, despite a lack of official support and despite other pressures militating against it. Because of the curriculum moratorium, this is likely to continue to be the situation for the next few years, but citizenship education does appear to be back on the agenda and being seriously discussed. It may therefore not be unrealistic to look forward to a time when its place in the curriculum could be more secure, and reinforced by schools inspection.

6 Values and Citizenship Education in Malaysia

Haris Md Jadi

Introduction

The educational reform that began in Malaysia in 1983 saw the introduction of values into the school curriculum. These values which were seventeen in number were prescribed for integration into the primary and secondary school curriculum[1]. Added to these seventeen values, Moral Education as a subject was also introduced for the non-Muslim pupils. The Islamic Religious Studies, which has been a subject in the Malaysian curriculum since independence, is offered to the Muslim pupils. The other addition to these values-related subjects is the introduction of Citizenship Education. However, Citizenship Education is not offered as subject per se but rather being taught as part of the history curriculum.

The passing of the Education Bill 1995, reinforced the position of these values and the values-related subjects in the national system of education. For instance, the Education Bill 1995, explicitly states that:

> the purpose of education is to enable the Malaysian society to have a command of knowledge, skills and values necessary in a world that is highly competitive and globalized, arising from the impact of rapid development in science, technology and information.

The Education Bill 1995 also states that education in Malaysia attempts to provide a balance between knowledge and skills on one side and the inculcation of values on the other. However, it is important to note that Malaysian education provides for the teaching of two kinds of values. One which is based on the universal human values as reflected in the content for Moral Education and the other is based on the values attached to the Islamic religion. Although values that are taught in Islamic Religious Studies overlap with the seventeen noble values of Moral Education, the subjects are offered to two different groups of pupils. For the Muslims it is mandatory for them to take Islamic Religious Knowledge. Non-Muslims must take Moral Education. In addition to these clearly stated values subjects, the whole national curriculum has to be imbued with the seventeen noble values. These values have to be taught across the national curriculum. As for citizenship values, History as a subject has to play its role in nurturing patriotism and loyalty to the country.

The statement of purpose, for education referred to above is also in line with the National Philosophy of Education which states that

Education in Malaysia is an ongoing effort towards further developing the potential of individuals in a holistic and integrated manner so as to produce individuals who are intellectually, spiritually, emotionally and physically balanced and harmonious, based on a firm belief in and devotion to God. Such an effort is designed to produce Malaysian citizens who are knowledgeable and competent, who possesses high moral standards, and who are responsible and capable of achieving a high level of personal well-being as well as being able to contribute to the betterment of the family, the society and the nation at large. (Ministry of Education, 1987)

To understand this new development it is imperative to understand the historical background of Malaysia and its influence on the country's system of education.

Historical Background

Much has been written about Malaysia's historical past. This includes writings on colonialism (Amin and Caldwell, 1977) and the emergence of a plural society which led to the development of the plural school system (Chang, 1973; Loh, 1975). Malaysian education is thus marked by its pluralism, a continuing heritage that it prolonged when it achieved its independence from Britain in 1957. Attempts to establish a single and unified education system with the national language as the main medium of instruction was only realized at the secondary and university level, after the ethnic crisis of 1969. Even today the issue over the language of instruction in school is still sensitive and controversial in Malaysia.

The pluralism in Malaysian education is traceable to the beginning of the British colonial rule in Malaysia. The British forward movement which began towards the end of the nineteenth century saw a large scale importation of labourers from China and India. These labourers became the backbone of the colonial economic machinery without which the exploitation of the states would be almost impossible. For instance, the last decade of the nineteenth century saw a tremendous increase in the revenue collected by the colonial government. According to Roff:

Between 1875 to 1900 the total revenue of the states under British protection rose from well under half a million Straits Dollars to fifteen and a half million, and the value of exports rose from three quarters of a million dollars to more than sixty million. (Roff, 1967, p. 13)

These immigrants who were initially transient became a permanent feature in the Malaysian demographic structure. On the eve of the Second World War, Malaysia's position as a plural society was well established and fitted into Furnivall's (1948, p. 304) definition *where different sections of the community living side by side, but separately within the same political unit. Even in the economic sphere there is a division of labour along racial lines.*

Along with them these immigrants also brought their social and cultural system reminiscent of that of their countries of origin. In the field of education schools were built independently by their respective communities. Out of these emerged the vernacular school system which remains a permanent feature in the Malaysian education system. These schools had no common elements that could make Malaysia as their common focus of loyalty and patriotism. Even the English schools which were supported by the colonial government did not provide a locally oriented curriculum. Instead, the curriculum adopted by English schools was similar to that available in any British public school.

On the eve of the country's independence in 1957, Malaysia inherited a polity which was ethnically divisive in terms of ideological orientation, religious beliefs and political loyalty. It was in this light that the Education Committee of 1956 (Razak Report, 1956) was formed with the view to establishing a national education system that would be acceptable to the population as a whole and at the same time could foster unity and provide common experiences among the future generation (Razak Report, 1956, la).

The *Razak Report* (Report of the Education Committee, 1956), which became an Education Ordinance 1957, was, however, reviewed by the Rahman Talib Report (Education Committee of 1960). The outcome of the Rahman Talib Report was the Education Act, 1961. Both the reports recommended among other things the setting up of a centralized national system of education which provided instruction in vernacular languages at a primary level. At the secondary level only two languages of instruction were allowed and they were the country's national language and English. The important features of the Act were the introduction of a common content curriculum for all schools, a common centralized examination and a common teacher's training program.

It is important to note that the model chosen in its educational structure, organization and its curriculum content were from the English school system. This was understandable considering the absence of any local model that could be used as a basis for the establishment of the new Malaysian system of education. Paradoxically, issues related to the curriculum content and the purpose of education per se did not attract much controversy. It was over the choice of the language of instruction in schools that polarized the indigenous and the immigrant communities. It was also this issue that became a 'single issue politic' in Malaysia for more than a decade after independence.

The indigenous-immigrant polarity could be attributed to the contradictory philosophies over the process of nation-building. Basically the contradictions were over certain constitutional issues related to the position of the indigenous community vis-a-vis the immigrants in the newly independent state. The Federal Constitution defined the special rights of the indigenous communities in the field of education and economy (Art. 153). Added to that the Malay language, which was indigenous was made the national language (Art. 152) and it was recommended by the *Razak Report*, 1956 that it was the ultimate objective to make the national language the main medium of instruction in school (para. 12). In the process, competing demands over political and cultural rights among the various ethnic groups became more apparent. It came to a climax in 1969 when large scale ethnic riots occurred and for a short period of time Malaysia was ruled by the National Operation Council.

It was during the period of the National Operation Council's administration that the New Economic Policy was launched and the RUKUNEGARA or the National Ideology was introduced. The two-pronged objectives of the New Economic Policy were the eradication of poverty and the restructuring of Malaysian society to reduce and eventually eliminate the identification of race with economic functions (Second Malaysia Plan, 1971, p. v). The introduction of RUKUNEGARA was to provide ethical and spiritual guidance for every Malaysian.

Both the RUKUNEGARA and the New Economic Policy were formulated following the ethnic crisis of May 1969. Following the turbulent decade of the sixties, it was realized that the institutional growth within that period had not been successful in inculcating a sense of shared interest in the new state. In short, the country had a long way to go in harnessing the various divergent values into a common national goal. As a result, the ethnic gaps became even wider, conflict potential became even more rampant, and the ethnic consensus that was formulated on the eve of the country's independence was collapsing (Haris, 1993). It was against this background that RUKUNEGARA was formulated.

Civics, Moral and Islamic Education

With such a fragile nation-state inherited from colonial Britain, it was imperative that the system of education aimed at reducing the differences and enhancing the common cultural traits and heritage among the country's diverse population. It was in this light that values were considered as an important component of the school curriculum. Although the Education Committee of 1956 did not specifically mention the need for the teaching of values in school, it did not take a position on the teaching of the Islamic religion. It clearly stated that 'in any assisted school where not less than 15 pupils profess the Muslim religion, religious instruction to them shall be provided at public expense' (para: 121). The official status given to Islamic education for Muslim pupils was in line with the Federal Constitution (Art. 3 (1)) which states that Islam is the official religion of the country.

The Education Review Committee of 1960, however, realized the absence of any values-related subject for the non-Muslim pupils. The Committee recommended that some form of moral education be provided for this group of pupils. The Committee recommended the teaching of 'civics' as an integral part of the curriculum. However, civics as a subject must be taken by all pupils irrespective of their religious backgrounds. The Committee defined the subject as 'good citizenship in the fullest sense of the word' (para. 368). As a subject in the school curriculum civics is being taught at both the primary and secondary levels of education.

The Education Act 1961, was also silent over the teaching of values in schools. However the Act (para. 36 (1)) reiterated the position of Islamic Religious knowledge in the national school system. The Act allowed religious instruction for non-Muslim pupils provided that their parents gave their consent and at the same time did not incur any cost to the government (para. 38).

However, the Cabinet Committee on Education (Ministry of Education, 1979) observed the inherent weakness in the values-related subjects being offered in the school curriculum. For instance there was no values-related subject for the non-Muslim pupils. Thus while the Muslim pupils were having Islamic religious instruction, the non-Muslim pupils were left on their own. The Cabinet Committee found this situation inappropriate. The Committee recommended that the non-Muslim pupils must be given instruction in morals and ethics, subjects which they must also sit for the examination (para. 127.1).

Before the implementation of the national curriculum, Civics Education as a subject was introduced in Standard IV and continues until Form V. Civics is a non-examination subject. The main aim of Civics education was to 'cultivate, instil and foster patriotism, the qualities of tolerance and being considerate, an independent attitude, self achievement and the desire and ability to understand the society's problems as well as be ready to act or contribute towards solving these problems' (para. 130).

The syllabus used for the teaching of Civics was based on the RUKUNEGARA, the Malaysian Constitution and the working of the government. However, there was dissatisfaction with the way this subject was being handled (Haris and Ahmad, 1987). Being a non-examination subject, it was considered unimportant. The Cabinet Report also mentioned that 'most teachers not only do not know how to teach Civics but also possess a negative attitude towards the subject. As a result, the pupils are not interested in the subject' (para. 131).

Values and Moral Education

The National Curriculum which was introduced in 1983 and 1989 for the primary and secondary level respectively, gave a new emphasis on the teaching of values. The integration of seventeen values in the school curriculum and the introduction of Moral Education for the non-Muslim pupils were a departure from previous practice where no values-related subjects had been offered to them. The subject was also made compulsory for the non-Muslim pupils and there was a final examination. However, the position of the Muslim pupils and the Islamic Religious Knowledge instruction remained unchanged.

It is important to note that the seventeen noble values that are to be integrated across the curriculum are also values used as subject content for moral education. As such, the reinforcing of the same values is carried out throughout the pupils' school years. The seventeen noble values thus have two functions. The first is in relation to Moral Education as a subject in the curriculum where they serve as 'subject content' and the second function is as 'noble values' that have to be integrated across all subjects in the school curriculum during the teaching learning process.

The aim of Moral Education for primary schools is to develop individuals with integrity and responsibility through inculcation, understanding and the practice of Malaysian values. The objectives of Moral Education for primary school are:

- To enable pupils to be conscious and understand the n(the society;

- To appreciate the values and use them as a basis for ma everyday life;

- To practice moral habits and behaviour in everyday life;

- To be able to express reasons that are rational when making decisions and taking action.

As for the secondary schools, the objectives of Moral Education are:

- To strengthen and practice habits, and behaviour in accordance with the moral attitude and values acquired at the primary school;

- To be conscious, understand and appreciate the norms and values of Malaysian society;

- To develop rational thinking based on moral principles;

- To give reasonable justification based on moral consideration when making a decision;

- To use moral consideration based on moral principles as guides in the practice of everyday life.

History and Citizenship Education

The position of Citizenship Education in the national curriculum on the other hand is vague and unique. The Education Bill 1995 did not mention the need for any form of Citizenship Education. The national curriculum, however, incorporates the subject in the history curriculum. The history curriculum has two broad objectives. One is for the teaching and learning of history and the other is for the inculcation of citizenship values. In the national curriculum, history education emphasizes on the proper intellectual, spiritual, physical and emotional development of individuals. It is therefore important to note that history education not only aims at developing the historical understanding of individuals but values associated with the subject matter are also being emphasized.

It is assumed that the introduction of citizenship values into the history curriculum is to fill the vacuum created with the omission of Civics Education from the national curriculum. It was felt that history being a core subject throughout the pupils' secondary education years could contribute towards the understanding of historical events that shape the development of the country and this would indirectly contribute towards their political understanding and socialization.

However, it is important to note that history as a subject in the national curriculum is only introduced at the secondary level of education. At the primary level, pupils are not exposed to history as a subject per se. Pupils at the primary level are only introduced to the subject of Local Studies at year four.

At the Lower Secondary Level the aim of history education is to inculcate the spirit of patriotism and the feeling of pride in being a citizen of Malaysia. Through the knowledge and understanding of the country's history, pupils will understand the conditions of the society and the country in creating the spirit of unity and *esprit de corps* towards society and country as a single unit, to create common memory towards history as a reference towards national consciousness and to strengthen the feeling of love towards the country (History Syllabus, Lower Secondary School).

The objectives of history education as stated in the curriculum are to enable pupils:

- To understand the political, economic and social development of society and country;

- To understand and appreciate the social and cultural characteristics of Malaysia and practice them in daily life;

- To appreciate the efforts and contributions of individuals who struggled for the sovereignty and independence, and individuals who contributed towards the development of the country;

- To possess historical consciousness in understanding the existing facts and conditions of the society and country;

- To analyse, summarize and evaluate the country's historical facts rationally;

- To enhance thinking ability and maturity based on the lessons from historical experience;

- To possess consciousness, sensitivity and the spirit of involvement in efforts defending the sovereignty, development and the progress of the country;

The curriculum content for the Lower Secondary School basically emphasizes the history of Malaysia and its development, from its early history until present time. The emphasis is on the acquisition of historical knowledge of Malaysia and the inculcation of the spirit of citizenship. In learning about Malaysia, pupils will be exposed to both the national, local and history of other countries outside Malaysia. As for the inculcation of citizenship values, the emphasis will be on values that could instil the spirit of citizenship. Through the understanding and appreciation of the country's history, emphasis will be given to efforts of building a common Malaysian identity.

As stated in the history curriculum, five main citizenship values are to be instilled and each of these main values carries a wide explanation and elaboration on its scope. The five main citizenship values are: proud to be Malaysian; patriotism; *esprit de corps*; discipline; industrious and productive.

The Pedagogical Issues

In any curriculum reform, the question of its effectiveness has often been the subject of discussion. The pertinent question often evolves around the process of implementation. For instance, how has the intended curriculum been operationally realized? Is the intended curriculum in consonance with the whole educational and social reality of the country?

As far as the national curriculum is concerned it has to be understood philosophically. The curriculum has to be understood in terms of its pedagogical implications. In this respect, teachers have a pivotal role in the whole process of curriculum implementation. As long as the philosophical underpinning of the curriculum is not properly understood, the subject matter of the curriculum could not be translated in the classroom as planned. It is in this respect that the intended curriculum has to be understood and implemented as envisaged by the planners.

In the case of the national curriculum, the intended curriculum is officially documented with elaboration on its philosophy, objectives, contents and even the process of its implementation. Being centrally planned and developed by the Curriculum Development Centre, an agency of the Ministry of Education, the curriculum had to be disseminated and explained to ensure that the implementation was in accordance with its intention. Currently, one of the methods used to disseminate the curriculum is through the *cascading model* where key personnel of specific subjects from each state are selected to attend national level in-service training. This serves to expose them to the new curriculum, its philosophy, contents and the various strategies of implementation (Haris, 1993).

The knowledge of the national curriculum was then disseminated by the state key personnel at the district level. It is from the district key personnel that the knowledge of the curriculum reaches the various subject teachers in school. One of the disadvantages of this model is that by the time the curriculum reaches the teachers, much information has been either *diluted or distorted* (Siti Hawa, 1986).

Another aspect of the curriculum which is rarely discussed is over its ideological underpinning. The philosophy of Malaysian Education is itself ideological in its implications. It explicitly expressed that education in Malaysia aimed . . . *to produce individuals who are intellectually, emotionally, spiritually, and physically balanced and harmonious, based on the firm belief and devotion to God*. In a similar tone the purpose of Malaysian education as stated in the Education Bill 1995, was for the development of knowledge, skills and values. In order that the intended curriculum is operationalized meaningfully there must be commitment in both the curriculum's philosophical and ideological underpinnings on the part of implementing it. As O'Neill (1981, p. 29) points out: 'An individual's beliefs and behaviour correspond to the extent that his professions of belief are corroborated by appropriate types of behaviour'.

From the above discussion, two things could be highlighted. First, the total understanding of the curriculum is imperative if it is to be implemented meaningfully as intended. This means that teachers who implement the curriculum must understand fully the content and the spirit of the curriculum. Secondly, it has been pointed out that the national curriculum is both philosophical and ideological in its application. Philosophically, the curriculum has to be perceived and understood clearly. The teachers have to create and develop a learning situation where the teaching and learning processes involve both the acquisition of knowledge and values. In this respect, the intended curriculum would fail if the commitment towards the expressed values, whether the seventeen noble values or the citizenship values, is absent among the teachers. Finally, the process of curriculum reform involves all the mechanisms and the structures in the educational system. There must be a synergetic movement towards the fulfilment of a common educational aim. In this respect it is of importance to note whether the national curriculum, beginning from its planning and development, dissemination, classroom implementation and the process of evaluation has that flow of coordination and does not exist in any contradictory pattern along the way.

Intention vs. Reality

It should be of note that values and value-related subjects were already in existence under the old curriculum. However subjects like Civics was not an examination subject. As a result schools were not taking the subject seriously. The time allocated for the teaching of Civics was usually used for the teaching of other important examination subjects like mathematics and science.

The national curriculum, in its attempt to create a balance between the cognitive and affective domain emphasized that the seventeen noble values must be integrated across the curriculum. In addition these seventeen noble values were also made the subject content for moral education. In history education, citizenship values were again being integrated as part of its curriculum objective. All these developments as prescribed by the curriculum planners had important implications for the teaching and learning process of the subject.

For any curriculum to be operationalized and its intention realized, there must be an understanding of its underlying ethos besides the understanding of its philosophy. It is in this light that Malaysian teachers are facing a dilemma over its implementation. On one hand they have to fulfil the requirement of the curriculum as prescribed by the central planners and at the same time they have to be aware and realize the social reality of Malaysian education and the demands from the school system.

Malaysian education is highly academic and competitive. Passing the public examination with excellent grades is the dream of all pupils and parents. Schools which produce a high percentage of passes are widely acclaimed while those which do badly are ticked, the teachers being at the receiving end. The announcement of these public examinations is an affair by itself, with the Minister of Education himself announcing the details of the examination results.

Basically, it could be observed that Malaysian education is content and examination centred. It is the highly centralized examination system that dictates the pedagogy of the classroom. In the system which rewards the highly successful pupils, based on the final year public examination, we find it difficult to see effective implementation of values and value-related subjects in the curriculum. In this respect the whole array of people involved in the education of the country know the prevailing paradoxes. They know the reality that the examination system emphasizes strongly the cognitive rather than the affective domain. They also know that society is more interested in scholarship rather than citizenship. Presumably, they are also aware of the flaws in the system.

Conclusion

The Education Bill 1995 attempts to give a new direction to Malaysian education. The new emphasis given towards the acquisition of knowledge and values shows the seriousness of the planners in attempting to provide a balanced education for pupils. The National Curriculum provides all the mechanisms to enhance the spirit as enshrined in the philosophy of Malaysian Education. However, what is being intended has also to be matched with the social reality of the society in general. As had been discussed the reality of Malaysian education is centred around the system of education which is highly competitive and academic in emphasis. Thus it is always difficult for subjects related to values if either the seventeen noble values, moral education or citizenship values are to be given priority in the national curriculum.

Added to this, teachers' understanding of the curriculum also plays a part in the mismatch between what is intentional and what is being operationalized. At the same time a question could also be asked whether the teachers are prepared and given proper training to teach these values-related subjects either in the form of moral education, citizenship values through history education or the inculcation of the seventeen noble values across the curriculum.

From the above discussion can also be observed that values and values-related subjects are important elements in the national curriculum. It is the intention of Malaysian education to equip pupils with knowledge and concurrently inculcate in them Malaysian norms, values and culture. Citizenship education for instance attempts to instil pupils with the spirit of patriotism and loyalty to the state. This is done through understanding historical events that influenced the evolution of Malaysian society. Of importance is the role of values in shaping the future citizens of the country.

The success of the curriculum therefore depends much on the teachers' understanding of the curriculum. Their philosophical orientation and their ideological stand have much influence on the way it is being implemented (O'Neill, 1981). At the same time idealism must also match the reality of the society. The reality is that Malaysians are not willing to sacrifice the scholarship of their children at the expense of any abstract form of idealism. Teachers implementing the curriculum are in a sense pragmatic and they respond well to the needs of the system and society.

Note

1   The 17 noble values are: 1. Kindness 2. Self-reliance 3. High principles 4. Respect 5. Love 6. Justice 7. Courageousness 9. Physical Cleanliness 10. Honesty 11. Industriousness 12. Cooperation 13. Moderation 14. Thankfulness 15. Rationality 16. Socialization 17. Citizenship (latest addition).

7   Civics and Citizenship Education in Hong Kong

Paul Morris

Introduction

This chapter examines the nature and role of civics education in the formal curriculum of schools in Hong Kong since 1945. It begins with a brief analysis of the diverse meanings associated with the concepts of civics, citizenship and political education and then provides an historical overview of the shifting role of civics in Hong Kong schools in the post-war period. Subsequently, the chapter focuses on the various cross-curricular guidelines which are currently the most explicit attempts to promote civic education, in its broadly conceived sense, within the curriculum. The impact of the guidelines is examined through an analysis of how they were interpreted by school principals. The chapter ends with an analysis of the role of the hidden curriculum and a more speculative discussion of what the future holds.

Before proceeding it is necessary to identify a number of Hong Kong's salient features which both distinguish it from the other societies analysed in this volume and which have had a major influence on the development of civics education. Firstly it is not a nation-state — it was a British colony which returned to the sovereignty of China on 1 July 1997, and it now has the status of a Special Administrative Region of China. This arrangement was agreed in the Sino-British Joint Declaration which was signed in 1984. Secondly, whilst Hong Kong displays some of the characteristics associated with the process of decolonization (Von Albertini, 1982), especially the tendency to not provide for fundamental political emancipation, it also displays a number of important differences (Lee and Bray, 1995). Those which have had an impact on the school curriculum include: the strong influence of China in Hong Kong's affairs — to the extent that the colony's existence required at minimum the acquiescence of its neighbour; decolonization is not leading to the creation of a sovereign independent state and the process has not involved an independence movement; the process of decolonization involved a relatively long time period of thirteen years; and this period has seen rapid moves towards democratization of the political system.

Civics, Citizenship and Political Education

The end of the second millennium has seen something of a renaissance of concern for civic education as governments see it as a potential means for addressing problems of social fragmentation, crime and for promoting 'values' ranging from entrepreneurship to patriotism. Whilst the creation and maintenance of nation-states was facilitated by the widening of access to schooling in earlier centuries (Green, 1991) it is again to schools that the state turns as part of the solution to contemporary social problems. Quantitative expansion of schooling is in many societies no longer an option, and the focus is on changing the nature of the curriculum to produce 'good citizens'. The question of 'what is the nature of a good citizen?' is problematic, as is the associated question of how it might be achieved. Central to these questions is the core of civic education — namely the attempt to establish the nature of the relationship between the individual and society.

The Spartan concept of a good citizen was of a 'warrior-citizen' who was committed to serve the military state. The classical Greek concept was based on the need for individuals to be equipped to fully participate in state and community affairs. Giroux (1980, p. 327) describes the classical Greek conception of citizenship education by saying: '. . . education was not meant to train. Its purpose was to cultivate the formation of virtuous character in the ongoing quest for freedom'.

This distinction between a conception of civic education which stresses commitment to the state and/or a preconceived set of values, and one which stresses participation in public and social affairs is one which is central to many attempts to analyse the purposes and approaches to civic education. Wringe (1992), uses this dichotomy to distinguish between citizenship and education for political literacy:

> Unlike those of political literacy, the goals of active citizenship are substantive and specific. They are spelt out in terms of belief and attitudes that are to be acquired and behaviours that are to be adopted. Skills, competencies, and above all understandings . . . do not appear among these goals. The preferred educational model appears to be inculcation.

Similarly, Heater (1990) distinguishes between indoctrination, political socialization, and political education or literacy. Davies (1994) distinguishes between citizenship education for the promotion of 'rights' or for the promotion of 'duties'. These conceptions are associated with very different assumptions about appropriate pedagogies, with a participative/literacy conception stressing the importance of contextualized social and moral issues and social action for the creation of a better society. Citizenship education, which stresses commitment to the status quo, focuses more on providing pupils with appropriate knowledge about the workings of the state, and stresses the responsibilities and duties of a model citizen. This paper uses the term civic education in its broadest sense to include each of these diverse perspectives.

The locus of civic education in the school curriculum is also not easy to identify. In some societies there is a subject called Civics, Citizenship Education or Moral Education. In others it takes the form of 'cross curricular themes' or 'guidelines' which are intended to permeate the whole curriculum. Elements of civic education are also evident in school subjects such as history and social studies, and both the informal and hidden curriculum of schools contain messages for pupils which are thought to contribute to their civic education. It is also necessary to recognize the extent to which precepts and practices might differ. As will be argued in this paper, the state's recent commitment to the promotion of a participative form of civic education in Hong Kong, and the pedagogies associated with that was more a form of symbolic action than designed to affect the implemented curriculum.

Much of the literature on civic education has emerged from scholarship in Western liberal democracies which are relatively well established in terms of political processes and the security of the nation-state. Within these societies the state is portrayed as playing a minimalist role, as operating in pluralist or corporatist contexts, and civil society is viewed as placing a clear demarcation between the rights of citizens and those of the state. There is, therefore, the potential of developing an analysis of civic education based on these precepts which produce portrayals of other societies which are, albeit unintentionally, negatively comparing them to the West in ways which contribute to a form of 'Orientalism' (Said, 1967). Many of the nation-states of East Asia have emerged in their current forms in the post-war period. They are the products of civil wars, many of which are effectively unresolved and the state plays a vital role in defining the nature of the society and the role of education. The tense relationship between former antagonists such as China and Taiwan, and, South and North Korea, has served as a powerful influence on the degree of control of the state over people and organizations generally and on the nature specifically of the curriculum and civic education (Scott, 1996; Marsh and Morris, 1991). Whilst Hong Kong does not pose a military threat to the government of China there has been a tense relationship between them as the respective states attempt to avoid subversion, spiritual pollution and any other threats to their status and survival. That has, as will be elaborated below, exerted a strong influence on civic education in Hong Kong as the state has sought to propagate its vision of civil society (Scott, 1996). The changing nature of civic education within the formal school curriculum in Hong Kong is in effect a portrayal of the shifting images of society portrayed by the state. By understanding the extent to which civic education in different societies is a reflection of its specific social, political, economic and historical contexts we can mitigate, but not avoid, the charge of cultural imperialism.

Antecedents

The role of civic education in Hong Kong since 1945 can be analysed in terms of three distinct periods. In the first, from about 1945 to 1965, the role of the state in defining the nature of valid knowledge relied on coercion and was primarily designed to counter any direct threats to the legitimacy of the colonial government. In the second period, from about 1965 to 1984, the nature of valid knowledge was primarily defined by the market but was also influenced by a desire to avoid offending the sensitivities of the People's Republic of China (PRC). In the final period, from the early 1980s onwards, the definition of valid school knowledge has continued to be defined by the market but has also been substantially influenced by the impending transfer of sovereignty and the resulting crisis of legitimacy for the colonial government (Scott, 1989). These periods were associated with very different approaches to the extent, role and nature of civic education in the school curriculum.

In the period since 1945 Hong Kong experienced a ten-fold increase in population and the emergence, from small beginnings, of one of the world's largest trading and financial centres. These changes have been overseen by a colonial political system in which the civil service has performed both the legislative and executive functions of Government and in which the approach generally adopted to public policy has been described as '*laissez-faire*' or 'positive non-interventionism' (Sweeting, 1995, p. 107).

Given a stable socio-political environment, this approach should have ensured that all, or most, of the requirements for services such as housing, schooling and health were satisfied through private provision. As a concomitant of the policy, the curriculum of privately run schools should have been their own concern and in the post-war period, different curriculum models co-existed, leading to a variety of qualifications and certificates, as has remained the case in neighbouring Macao (Bray and Hui, 1991). However, the socio-political environment did not remain stable, and the response of the government to threats to public order and to its own tenuous legitimacy has been to expand public provision, particularly of schools and housing, and to strengthen its control of the curriculum (Sweeting and Morris, 1993).

Within the area of schooling, which was mainly provided by the private sector, early provision included schools sponsored by one or other of the warring factions in China, the Chinese Communist Party and the Kuo Min Tang, neither of which viewed Hong Kong's colonial status in a favourable light. To counter the influence of such schools, which had developed their own curricula, the government built its own rival schools in their vicinity and encouraged the many missionary societies which had fled the civil war in China to establish schools in Hong Kong. It also enacted a complex range of regulations which allowed it to suppress anything perceived as subversive in both the government and private school curriculum. Regulations were introduced in the late 1940s which gave the Director of the Department of Education control over school subjects, textbooks and all other teaching materials, and over any activities in schools which might be thought to be political in nature (Morris and Sweeting, 1991). These regulations were used to deregister teachers and to close a communist school in 1949. This was further reinforced by the production of 'model' syllabuses and the establishment of a common system of public examinations and certification.

The outcome of this process was the emergence of a highly centralized and bureaucratic system of control of the curriculum in which schools were provided with syllabuses for permitted subjects, textbooks which have been vetted by officials, recommended teaching guides, and official examination syllabuses. The key purpose of this system of control was to ensure that the content of syllabuses and textbooks was depoliticized. This was achieved by avoiding any content which was concerned with contemporary China, the local context or any 'sensitive' topics. The effect of this policy was that pupils studied the history, geography and literature of other cultures or of distant time periods: in other words, a decontextualized and remote curriculum. Luk (1991, p. 668) elegantly describes the consequences of this for Chinese culture subjects (language, literature and history):

> Thus generations of Hong Kong Chinese pupils grew up learning from the Chinese culture subjects to identify themselves as Chinese but relating that Chineseness to neither contemporary China nor the local Hong Kong landscape. It was a Chinese identity in the abstract, a patriotism of the 'émigré', probably held all the more absolute because it was not connected to a tangible reality.

Consequently the curriculum, as experienced by most students, consisted of abstract academic content, taught by transmission and examined in English by means which emphasized memory and reproduction over application to real problems. Within this context civic education was developed as a school subject, and examined in the school leaving certificate from 1950. Its purpose was to counter communist propaganda. The content of the syllabus required pupils to understand the workings of local government, its links to the UK, how local problems were solved and the nature of international organizations such as the UN and IMF. It avoided mention of local issues or controversies and was thus similar in its orientation to that evidenced in other subjects which stressed remote and abstract content. The emphasis was strongly on promoting the duties and commitments of a citizen to the status quo.

The 1960s heralded a significant shift in the nature of the political and economic conditions prevailing in Hong Kong. On the political front it became increasingly evident that Hong Kong existed because it was tolerated by the PRC and the riots of the mid 1960s served to underline Hong Kong sensitivity to events in the PRC. In terms of curriculum policy making this served to place a premium on maintaining a curriculum that avoided sensitive content and issues. From about 1965 rapid industrialization placed the territory in the forefront of the dynamic Asian economies. This was subsequently followed by the emergence of a middle class and growing levels of affluence, and an increase in the numbers of refugees from the PRC. As the economy grew, so access to well paid employment was provided by educational qualifications in this transient society, where mobility was based on achieved rather than ascribed criteria. This placed a premium on the selective and allocative role of schooling and created public pressure for the expansion of educational provision. In 1969 nine years of compulsory education became government policy and was fully implemented in 1979. The shift from an elite to mass system of education served to highlight the inadequacy of the prevailing curriculum and saw the government promote a series of reforms designed to achieve a broadly based and balanced school curriculum which is portrayed in terms akin to an integrated code, open systems and personal knowledge.

Civics education in this period can best be characterized as dormant and maintaining the role it had played in the previous period. Throughout the 1970s, neither the annual Education Department Reports nor the various white papers on education made any reference to civics education (Bray and Lee, 1993). Schools busied themselves with the task of preparing pupils for the highly academic public examinations which determined both whether a pupil continued to stay in the educational system and the nature of the school they were allocated to. Whilst pupils (and parents) competed to get into the best schools, the schools competed to attract the best pupils. In effect the political depoliticization of the curriculum and consequently the neglect of civic education was achieved in the period from 1945–1965 by direct government intervention whilst in the subsequent period it was more a by-product of the curriculum priorities in schools.

Civics ceased to exist as a school subject in 1965 and was replaced by a subject called Economic and Public Affairs (EPA). This was deemed necessary because Civics was insufficiently academic, did not have an equivalent subject in the UK 'O' level system (with which Hong Kong examination results were moderated) and was not linked to a subject at the matriculation level. The addition of an economics component was seen to rectify these problems. The new subject was essentially descriptive, stressed the duties of a citizen and was laudatory of the government's role. Where potential social issues were addressed, such as homelessness, pollution and crime, the essential logic employed was: to briefly identify the nature of the problem, ascribe this to deviant or antisocial behaviour and describe in detail the various policies enacted by the government to solve the problems. Controversial political questions and any mention of China comprised the core of the null curriculum for they were consciously avoided both in EPA and other subjects.

Only in the last period from the early 1980s, have the culture and contemporary politics of Hong Kong become valid items for inclusion in the school curriculum. Given the impending transfer of sovereignty in 1997, the government changed the criteria for the selection of valid curriculum knowledge. The study of previously sensitive issues, politics and of aspects of the PRC became acceptable components of the formal curriculum. This shift was manifested in three ways: changes were made to the content of existing school subjects, new subjects were added which had the potential to explore critical social, political and moral issues, and in 1985 and 1996, Civic Education was promoted as a cross-curricular theme within the school curriculum, along with moral, environmental and sex education. The EPA syllabus was amended in 1984 with an increased focus on systems of government, especially those involving representation and consultation, and on the principles of law making. The history syllabus changed in 1988 so that pupils now studied Chinese history up to 1970, rather than only up to 1949 as had previously been the case, and the study of British colonial and commonwealth history was deleted. More recent changes have resulted in pupils studying Hong Kong's local history. The social studies syllabus was revised in 1989. Prior to the revision it was descriptive and avoided mention of China. The new syllabus retained its descriptive orientation but included extensive coverage of information about China (Morris, 1988, 1996).

The new subjects introduced in this period were Government and Public Affairs (GPA) and Liberal Studies. In contrast to EPA, which focused on describing the institutions and processes of government, GPA emphasized concepts which were central to Western liberal democracy (such as the rule of law, representation, consultation and elections) and the study of political processes in China. Liberal studies was introduced as a subject to broaden the highly specialized sixth form curriculum. The subject attempts to promote a more conceptual and critical orientation and includes content which relates to the transition of sovereignty and to an analysis of socialism versus capitalism, the modernization of China, its legal system and the roles of the Communist Party and the People's Liberation Army.

These changes to the content of subjects and the introduction of new subjects heralded a shift in the role of civic education in schools. Concepts and content relevant to civic education are now included in a variety of subjects, new and old, and the formal curriculum now promotes the study of political concepts and controversial issues, especially those relating to China. A note of caution is necessary before any conclusions are drawn from this. The subjects which have been primarily affected by this process of politicization are low status subjects and/or unpopular ones. EPA has declined rapidly in popularity following the introduction of Economics in 1975. GPA is studied by a handful of pupils. Social studies is officially part of the core curriculum but is offered in less than 20 per cent of schools, whilst liberal studies is offered in about 10 per cent of schools. There is thus a need to distinguish between the nature of the intended and implemented curriculum. This is explored below through a more detailed analysis of the impact of the cross-curricular guidelines on schools.

In spite of this high degree of central control over the content of the curriculum, a significant set of key decisions is left to be taken at school level, including: the specific combinations of subjects to be studied; the time devoted to specific subjects; the mechanisms for the streaming and selection of pupils up to secondary year 5; the language of instruction; and all aspects of pedagogy. These issues have become increasingly critical with the advent of universal junior secondary education in 1979 and the growth of the range of available school subjects (especially computer studies and Putonghua/Mandarin).

However, the most critical influence on the curriculum has been the emergence of an allocative mechanism which has encouraged the operation of a market in which schools compete for pupils. The impact of this market has effectively superseded direct control by the state. This has allowed the government to revert to its traditional *laissez-faire* role and allowed it to minimize its statutory control of missionary and benevolent bodies whose willingness to provide education has partly depended on their freedom to promote their specific beliefs. The effect of the emergence of a market for pupils has been to ensure that issues of valid knowledge, valid transmission of knowledge and valid evaluation affect schools at the individual level rather than reaching them more diffusely through decisions taken at national level. The combination of these two considerations — the control by schools over which subjects are taught and the impact of the market on schools' decisions — exert a strong influence on the role and impact of civic education. This will be explored in more detail later in the paper.

These changes to the influences on the curriculum and civic education specifically were accompanied by significant shifts in the nature of the political system and of the attitude of the population towards politics, especially during the last period. Each period was associated with a relative increase in the degree of openness of, and public participation in, both local and central government. This trend was accelerated with the signing of the Sino-British Joint Declaration and the Tienanmen Square debacle in 1989, as the government belatedly attempted to develop a system which would allow the people of Hong Kong to establish and assert their identity within the 'one country, two systems' formula. Thus the proportion of directly elected members of the Legislative Council (Legco) increased from one third in 1991 to half in 1995.

In parallel, social attitudes to public participation in political processes has shifted away from what has been described as 'politico-phobia' (Choi, 1990) and 'political aloofness' (Tsang, 1996) which prevailed in the first two periods identified earlier. The reasons for this acceptance of depoliticization in the first two periods are complex but salient factors include: the fact that the population of Hong Kong is made up of immigrants, many of whom were refugees from China; the rapid economic growth of the colony allowed some aspirations to be satisfied; and the tendency of the government to adopt a minimalist role. This is not to suggest that the increased levels of public participation are evidence of support for or acceptance of the government. Lau and Kuan's (1988) work indicates low levels of trust of the governments of both HK and China by Hong Kong citizens. They also described the local political culture as 'group based, unconventional and confrontational' and argue that the foundations of Hong Kong society had shifted from an emphasis on 'utilitarian familism' to a combination of 'egotistical individualism' and 'utilitarian materialism'.

The changes outlined above were consistent with the shifting policy of the government towards the role of civic education in schools. This saw the active pursuit of a depoliticized curriculum in the first period to the promotion of the need for the inculcation of civic and moral values which stress the individual's commitment to the status quo in the second period, and the current promotion of a more participatory form of civic education. Insofar as the first and third periods described above were a product of direct threats to the stability and legitimacy of the state, this supports Scott's (1996) assertion that such threats result in the state using its institutions, in this case education, to propagate its own version of society (and the model citizen) in an attempt to maintain control.

The analysis to date has focused on the planned or intended curriculum which in Hong Kong is effectively defined by the government. That has served to set the parameters within which schools operate — it does not determine how schools interpret these policies nor how they are implemented. These issues are addressed in the next section which focuses on how schools interpreted the key policy documents which served to describe the rationale for, and means of implementation of, four cross-curricular themes, each of which was designed to contribute directly or indirectly to promoting aspects of civic education.

The Cross-curricular Themes: Civic, Moral, Environmental and Sex Education

The unpopularity of subjects such as social studies, EPA and liberal studies effectively meant that most pupils' exposure to civic education in the formal school curriculum was through the implementation in schools of the cross-curricular themes. The intentions and impact of these initiatives is analysed below through an examination of the features of the guidelines and how they were interpreted by school principals.

The Planned Curriculum

In Table 7.1 a summary is provided (Morris and Chan, 1996) of the nature of the four official cross-curricular guidelines: moral education (Education Department [ED], 1981); civic education (Curriculum Development Council [CDC], 1985), and Education Department (1996); sex education (CDC, 1986); and environmental education (CDC, 1992), with regard to the following features: the manifest source of change; their aims; the form of curriculum organization advocated; their content; their recommendations on pedagogy, assessment and evaluation; and the key learning competencies promoted. From the table it can be seen that they exhibit a number of common features which are summarized below.

First, each of the guidelines portrays its rationale in terms of a planned governmental response to a community need which has arisen from a rapidly changing socio-political environment. The need for moral education is linked to the rise in juvenile delinquency. Civic education was initially associated with 'the need for the public to be educated more effectively to cope with the implications arising from proposals for developing the local system of government' (CDC, 1985, p. i) and more recently its rationale derived from China's resumption of sovereignty in 1997 and the resulting 'special need for schools to strengthen civic education, with a view to preparing students to become rational, active and responsible citizens' (ED, 1996, p. 1). Sex education is portrayed as necessary given changing social attitudes which have resulted in a society which is deeply divided over moral and social issues. Environmental education is necessitated by environmental deterioration in Hong Kong and the resulting need for schools to produce 'well informed, environmentally aware and responsible citizens' (CDC, 1992, p. 5).

Second, all the guidelines promote what is described as a 'permeated' or 'whole school' approach to curriculum organization which means that their goals are designed to be achieved through their inclusion in and across existing school subjects. This has parallels with the 'cross-curricular elements' in the UK national curriculum (Whitty et al., 1994) and the 'infusion approach' to the promotion of Asian Literacy in Australian schools (Williamson-Fien, 1994). In effect, this requires that existing subjects broaden their goals to achieve the personal and societal aims promoted by the cross-curricular guides. This permeated approach or strategy is portrayed, somewhat paradoxically, as a reflection of the high priority given by the government to the broadening of the curriculum. The Civic Education Guidelines (CDC, 1985, p. 4) explain:

> These guidelines reflect the strongly held view that civic education is everybody's responsibility and that within the context of the school it should not be treated *as*

Table 7.1: *Comparison of key features of the four cross-curricular guidelines for schools in Hong Kong*

Features of the Guidelines	Moral Education 1981	Civic Education 1985	Civic Education 1996	Sex Education 1986	Environmental Education 1992
Change forces (i.e. the reasons identified in official documents for introducing the Guidelines)	The introduction of universal and compulsory education for 9 years had given rise to students with mixed abilities and family backgrounds; and an increase in juvenile delinquency	Political changes (e.g. 1984 White Paper on *The Further Development of Representative Government in Hong Kong*; signing of the Sino-British Joint Declaration which planned for the return of the sovereignty of Hong Kong to China in 1997); need for a stable and prosperous society in the period of transition to 1997	In the transition to the 21st century and the resumption of the exercise of sovereignty by China over HK in 1997, there is a special need for schools to strengthen civic education	A society which is deeply divided over moral and social issues; changing social values and influences of the mass media	Government 10-year plan on environmental policy given in the *White Paper on Pollution in Hong Kong — A Time to Act*
Aims	Cultivating pupils' moral attitudes and social values through the development of reflective or critical thinking	To renew their commitment to the preservation of social order and the promotion of civic awareness and responsibility and these guidelines are designed to facilitate this renewal	To prepare students to become rational, active and responsible citizens in facing challenges arising from the above changes	To educate pupils so that they can experience personal fulfilment, well-being and enjoyment through a growing awareness of their sexual identity and a developing regard for interpersonal responsibility	To promote in pupils a lifelong and forward-looking concern for the environment and to prepare them for making well-informed, justifiable and practical decisions regarding the conservation of environment so as to enable them to live as useful and responsible citizens
Approach to curriculum organization	Permeated approach, school ethos	A 'system' curriculum model. Permeated approach	Schools to select from 3 modes: permeated, specific subject and integrated	Permeated approach in the formal and informal curriculum, school ethos, in conjunction with moral education	Permeated and whole school approach in the formal and informal curriculum, school ethos; in conjunction with civic education

Framework of content/topics	Unavailable	Provided for Kindergartens, Primary and Secondary Schools	Provided for Kindergartens, Primary and Secondary Schools	Available for Secondary Schools	Unavailable
Recommendations on pedagogy	Suggested activities like story-telling, dramatization and role-play, discussion, case study, project method, outside reading; emphasis on extra-curricular/other school activities	Exemplar activities for knowledge acquisition like observation, manipulation of materials, collection, interpretation and presentation of information; exemplar activities for value orientation like story-telling, case study, simulation and role-playing; class or group discussion; suggestions for extra-curricular activities	Encourages a focus on 'controversial issues' and on developing critical thinking	Ideas for learning activities are provided for all topics in the scheme of work such as film shows, seminars, questionnaire survey, discussion	Guiding principles including experiential learning, development of balanced viewpoint, emphasis on formation of attitudes, encouragement of individual contribution and participation. Suggested activities such as brainstorming, debate, designing/drawing, diary keeping, discussion, fieldwork, experiment simulation/role-play/game, model making
Assessment and evaluation	Teacher's assessment in school report	Largely informal at the school level	School based evaluations of pupil learning outcomes and of the School Programme	Programme-based at the school level, suggested techniques like observation, surveys, self-appraisal device	Programme-based, different methods for different aims and objectives (knowledge, skills attitudes/values) only at the school level
Key learning competencies/skills	Reflective and critical thinking	Critical and logical thinking, the spirit of inquiry	Critical thinking, wise decision making, creative thinking, independent judgments, self reflection, uphold principles	Decision making and communication skills, a consistent system of values	Open mindedness, balanced viewpoints, informed and critical understanding/reflection

(*Source:* Morris and Chan in press)

> *just* another subject for which exclusive responsibility rests with a particular member or members of staff. Rather, a whole school approach is advocated . . .

Third, the goals of the cross-curricular themes are described in terms consistent with a reconstructionist vision of schooling. Moral education is associated with the promotion of reflective and critical thinking, civic education is linked to the need to develop critical, creative and logical thinking, self reflection, independence and problem solving. Environmental education is portrayed as necessitating open mindedness, reflection, balanced viewpoints and critical reflection consistent with an amalgam of progressive and constructivist views of schooling and learning. Dramatization, role-play, data based analysis, issues based teaching, experiential learning and brainstorming are examples of the range of recommended techniques.

Finally, in terms of content and assessment, the advice of the guidelines is more varied. Three of the guidelines leave it to the schools to select an appropriate body of content whilst in two of them this is provided. Assessment in all of the guidelines, is defined as a task to be undertaken wholly by and within the school.

Interpreting the Plan

A substantial body of evidence indicates a low level of implementation of the guidelines in the formal school curriculum and specifically of those topics which lay outside the content of existing school subjects (Tang and Morris, 1989; Fung and Lee, 1993; Ng, 1995; Leung, 1995). Given the tendency of school subjects to focus on abstract, non-controversial and established knowledge, this results in an avoidance of those topics designed to focus on issues, controversies, moral questions and uncertainties. This is best illustrated by recent reports on the implementation of sex education (Curriculum Development Institute [CDI] 1994) and civic education (CDI, 1995). The former notes that pupils were generally well informed about bodily parts and functions, except with reference to more 'sensitive topics' (e.g. menstruation and masturbation). Approximately 75 per cent of pupils reported that the following had not been covered in the formal or informal school curriculum: masturbation, AIDs, family planning/birth control, parental preparation, sex diseases, homosexuality and abortion. Similarly, the latter study noted that the impact of civic education programmes in schools had focused on the provision of 'civic knowledge', rather than on themes related to 'moral judgments' and 'social justice'. Other studies would seem to confirm the low level of implementation of the themes. Lau and Kuan (1988) have described Hong Kong's youth as tending to identify with narrow familial and parochial interests, and having a weak sense of communal solidarity. Bond (1993) argues that Hong Kong students display a complex identity which is characterized by a low level of identification with Hong Kong and a tendency to ascribe to themselves the more desirable features of traditional Chinese and modern Western identities. This lack of a coherent sense of civic identity or community values is especially pertinent given Hong Kong's return to Chinese sovereignty.

This scenario is a result of schools deciding that the cross-curricular themes warranted a low priority and that little effort was to be accorded to including them in the formal curriculum. It is the result not of teachers attempting to address these topics but failing to have an impact on pupils' learning.

The documents which promoted the themes contained a subtext which provided a clear set of clues for principals and teachers which served to define the status and priority which should in practice be accorded to the themes. To identify the clues or signifiers which school personnel used to determine the status and the priority to accord to the implementation of the cross-curricular themes in-depth interviews were conducted with twenty school principals.

What emerged clearly was the view that the guidelines were uniformly perceived to be promoting important and worthwhile educational goals, but they were not seen as requiring significant changes to schools' existing priorities in general, and specifically the subject oriented curriculum. This was because the guidelines were seen to contain a combination of internal contradictions and impractical features which served to define them as having a marginal status and not designed to seriously challenge the prevailing collection code curriculum. These features relate to: their non statutory and ad hoc status, the administrative structures designed to support the themes, their linkages to the existing curriculum, and the coherence of the government's policy and the resources devoted to support policy. Consequently, in most schools the promotion of the themes was assigned a low priority and few resources were devoted to support implementation.

By their very nature the advisory, discretionary and non statutory status of the guidelines sent clear messages that they were optional and not designed to disturb the status quo. These messages were reinforced by a number of features. All but one of the guidelines claimed, somewhat paradoxically, that their goals were an integral part of the existing core curriculum of schools and constituted an elaboration of current practice in schools and, thus, did not require significant adjustments. This reflects a fundamental tension which faces the colonial government in all areas of policy making, namely, that reforms cannot be primarily justified by reference to the deficiencies of the existing system, for to do so is to criticize the government's own past record. For example the Moral Education Guidelines (ED, 1981) explain that moral education is already one of the aims of education in Hong Kong and:

> ... the secondary school curriculum has been developed so that stress on moral education is apparent in nearly all subjects. An examination of the stated aims and objectives of the subject syllabuses will confirm this point. (p. 12)

and:

> If one goes through the aims and objectives of subjects in the primary curriculum, one will also find that they include various aspects of moral education. (p. 9)

The non statutory and discretionary nature of the guidelines was reinforced by many of the consequences of their non subject status. Specifically, they did not need to be timetabled or staffed. In terms of a school's relationship with the government this meant that they were not directly resourced and were not subject to direct inspection. In brief, the consequences of not implementing the policy were not readily transparent.

The guidelines were also perceived to have emerged as ad hoc and uncoordinated governmental responses to emerging socio-political contexts. For example, the Civic Education Guidelines were perceived as an instantaneous and superficial response to questions asked in Legco which focused on the need for greater civic and political awareness in view of the impending transfer of sovereignty. Consequently, the guidelines were seen as precursors to similar fragmented initiatives in areas such as drugs, consumer and health education. This encouraged an attitude which involved a mixture of pragmatic scepticism and a 'wait and see' attitude to the adoption and implementation of the themes.

Second, the guidelines were seen to have failed to link directly or meaningfully to the existing curriculum. By expecting schools to identify appropriate content to support moral and environmental education, to develop resources and devise their own methods of assessment the guidelines serve to underline the difficulties affecting change. The schools interpreted the unwillingness of the government to try to provide these curriculum components as evidence of the immutable, sacred and 'taken for granted' status of the prevailing curriculum. The impact of assessment is critical. Whilst schools see themselves as competing with other schools for pupils the key determinant of a school's intake is the quality of public examination results, especially in the key high status subjects, English, Mathematics and Chinese. This exerts, as noted earlier, a powerful pressure on schools to maintain a curriculum oriented to maximizing examination results. Time spent on worthwhile, but non examined, areas such as personal, social and moral education means less time spent on the high status subjects which account for about 70 per cent of a pupil's timetable.

The same problem manifests itself in curriculum resources, especially textbooks, which are the key definers of curriculum content. All textbooks used in Hong Kong schools have to obtain government approval and this necessitates that they closely follow the content specified in the central examination syllabuses. Essentially, when the syllabuses of school subjects have not been adjusted to include cross-curricular themes then they have not been included in textbooks. Since the most popular resource for student learning in Hong Kong is still the textbook, this means that key components of the curriculum continue to embody a strong orientation to curricular knowledge which is insulated, established and abstract.

Where the guidelines did provide a detailed description of the content of the curriculum, as was the case with civic education, the suggestions as to how some subjects, especially in science, were expected to promote the themes were seen to constitute a mixture of the bizarre and impractical. The two examples provided to illustrate this were the suggestions that the teacher introduce the idea of 'moral standards' when teaching Einstein's theory of relativity and that chemistry teachers talk about social harmony when they are explaining why chemical elements bond together. As one Principal (Interview: School Principal) concisely explained:

> It would be ridiculous to expect the Physics or Chemistry teacher to incorporate a lot of civic and moral education elements in their teaching . . . they have already a big syllabus to cover.

Third, the internal structures and administrative mechanisms used by the government to develop and promote the themes, similarly served to reflect their status as subordinate to that of discrete school subjects. Responsibility for the guidelines was originally vested in the Advisory Inspectorate (AI) and since 1992 in the newly created Curriculum Development Institute (CDI). In the Advisory Inspectorate, the responsibility for the development of each cross-curricular area belonged within the territory of subject based sections which closely parallel the organization of subjects in schools. For instance, sex education was associated with biological sciences; environmental education with geography; moral education with religious studies; and civic education with government and public affairs. There is no group or agency that has responsibility to oversee the broad area of personal, moral and social education and give consistent advice of a cross-curricular nature and this serves to maintain the themes as supplements to cognate school subjects. In the CDI the administrative organization of the four areas is potentially more integrated than was the case in the AI, as they are all incorporated in the Humanities Section. In neither the AI nor the CDI were the cross-curricular themes linked with resources and status in the manner associated with school subjects. For the personnel involved, the reward structure, in terms of recognition and promotion was associated with the production of the guidelines, not with their dissemination or implementation. These features were reflected in the lack of enthusiasm which accompanied the promotion of the themes and the priority they were accorded by those responsible for them.

A fourth feature derives from what was described as the government's 'sincerity' or consistency towards the promotion of social, personal and moral education. As noted earlier, the guidelines promote a movement away from a curriculum with a strong collection code to a more integrated one which is characterized by a greater focus on personal and problematic knowledge and on developing critical, reflective and independent thinking skills. The government's response to two critical issues were cited as evidence of the persuasiveness of a view of school knowledge as an established and unproblematic entity, and of the government's lack of 'sincerity'. The first issue was addressed in the Civic Education Guidelines and involved the question of whether the concept of 'democracy' should be addressed. The guidelines explained that because:

> Democracy means different things to different people . . . So education for democracy per se would be difficult to interpret . . . for the purpose of these guidelines the term civic education will be used. (CDC, 1985)

The outcome was that as the concept was controversial the guidelines avoided any further mention of the concept.

The second issue related to the question of how the curriculum in Hong Kong would deal with what was one of the most problematic and critical issues for the people of Hong Kong in recent years: namely, the suppression of the student movement in Tiananmen Square in 1989. Textbook publishers were encouraged to avoid the topic or treat it in ways which were uncritical of the government of the PRC. When it was referred to in a school history text, criticisms of the government's attempts to have the text changed were countered by the Director of Education with the argument that it was necessary for twenty years to elapse before an 'accepted' version of the incident emerged. What these responses indicate is that the desire to develop a curriculum which incorporates personal and problematic knowledge is at best rhetorical, for when controversial issues emerged they were effectively excluded from the curriculum on the grounds that they were problematic and not sufficiently established.

These two issues reflect the changing patterns of influence on the school curriculum in the post-war period. The period up to about 1985 saw the government consciously pursue an apolitical curriculum in an attempt to avoid raising the political consciousness of a population who might begin to question Hong Kong's colonial status. The signing of the Joint Declaration made this concern less pressing given the rapidly decreasing tenure of the government. The current concern is to appease Hong Kong's future masters, and the result is a continuation of the avoidance of controversial issues and problematic knowledge alongside the insertion of new elements designed to promote 'nationalistic' and 'patriotic' education under the aegis of civic education.

This same ambivalence towards problematic knowledge is also evident within the guidelines themselves. For example, the only guidelines which directly attempt to provide advice on how teachers should handle 'controversial issues' explains:

> Some teachers find controversial issues in civic education difficult to handle because these issues are not matters of absolute truth or fallacy, ethical or moral, right or wrong. (Education Department, 1996, p. 70)

However in their advice to teachers they qualify the range of issues which can be discussed and underline the role of facts. They explain:

> Avoid issues that invite over-emotionality or get pupils and parents too wrought up . . . Be careful not to thrust adult concerns upon young children, such as discussing homosexuality with primary school children. (p. 71)

and, with regard to teaching tactics, it advises: 'Set ground rules for discussion . . . statements must be supported by facts' (p. 71).

In the case of the environmental education guidelines a conscious decision was made not to provide a framework of contents. This was based on the earlier experience with the civic education guidelines which provided a framework of curriculum content which was subjected to extensive public criticism partly because it focused on civic knowledge and avoided critical issues. This problem was exacerbated by the fact that the content of existing subjects had been decided prior to the emergence of the guidelines and subsequent revisions made little attempt to incorporate the topics and themes suggested by the guidelines. Accordingly, it was decided that the best way to avoid the environmental education guidelines being subjected to similar public scrutiny and criticism was to avoid providing a body of content.

Finally, the status of the themes was also underscored by the extent of support they were accorded by the government and the strategy used to develop the policy. The main strategy used to develop the policy and support their promotion was the production and distribution of the respective guideline document. There was no large scale systematic attempt to involve teachers in their development, to provide in-service programmes or a range of classroom resources. In terms of the link between career prospects and the promotion of the themes the only area in which the role of school co-ordinator was linked to a promoted post was civic education. This was reflected in the higher profile which was given to this area in the schools. This pattern is in marked contrast to the support which has been provided to a recent curriculum reform, the Target Oriented Curriculum, which has received a massive input of resources.

The foregoing analysis indicates that the state's attempts at reforms designed to promote civic education in its broadest sense are classic examples of what Cuban (1992) describes as 'symbolic action' which serves primarily as a legitimating device which demonstrates concern for the perennial dilemmas of schooling rather than an attempt to change the implemented curriculum. The outcome is a façade of change, a substantial gap between the rhetoric of policy and the reality in schools, and a general failure to achieve any significant impact on schools. Thus Leung (1995) argues that the guidelines contributed to the trivialization of civic education in Hong Kong. Nevertheless, to dismiss such policies as essentially superficial and unimportant is inappropriate for they also serve a more subtle and powerful function through the creation of a discourse which placed the role of interpreting and operationalizing the policy within the schools. This serves to locate the focus of the discussion about the nature and reform of the curriculum within schools and assigns the power and responsibility to teachers for any problems of implementation or curriculum imbalance which subsequently emerge. That has ensured that civic education plays a minimal role in schools, for their power to change the curriculum is severely constrained by the need to survive within a market within which schools compete for pupils.

Civics Education: The Informal and Hidden Curriculum

The extent to which pupils' values, attitudes and skills in areas such as participation, decision making, co-operation, tolerance and inter-personal relationships are influenced by the informal curriculum (e.g. assemblies, form periods and extra curricular activities) is more difficult to determine. There is evidence that many schools (CDI, 1994) did attempt to address topics in the area of civic and moral education through school assemblies. This often took the form of a guest speaker who addressed the whole school and tended to involve: a minimal degree of participation, an absence of any follow up and a tendency to the prescriptive and normative.

There is little evidence to suggest that the culture of Hong Kong schools would support the development of skills associated with active citizenship. Various writers have described schools as highly autocratic (Visiting Panel, 1982; Tsang, 1985) and a government document (Education and Manpower Branch and Education Department EMB ED, 1991) even describes some principals as operating like 'little emperors' (p. 14). The standard portrayal of Hong Kong schools and classrooms is in terms of the prevalence of strong hierarchical structures, rote learning, memorization and teacher centred instruction. This would suggest that patterns of classroom interaction would reinforce the depoliticized and descriptive approaches to civic education in which pupils were encouraged to recognize their duties and accept the status quo. However such a depiction of Hong Kong classrooms tends to be based on cultural preconceptions that fail to recognize the culture of the classroom in East Asian societies. Thus for example Hamilton et al. (1984) argue in their comparison of citizenship education in Japan and the USA that classroom interaction in Japan stresses a morality of aspiration (encouragement of top performance) whilst that in the USA stresses a morality of duty (minimal standards that must be met to avoid punishment). The Japanese teachers achieved this through an emphasis on positive feedback, stress on persistence to achieving goals and attributions to effort. Chen (1994) also argues that the civic education programme in Taiwan stresses personal morality and the duties of the individual to society. Similarly Biggs (1995) argues with reference to HK that what is taken for rote learning is better understood as repetitive learning which involves the rehearsal of tasks. He also portrays teachers and pupils as holding high and positive levels of expectations of each other, teachers and peers providing high levels of support to pupils within a mentor/mentoree relationship, and, a climate of positive interpersonal relationships. These observations support Ichilov's (1994) contention that:

> While in the West civic education emphasizes instruction in the values guiding the relation of individuals to the state and polity, in much of Asia . . . the stress is on interpersonal or moral values . . . Asian countries rely on education to teach a code of behaviour for everyday life along with loyalty to the state.

Evidence indicates that levels of loyalty to the state (both the colonial and mainland varieties) are extremely low in Hong Kong and this is consistent with the promotion of a depoliticized curriculum. However, the patterns of classroom interaction do seem to have served to promote a range of interpersonal and moral values which allow a society to operate.

The Future

Formally, according to the Joint Declaration, the educational system of Hong Kong is not supposed to change for fifty years from 1997. In reality change will occur as improvements are introduced, and the Chinese government has made a number of statements indicating that aspects of the curriculum relating to civics, politics and history will be changed. Given the very close link that prevailed before 1997 between civics education in Hong Kong and the governments of both Hong Kong and China this will in effect merely continue that linkage, albeit without the depoliticizing tendency of the colonial government. Some of the proposed curriculum changes which have been heralded involve appropriate factual changes to reflect a new system of government and a change of sovereignty. Other changes refer to the need to display a love of the motherland, patriotism, healthy moral values and to avoid sensitive topics. This will not require significant changes to most syllabuses and textbooks, which have anticipated this expectation and removed reference to problematic topics, especially the Tienanmen Square massacre and the status of Taiwan.

In the earlier quote, Ichilov (1994) noted that in China civic education has focused on promoting a moral code of behaviour and loyalty to the state. In terms of the classical Greek conception this suggests that the development of a virtuous character has been at the centre of civic education in East Asia but that the quest for freedom has been replaced by the quest for loyalty and commitment. Similarly Meyer (1988) notes that from 1979 China moved away from emphasizing equality and redistribution towards the promotion of more hierarchical values. During the late 1980s schools offered courses on communist ideology and morality which stressed 'correct attitudes' and the ability to distinguish between right and wrong. This chapter would suggest that Hong Kong schools have provided pupils with a moral code of behaviour, especially through the hidden and informal curriculum. However, loyalty to the state or the promotion of a sense of national identity have not been key goals of schooling, as is the case both in China and other East Asian societies such as Japan (Cummings et al., 1988) South Korea (Suh, 1988) and Taiwan (Chen, 1994). Evidence does suggest that this is in the social psyche of Hong Kong citizens which, as noted earlier, has been described as: defiant to both the governments of Hong Kong and China (Tsang, 1996), lacking a sense of community and individualistic (Lau, 1988) and lacking a clear cultural identity (Bond 1993). Its aspirations to democracy have also been heightened by the colonial government on the eve of its departure. As Leung (1995) notes there is an inherent problem with regard to the promotion of democracy and the increased politicization of Hong Kong society for in parallel the school system is failing to provide pupils with the appropriate knowledge and skills. He explains: 'They simply do not have the requisite knowledge, concepts and skills to meet the challenge posed by the political transition of Hong Kong' (p. 302).

This combination of conditions, especially the instinct of governments to promote forms of civic education which are perceived to ensure the survival and legitimacy of the state suggests that civic education in Hong Kong will in future exhibit both change and constancy. The role and nature of civic education promoted in school curricula will change as the state promotes its view of a model citizen but it will continue to reflect the prevailing socio-political conditions within the society.

8 Phoenix or Shooting Star?: Citizenship Education in Australia

Murray Print

Introduction

Over the past few years citizenship education has experienced a vigorous renaissance in selected aspects of Australian education, reflecting in part a strong international resurgence in the field. But is this a truly awakening phoenix or merely a shooting star? From negligible interest and support but a few years ago, citizenship education in Australia has quickly become an important focus of national educational attention. Over the past three years a major inquiry has been conducted, curriculum projects initiated, research projects commenced, national conferences held and the literature expanded at a rapid rate. The vital question facing Australian educators is — will revitalized citizenship education be sustained or will it fade like a shooting star?

Within Australia the renaissance in citizenship education is found almost exclusively within three educational levels — national government, academia and state educational bureaucracies. Interest is not widespread in Australian schools or amongst teachers and students. Neither teachers nor their organizations are clamouring for information, resources or assistance on citizenship education. This is the next important phase — the process of transformation of schools, of curriculum, of school vision, of teacher pedagogy and of assessment and reporting procedures. Consequently, Australia is at a critical stage in the implementation of citizenship education as a curriculum innovation in our schooling system. Despite current levels of interest and activity, there is no guarantee that the innovation will be successfully adopted and consolidated to the point of institutionalization within the school curriculum.

Where has this interest come from? What form has citizenship education taken in recent times? What is it trying to achieve in Australian schools? What are the issues facing citizenship education in Australia? These are important questions to address as citizenship education faces its next major hurdle in its movement to become an established component within the Australian school curriculum. Before these questions are addressed it is important to understand some historical context for the development of citizenship education in Australia.

Historical Context of Citizenship Education in Australia

The first six decades of the Commonwealth of Australia since federation in 1901 saw citizenship education as an integral part of Australian schooling. Focus was placed upon teaching features of civic virtue and 'good' citizenship to young Australians, especially their duties and rights, as well as Australia's role in the British Empire/Commonwealth. In part this helps explain why hundreds of thousands of Australians rushed off so willingly to serve valiantly overseas in both world wars. Through the school curriculum students also learnt about the functions of government including the civil service and cabinet, order and justice, the electoral system, and more practical activities such as work, housing and the care of people (Musgrave, 1994; Thomas, 1994; Kennedy, 1995).

In this time both teachers and students were viewed essentially as receptive participants in a civic mission. They were to benefit from understanding their rights and responsibilities as citizens in a democratic ideal, especially through voting, paying taxes and military service. In schools teaching was fundamentally didactic, with the subject matter of citizenship education essentially contradicted by authoritarian school practice. Texts and resource publications were readily available including such standard fare in primary (elementary) schools as *The School Paper* and the *Victorian Readers* (Musgrave, 1994). In high schools, particularly from World War I onwards, references such as Hoy's *Civics for Australian Schools*, Murdoch's *The Australian Citizen*, Marshall and Hoy's *Australasian Text Book of Civics*, as well as Thorn and Rigg's *Handbook of Civics* (Thomas, 1994; Kennedy, 1995) were regularly used. Throughout this period it was difficult to identify citizenship and civics as an independent subject in school curricula. More commonly, citizenship education was interwoven within history, moral training and, later in the 1930s and 1940s and beyond, in the new school subject called social studies. In this subject citizenship learning focused on information about political structures and processes, citizen rights and responsibilities and the values of civic participation (Thomas, 1994). Additional components included understanding the constitution, the roles of the civil service and cabinet, order and justice, the electoral system and the three-tier system of government. While these learnings were important and valued, it is this lack of independent subject identity which some authors suggest contributed to the later demise of civics (Thomas, 1994; Connell, 1971).

From the 1960s onwards, however, Australia experienced a significant decrease in the formal teaching of citizenship education within the education system (Thomas, 1994; Civics Expert Group, 1994; Kennedy and Print, 1994; Macintyre, 1995; Print, 1995c). Surprisingly, this occurred in a period of a rapid influx of migrants from Britain and Europe which saw over two million migrants arrive within two decades of the end of World War Two. Although the technicalities of citizenship were important components in educating the new arrivals, by the 1960s little citizenship education was being translated into the school curriculum. Issues of growth, development and prosperity were far more significant for Australian society. Instead of continual demands to address citizenship within the school curriculum, it fell away.

Partly the demise of citizenship education was a reflection of the significant social revolution of the 1960s in the Western world. Change, prosperity, new values and a focusing on youth saw little need to address issues of citizenship. Partly the explanation may be found with a significant trait of Australian society — its 'laid-back' nature and 'acceptance' of things new and different as long as all was going well. These factors help explain why citizenship education was less popular from the 'sixties' onwards, but further research needs to be conducted to critically analyse these assertions.

By the late 1980s interest in reviving citizenship education within the school curriculum was increasingly evident. Several attempts were made to invigorate participation in citizenship-related subjects. In Western Australia, for example, a subject called Politics was available for upper secondary students, though few subsequently studied it. For students in New South Wales, Australia's most populous state, a small component of government could be studied in Commerce (at Year 9 or 10), and later, in Legal Studies (Years 11 and 12). However, the government component failed to attract large numbers of students to those school subjects. Broadly-based concerns about the lack of direction of Australian education led to attempts for more sharply focused policy and vision. In 1989 all Australian Ministers for Education adopted a set of national goals for schooling. Within this vision active citizenship education was highlighted as a key objective for the curriculum (Australian Education Council (AEC), 1989). The only nationally accepted statement of curriculum intent in Australia, the *Common and Agreed National Goals for Schooling in Australia* (1989) states the agreed position towards citizenship explicitly through two goals.

Goal 7: To develop knowledge, skills, attitudes and values which will enable students to participate as active and informed citizens in our democratic Australian society within an international context.

Goal 6: To develop in students . . . a capacity to exercise judgment in matters of morality, ethics and social justice.

These goal statements, while visionary, and yet acceptable to state and federal governments alike, were of little value until translated into policy. At the state level, where the legal control of schooling is held, little evidence exists of specific policy to address citizenship education some seven years later. This is currently changing as the various state governments address the citizenship education initiatives of the Federal Government.

Important examples of federal attempts to stimulate an active policy response for citizenship education are the investigations of citizenship by the Australian Senate. The inquiries and their subsequent reports, *Education for Active Citizenship* (SSCEET, 1989) and *Active Citizenship Revisited* (SSCEET, 1991) had the effect of heightening awareness and concern at the condition of citizenship within Australian schools. The Senate also established a Standing Committee on Legal and Constitutional Affairs and it is examining the development of national indicators that might assist planning and monitoring progress in relation to specific citizenship goals (SSLCRC, 1995).

A valuable innovation in the late 1980s was the Senate funded Parliamentary Education Office (PEO). Believed to be unique amongst Western democracies (Carter, 1993), the PEO was designed to actively promote effective understanding of parliamentary processes amongst Australians, particularly amongst school students. This office has produced several major reports which have demonstrated the need for active citizenship education, run an extensive parliamentary visitor program and produced numerous curriculum resource materials in the latest technological forms. By any standards the PEO has been most effective in stimulating interest and understanding of Australia's Federal Parliament.

In 1991 the Constitutional Centenary Foundation was formed (Boston, 1996) to encourage public discussion and understanding of arguably the least understood document in public life — the Australian Constitution. Similarly, the 1994 report of the Centenary of Federation Advisory Committee included an analysis of the forthcoming centenary celebrations as well as the encouragement of understanding and review of Australia's history and its constitution (Pascoe, 1996).

Despite these numerous attempts to foster interest in citizenship education they were unable to raise its profile to one of national importance. Individually they had merit, but collectively they failed to make a significant impact on the school curriculum in the Australian states. Most notably, these initiatives in citizenship education were unable to create a critical mass of interest amongst students, teachers, parents or educational bureaucrats. Australians, especially young Australians, remained largely ignorant about their political and government systems and their role as citizens with their country (CEG, 1994; Doig et al., 1994; Print, 1994, 1995a, 1995b).

All that changed in 1994 with creation of the Civics Expert Group (CEG) by the Federal Government and the release of its report *Whereas the people . . . Civics and Citizenship Education* (the beginning words of the Australian constitution) later that year. From that time citizenship education has been a prominent feature in Australian education policy making, media participation, and pressure group activity. But why? How has a critical mass of interest and support for citizenship education been achieved in such an apparently short time?

The factors which achieved a critical mass of support for citizenship education in Australia were already evident. What they lacked was the catalyst to unify them, to galvanize them and inform the wider community. This was found in the role of the Prime Minister, Paul Keating, and the formation, largely on his initiative, of the CEG.

During the 1990s several other broadly-based factors had affected interest in citizenship issues within Australia. Increased educational awareness of citizenship issues through publications and media reports was gradually occurring within the education field; the changing international scene especially in the former Yugoslavia, Germany, and Africa was impacting on concepts of citizenship and countries; Australians were manifesting increasing concern and political disenchantment; the activity of indigenous peoples to address their identity had heightened interest in citizenship; the inexorable refocusing of Australia's identity towards Asia forced

Australians to reconsider their national identity; and the timing of several serendipitous events.

The turning point created by the CEG report was reinforced by a set of
serendipitous factors which have encouraged Australians to reflect upon their identity and in what directions their citizenship may continue. Coming together in
Australia in the mid-1990s, these factors include the approaching centenary of
Australian federation, the Olympic Games in Sydney in 2000, initiatives such as the
Centenary of Australia Advisory Committee and the Ideas for Australia program as
well as the increasing pressure for an Australian republic which has acted as a
vehicle for debate. It is not unreasonable to assert that Australia stands at the beginning of a new age, ready to take on a new set of values that will underpin new
directions and new ideals for what it means to be an Australian. In a sense, Australia is poised, as was the US in the eighteenth century and many Asian and
African nations after 1945, to shape an identity that is unique and distinctive. In this
exercise the role of the school, particularly what is offered as citizenship education
through the school curriculum, will be of vital importance.

Status of Citizenship Education in Australian School Curricula

Despite high levels of interest in matters civic within Australia, citizenship education is largely unknown outside of academia and the educational bureaucracies.
There is little evidence of significant support (or opposition for that matter) from
teachers, students or parents for citizenship education programs in schools. Community groups, with the exception of the non-representative republican and constitutional monarchy supporters, have displayed a remarkable lack of interest in
citizenship education issues. There appears to be a belief that the system of Australian government created by the constitutional makers has worked remarkably
well. Australians identify themselves as participants in one of the most robust,
stable and successful constitutional democracies in the world.

However, when asked by researchers if learning about civics and citizenship
was important for young people, adults quite naturally agreed (Civics Expert Group,
1994). Similar research suggests that Australians, young and old, believe that learning about government, rights and responsibilities and other aspects of citizenship is
important (SSCEET, 1991; Doig et al., 1994; Print, 1995a, 1995b; Bowes, 1995).

Other literature has identified the weaknesses of an ill-informed, or perhaps
under-informed, citizenry (SSCEET, 1989, 1991; Civics Education Group, 1994;
Kennedy and Print, 1994; Musgrave, 1994; Print, 1994; 1995c; Phillips, 1995;
SLCRC, 1995). It is this support, and its manifestation in government policy and
bureaucratic implementation, that argues for representation of citizenship education
in the Australian school curriculum. In this process the single most important factor
has been the inquiry, report and subsequent active government acknowledgment of
the Civics Expert Group.

Civics Education Report

The formation of the Civics Expert Group early in 1994, acting as both a unifying agent and a catalyst, precipitated a critical mass of support for citizenship education. Concern about levels of political literacy had mounted in the late 1980s and early 1990s with the two Senate reports (SSCEET, 1989, 1991) and the release of research data on the political literacy of Australian students (Print, 1994). Increasingly strident media reports called for action. Building upon earlier inquiries and research findings, the CEG report placed this information in a position of political prominence. With bi-partisan support and particularly strong endorsement from the Prime Minister, the CEG had the imprimatur for success.

Presented in December, 1994 the Report was widely endorsed by the Australian education community. Education system and community responses alike were favourable, particularly to the central thrust of the Report and its recommendations for active encouragement of citizenship education in Australian schools. The report was a bold attempt to identify the main directions for civics and citizenship education in Australia and particularly for schools. It briefly examined the history of citizenship education and found it, over the past half century, both sparse and problematic. Researchers will take some time to disentangle the confusing story of civics and citizenship education in Australian schools over that time.

Probably the boldest feature of the report was its suggestions for comprehensive curriculum materials in civics and citizenship education (Civics Expert Group, 1994; Boston, 1996). While emphasizing a government/political/democracy perspective to the materials, the report was quite expansive, encompassing such diverse aspects as our heritage, Australia's multicultural population, active participation of citizens, international relations, and acquiring values including social justice, democratic processes and ecological sustainability. Implementation of engaging curriculum materials will play a major role in achieving the report's goals.

The report did not recommend the creation of new school subjects, accurately realizing the problems this would cause for schools with overcrowded curricula as well as the need to address the participatory nature of citizenship education (Pascoe, 1996). Significantly, the report recommended that citizenship education be taught in the compulsory years of schooling in Australia, with emphasis on Years 5–10 (Civics Expert Group, 1994; Pascoe, 1996). Given the power of the external examinations in Year 12, and their assessment-driven influence over the school curriculum, citizenship education was not recommended for the upper years of secondary schooling (Civics Expert Group, 1994). While this was a realistic recommendation, it has lessened the possible status of citizenship education in schools as well as established a gap between formal learning and use of citizenship skills.

Heartened by the widespread support for the report, the Federal Government took purposeful action through a substantial allocation of targeted funding. In June 1995, some $25 million was directed to support the report's recommendations, with the bulk of funding targeted specifically for school initiatives. Funding was also tied to specific organizations which suited other government agendas:

1   The Curriculum Corporation was allocated $10.6 million over four years to develop curriculum materials for use in lower secondary schools and upper primary schools.

2   Over four years, $6.3 million was directed to enhance teacher effectiveness in citizenship education through professional development under the control of the federal Department of Employment, Education and Training (DEET).

3   The higher education community, through the Open Learning Agency, and TAFE, received small amounts for professional development of teachers.

4   The Attorney-General's Department and the Department of Immigration and Ethnic Affairs were allocated nearly $5 million for community education on citizenship.

5   Government-sponsored forums were identified to inform the educational and broader community about materials and directions in citizenship education.

On the release of this affirmative response to the report, the government moved quickly to consolidate support. A small civics education section was created within the Quality Education Branch of DEET. Its task was primarily policy creation and advice to the Federal Government and, vitally important, allocating funding to activate the government's initiatives. The government has also agreed to a monitoring function over citizenship education including eventual evaluation of all programs emanating from federal funding of citizenship education.

In allocating responsibility for the development of citizenship-oriented curriculum materials to the Curriculum Corporation, the Federal Government ensured a major role for that organization in citizenship education. Arguably, since the CEG report, the production of these curriculum materials, based on federal funding, has placed the Curriculum Corporation at the forefront of initiatives in citizenship education within Australia. The nature of the materials, particularly how they relate to curriculum statements from the states, will be the most significant factor in determining the direction of citizenship education within Australia.

Despite this level of interest and support for citizenship education within educational circles, nowhere has this been manifest as a new school subject. Unlike the United States, resistance to create a new subject by curriculum agencies, such as the NSW Board of Studies, is clearly evident. When curriculum decisions are finalized, the form through which citizenship education is to be studied in Australian schools will be as an integrated part of existing school subjects. This raises significant problems for curriculum implementation and pedagogy in schools.

Furthermore, despite the level of academic and education system support, the current state of citizenship education is characterized by a lack of interest by teachers, both primary and secondary. Given that in the past few years Australian schools have experienced profound and relentless changes to school procedures and curricula, it is not surprising that teachers are resistant to the promise of further change with its consequential implications for teacher change. While some limited evidence of teacher activity exists, such as examples of best practice in citizenship education within schools, a groundswell of teacher support is not evident and will take considerable effort and funding to engender.

Issues Characterizing Citizenship Education in Australia

Australia has moved from a period of rapid development in citizenship education, with relatively high levels of unanimity due to a lack of contestation, to one of greater controversy. Issues characterizing and shaping the citizenship debate during the mid-1990s include conceptions of citizenship education; the republic debate; what values education to incorporate; the role of teachers; and the place of citizenship education within the school curriculum.

Emerging and conflicting conceptions of citizenship education and the degree to which these are inclusive, particularly of gender, ethnicity and indigenous peoples, will be a significant feature of the on-going debate in Australia. Certainly there are increasingly diverse conceptions of citizenship education emerging within Australian literature (Gilbert, 1993; Kennedy, 1995; Macintyre, 1995). One view sees citizenship education concentrating on government, democracy and citizen rights and responsibilities for all Australians (Carter, 1993; Civics Expert Group, 1994; Boston, 1996). At the other end of a curriculum continuum is a view which includes a wide diversity of learnings including additional issues of environment, community, school management and civic virtues (Newell, 1995; Stubbs, 1995). Another conception sees citizenship education focused on issues of gender, ethnicity and particularly indigenous people (Yates, 1995; Kalantzis, 1994; Craven, 1995). These debates are largely confined to the academic literature, and although discussion has intensified dramatically in the last three years through forums, conferences and the media, they have largely failed to affect teachers and schools.

Under the tutelage of the former Labor Government, the issue of Australia as a republic received high profile media attention in recent years. Despite the activities of a counteracting group of constitutional monarchists and calls to maintain traditional loyalties, the march towards a republic moved inexorably along. There is now a new Federal Government that has successfully slowed that momentum, but for how long? As the older, British-oriented proportion of the Australian population diminishes, it is largely replaced by those without such ties and loyalties. And while the republicanism of the early 1990s was more a reflection of intense media attention focused on the Prime Minister rather than a strong tradition, it will surely reappear. The resolution to republicanism will be found in attempts to address the increasingly controversial issue of 'the' Australian identity and what it means to be an Australian in the twenty-first century.

For teachers, educational systems and curriculum agencies, let alone parents and community groups, a significant issue of citizenship education is the deliberate inclusion of a values education component. Recognition that values education is increasingly an integral component of citizenship education, is widespread. But which values? How widespread? Initial response to values inclusion has been largely positive because the representation of values within citizenship is characterized in the most general terms — 'social justice', 'ecological sustainability' and 'democracy'

(Civics Expert Group, 1994). As the disentangling of these values concepts continues increasing concern and controversy is becoming apparent (Gilbert, 1993; Kalantzis, 1994; Pascoe, 1996). The conservative state government in Victoria (Australia's second most populous state) for example, has already removed 'social justice' from its discussions of citizenship education. As curriculum documents are devised by curriculum agencies and applied by schools, the controversial nature of values education will become more pronounced.

Recognition that teachers hold the key to effective implementation of citizenship education is widespread in Australia (Civics Expert Group, 1994; Musgrave, 1994; Print, 1995c, 1996; Boston, 1996). Given that no separate citizenship or civics subject is being developed for Australian schools, how teachers address citizenship education within existing subjects will be crucial. Similarly, the pedagogical strategies teachers select will be of considerable importance for the success of citizenship education within the school curriculum. Consequently teachers will play an even more significant role in the translation of government policy into school reality in the case of citizenship education.

The effective preparation of teachers is acknowledged as crucial to effective implementation of citizenship education in Australian schools (Civics Expert Group, 1994). Conventional wisdom, supported by some research, suggests that Australian teachers are inadequately prepared for teaching citizenship education (Phillips, 1989; Civics Expert Group, 1994; Print, 1995a, 1996; Boston, 1996; Pascoe, 1966). The only way to address this issue is through extensive teacher professional development. The Civics Expert Group report acknowledged this, and the Federal Government allocated support, but this will only commence the process. A major issue for the remainder of the 1990s is what contributions state education systems, schools and teachers themselves, will make to ensure an adequate pedagogical base for citizenship education.

In curricular terms they have an uphill battle. Current student opportunity to learn (OTL) about civics and citizenship is severely limited. A minimal component of citizenship education can be found within one or more lower secondary social studies courses. Some senior secondary subjects, such as Legal Studies, also offer a component of civics and citizenship education. However, given the choice, Australian students have avoided the study of civics and citizenship at any level of secondary school.

Curriculum policy documents such as the *Common and Agreed National Goals for Schooling in Australia* and the curriculum statements and profiles devised as part of the national curriculum initiative in 1993, sought to provide reasonable OTL for students. Without exception these policy documents have failed to be translated into a presence for citizenship education within Australian schools. In the future offerings in citizenship education will be highly dependent on the successful implementation of effective curriculum materials from the Curriculum Corporation and their articulation with respective state curriculum frameworks. At this point in time the most advanced is the NSW Board of Studies, with responsibility for some 750,00 students in Australia's most populous state. The draft citizenship education framework, currently under consideration, is to become operational from 1998.

Within the school curriculum a major issue in this process will be the 'subject battles' for 'ownership' and location of citizenship education. Over the past decade the humanities have been the major loser of status and students within the secondary school curriculum. The mathematics–science–technology triumvirate have been considerably more successful than humanities or the vocational and applied subjects. Within the humanities, history and geography, the traditional 'academic' school subjects, have felt the swing of student attitude against them. Evidence suggests that these subjects will strongly support the concept of including any learnings in citizenship education within their subjects.

Future for Citizenship Education

The immediate future for citizenship education in Australia is dominated by the yet to be finalized Commonwealth's position. After the election early in 1996, the Federal Government reviewed its commitment to civics and citizenship education as part of its general expenditure review. This was part of a drive to balance the budget in the near future and second to ensure that Australians are not swamped with republican sentiment. The outcome of this review, as yet unknown, is absolutely crucial to a successful future for citizenship education in Australia. If support continues, even in a modified way, its future is secured. Through the vehicle of the Civics and Citizenship Education School Curriculum Material Project (CCESCMP) it will become integrated within school curricula around Australia and probably institutionalized in state curriculum documents and practices. This is the most likely scenario.

If not supported federally, it is highly problematic that citizenship education will survive the ensuing financial wasteland. Cash-strapped states are unlikely to continue with initiatives in civics and citizenship education. While waiting for directions from the Federal Government amidst the budget review, the states have successfully avoided any manifestation of strong commitment, and development of curriculum materials, a crucial linch-pin in citizenship education, is unlikely to occur by the states collectively or individually independent of federal funding. Furthermore, as a strong tradition of private sector funding of such projects in Australia is unknown, this is also an unlikely possibility. Consequently, denial of federal funding would undoubtedly spell the end of current citizenship education initiatives and particularly the CCESCMP, the single-most important curriculum initiative in citizenship education. Given its limited funding base, the Curriculum Corporation, which has responsibility for the CCESCMP, would be unable to support such a multi-million dollar project. And without the project, curriculum materials for citizenship education will be severely limited, haphazard and subject to affluent pressure groups. In effect, the current citizenship education will collapse.

Some developments will not fade if federal funding is not forthcoming. Many university research projects will continue as would some university teaching, though the priority status of citizenship research from the Australian Research Council would disappear. The activities associated with the centennial celebrations will continue, though whether they would retain a strong citizenship emphasis is questionable. At best these activities would have a short term impact on schools. Without a driving need created through school-level curriculum application and demand for teacher professional development, interest in citizenship education will revert to unsustainable pre-1994 levels.

Assuming some level of federal support, earlier initiatives reinforced by state level curricula and professional development activities will drive citizenship education into the next crucial stage of implementation. This consists of two parts. First it will seek a considerably higher profile in schools in order to establish itself within the school curriculum. In 1996 it is fair to say that citizenship education is essentially a non-issue in Australian schools and teachers cannot teach what schools do not acknowledge. Second, along with a higher profile will be greater contestation of citizenship education, its nature, its school manifestation, and how it should be taught. As the imperative to include citizenship education becomes greater, so teachers and schools will purposively address its application to the school curriculum.

As these developments become consolidated within schools and educational systems, so the significant issues of accountability and evaluation will arise. Although many Australian educational programs do not have evaluation as an integral component, one has been in-built within the parameters of the CCESCMP. In turn this will produce research and evaluation of programs more broadly to determine, through student outcomes, if citizenship education has made any difference to learners. Boston (1996) asks the important question — How will we know whether we've been successful? Unfortunately this issue has not been raised by many school systems, though the NSWDSE will address Boston's question.

One of the most promising features of the citizenship education revival is the opportunity to identify and apply appropriate pedagogies. In part, this information is already available (Dynesson, 1992; Newell, 1995; Stubbs, 1995; Kennedy, 1996; Print, 1996) and in part future practice and research will ascertain what works best for teachers in Australian schools. Valuable strategies may be found through three recently funded federal projects within the National Professional Development Project. Similarly, a project on citizenship education funded through the Open Learning Agency may offer other promising prospects in distance education.

The profile of citizenship education in Australia is also enhanced through greater international recognition. The CCESCMP and associated Federal Government initiatives have generated considerable international interest and an international conference in Sydney in mid-1997 will provide a valuable fillip to the status and perceived relevance of citizenship education. Many countries are watching Australia's experiment with citizenship education very closely.

After many years of obscurity, citizenship education experienced a rapid renaissance in the first half of the 1990s. Just as the educational community was moving into top gear in policy, curriculum development, professional development, research and conferences, a newly elected Federal Government has placed that renaissance in jeopardy. As government policies emerge and priorities are adjusted, the future for citizenship education in Australia can only be described as hopeful, if somewhat perilous.

9 Citizens for a 'New World Order': A Historical Perspective of Citizenship Education in the United States

Sherry L. Field

Since the beginning of public schooling in the United States, a guiding precept has been to educate young pupils to be good citizens. There is unprecedented agreement about the importance of citizenship education, and it has been established as the single most important element of social studies instruction (Longstreet, 1985; Engle, 1982; Jarolimek, 1982; Remy, 1977). Though the import of citizenship education has been widely accepted, the practice of citizenship education has not been without debate. Considerable confusion over the role and nature of citizenship education practice has transpired. One problem seems to have been the difficulty of defining the social studies and the elements of the social studies necessary for citizenship education (Metcalf, 1963; Barr, Barth, and Shermis, 1977; Engle, 1982; Longstreet, 1985). Another problem that educators, researchers, and theorists have faced is the difficult task of documenting widespread classroom practice emanating from calls to advocacy for citizenship education. Because the United States lacks a prescribed National Curriculum, each state and each individual school district in the nation, is autonomous and may prescribe its own curriculum.

Recently, researchers have reenergized the debate about the current role of citizenship education in the United States as it relates to the content areas known as the social studies (Barth, 1996; Shaver, 1996; and Davis, 1993, 1996). Barth (1996) suggested that the present, confused status of citizenship education is a result of four distinctive purposes and rationales for teaching about citizenship from the past:

1 that citizenship education builds upon the traditional teaching methodologies of patriotic history;
2 that citizenship education promoted by the teaching of patriotic history was reformed by adding elements of an 'analytical scientific approach' recommended by reports from the 1893 National Education Association (NEA) Committee of Ten and the 1899 American Historical Association (AHA) Committee of Seven;
3 that 'effective democratic citizenship' (Barr, Barth, and Shermis, 1977, p. 19) should be fostered in addition to teaching history through the scientific approach, as recommended by the 1905 AHA Committee;

4   that 'social studies sought to reform nineteenth-century citizenship education. . . . which had much to do with inculcating patriotism but little to
do with developing thoughtful, decision-making citizens in a democratic
society.' (Barth, 1996, p. 13)

Various goals and standards have been set for education in America over the last
two centuries, and ideas about who should teach the nation's children, when they
should be taught, and what should be taught, have been a lively subject for discussion among educators. Often, a prevailing political trend is mirrored in school
curriculum rhetoric and practice. An overarching goals or objectives statement
describing the type of civics education in which pupils should engage is typically
included in curriculum materials. According to Earl F. Butts,

> for two hundred years, the American people have struggled with the dilemma of
> politics and education. On one hand, they believe that education is fundamental to
> the health and vitality of a democratic community, but, on the other hand, they do
> not believe that schools in a democracy ought to be involved in something called
> 'political education'. We have gone to enormous lengths to provide universal, free,
> compulsory, common schools in response, at least in part, to the rhetoric that civic
> education should be available, even required, of all students; yet we draw back
> from the precipice of political indoctrination or inculcation of political ideas. (Butts,
> 1980, p. 51)

An introspective survey of the successes and failings of programs designed to help
students achieve the skills and attitudes necessary for good citizenship is important.
A brief look at some of the issues surrounding the evolution of citizenship education in the United States may help illuminate some of the critical choices facing
contemporary educators and schools today.

The Early Years of Citizenship Education

The notion of educating children for citizenship in a democratic society has enjoyed
a rich history in early American public schooling. The founders of the Republic
agreed that education in America should be focused upon the ideals of liberty,
democracy, equality, popular consent, and understanding of the common good. Free
public schooling for the common citizen was determined to be the 'best means of
educating the citizenry in the cohesive civic values, knowledge, and obligations
required of everyone in a democratic republican society' (Butts, 1980, p. 54). Following the American Revolution, the first textbooks about American history, government, and civic education were published around 1790. Early textbook writers
promoted moral and religious themes, as well as patriotic beliefs and an overwhelming devotion to the 'American way of life'. Noah Webster's reading and
spelling books included didactic character education themes and the promotion of
a sense of loyalty, duty, and love of country. American leaders and ideals were

exalted in early American textbooks. For example, Ruth Elson noted an early textbook's deification of George Washington, described as 'The most unexceptionally, the most finished, the most Godlike human character that ever acted a part of the theatre of the world' (1964, p. 195). Children who studied these textbooks were to be loyal to the nation, patriotic, and virtuous.

By the 1830s, teachers routinely engaged children in recitations, lessons, and activities in order to promote the inculcation of good character, virtue, morality, and citizenship. For decades a fixture in classrooms was the McGuffey Readers series and others similar to it, such as Uncle John's Second Reader (Rudnitzki, 1995). Popularly used from their first publication in 1836, the McGuffey Readers posited stories from the Bible, larger than life stories of heroes, poems, and universal truths to help young Americans become good citizens. While undeniable in their religious overtones, McGuffey Readers also advocated values such as frugality, cleanliness, honesty, hard work, dedication, patriotism, and obedience (Field, 1996a).

Barth (1996, p. 13) argued, however, that critical discussions in schools about a 'citizens' individual values and beliefs and their consequences, social/personal problems and issues, and the practice of democracy' were not fostered by the type of citizenship education 'that taught moral lessons from McGuffey's Readers or patriotic history because both are based on indoctrination, which discourages the practice of reflective decision making' (Barth, 1996, p. 13). For the first years in the American republic:

> civic education put preeminent stress upon the inculcation of civic values, relatively less on political knowledge as such, and made no discernible attempt to develop participatory political skills. Learning to participate was left to the incipient political parties, the town meetings, the churches, the coffee houses, and the ale houses where men gathered for talk and conviviality. (Butts, 1980, p. 56)

Horace Mann emphasized the concept of free schooling being made available to all American children in the mid-1800s, and, by doing so, added fuel to the fiery citizenship education debate. Schooling had previously been the domain of private schools and religious schools for those who could afford it, and charity schools for a small number of needy students. Mann asserted that all students, including a large, formerly disenfranchised population of poor or immigrant children, should be entitled to a civic education and learn about the government of America. Teachers were encouraged to initiate 'children into the political community by literacy in English, didactic moral injunctions, patriotic readers and histories, and lessons that stressed recitations of the structural forms of the constitutional order' (Butts, 1980, p. 61). Apparent, too, was evidence that the values and character education ideals being promoted in schools were very different from the values evident in the day-to-day application of civic practice. The gap seemed to widen between perceived best practice and reality. While immigrant children began to learn about their civic and moral responsibilities to their new country, 'the goal of civic education embraced rapid assimilation to an ideal American political system' (Butts, 1980, p. 62).

The Twentieth Century and Citizenship Education

Citizenship education as practiced in public schools from the late 1800s to the early 1900s had a primary focus of socializing American children and assimilating immigrant children into the mainstream culture as quickly as possible. One popular tool used by teachers, clubs, and parents was the 'Children's Morality Code', which was a four-page brochure that consisted of ten major desirable character traits: self-control, kindness, self-reliance, reliability, truth, good workmanship, teamwork, duty, sportsmanship, and good health (Hutchins, 1917). The formation of clubs for children of 'good character' abounded, with the assumption that peer pressure might help children practice such character traits from the 'Children's Morality Code'. The extant patriotism expressed in schools during the Spanish-American War and World War I heightened to a nationalistic furor, and citizenship education was considered to be of utmost importance. In addition, waves of immigrants continued to pour into the country, and many politicians and laypeople considered their presence to be a threat to the mainstream culture. Increasingly, civic education took on a nationalistic and boastful tenor that sang the praises of the United States as a superior nation and demanded blind loyalty. According to Butts (1980), this shift in the emphasis led to notions of manifest destiny, an attempt at the instant Americanization of immigrants, and to an emphasis on self-made men.

Many Americans worried that the didactic, moralistic approaches of previous character and citizenship education programs were not appropriate. In 1916, a committee of the American Political Science Association argued that citizenship education should have a different focus, toward 'community civics', placing an emphasis for civics education close to home. Also during this time, the responsibility of 'citizenship education' fell to the social studies. According to Hertzberg, 'The Report of the Committee on Social Studies [of the NEA's Commission on the Reorganization of Secondary Education] had a significant impact on the direction of educational reform. . . . Instruction in the social studies should be organized around concrete problems of vital importance to society and of immediate interest to the pupil rather than on the basis of the formal social sciences' (1981, pp. 11–12).

The 1920s and 1930s spawned an outpouring of social reform and progressive education movements. Fears about the moral decline of America's youth generated during the Roaring Twenties spawned even more serious attention to character education during Prohibition (Kirschenbaum, 1994). Most school districts in the nation reflected a concern for a strong character education program by offering such programs in their elementary and secondary grades. Researchers began to question the success of American schools' character education programs. A major study by Hartshorne and May (1928–1930), the *Character Education Inquiry*, sought the answer to this query from over 10,000 young people in twenty-three areas across the United States. The study revealed that students who had been engaged in traditional character education programs displayed no more desirable character traits than did the rest of the population.

By 1930, courses specifically designed to teach civics and government were widely added to the curriculum. Especially in junior high schools, usually in the upper grades, and in high school, at the 11th or 12th grade level, these courses tended to follow NEA (National Education Association) and APSA (American Political Science Association) guidelines set forth in the previous decade which called for 'substantial treatment of the institutions of constitutional government in concert with studies of citizenship in local communities' (Patrick and Hoge, 1991, p. 428). 'Citizenship' readers became widely available during this time, although the number of formal programs to promote them lessened as the policies of the New Deal began to provide stability and hope. Education reform proposals recommended by the progressives and social reconstructionists, abandoned as radical, led to a 'movement back again to the more traditional emphasis on the structure of government and on patriotic values' (Shaver and Knight, 1986, p. 73).

While many programs of the New Deal shaped the nation's economic transformation, citizenship education for a nation on the verge of World War II encompassed several major themes. These included promotion of character education, inculcation of patriotism and symbolic rituals, endorsement of community activities, understanding of democratic principles, focus on American heroes and historical figures, and participation in patriotic pageants. Interest in citizenship education increased dramatically as documentation surfaced of life in the German dictatorship and totalitarian state in the early stages of European conflict and Japanese military expansion during the 1930s (Field, 1992, 1994).

The National Council for the Social Studies published three documents during World War II designed to help teachers carry out their wartime civic duties in school classrooms and to help students carry out community service projects (Field, 1996a). These were *The Social Studies Mobilize for Victory* (National Council for the Social Studies, 1942), *Wartime Social Studies in the Elementary School* (Chase, 1943), and *The Social Studies Look Beyond the War: A Statement of Postwar Policy* (National Council for the Social Studies, 1994). Social studies educators were urged to expand classroom emphasis on citizenship. The *Wartime Handbook of Education* (National Education Association, 1943) exhorted, 'the democratic way of life must be understood and appreciated by all citizens of a democracy'. Elementary and secondary school students were to learn about 'dramatic, key episodes in the history of American democracy, biographies of men and women whose lives have advanced or personified the democratic tradition; great documents in American history; contrasts between democracy and dictatorship; civil liberties and the responsibilities and self disciplines as well as the privileges of citizenship' (1943, p. 18).

Teachers selected many of these suggested emphases in order to increase attention to citizenship education during World War II realizing the importance of allaying normal fears of their students and they undertook this responsibility. Educators recognized the need for children to understand problems enlarged by war, such as the necessity to conserve war materials and accept substitutes willingly, to appreciate the huge financial costs of war and the consequent necessity to buy savings bonds and stamps, and to accept and understand the necessity for wartime rationing willingly. In addition to teaching about the economics of war as a patriotic and civic duty, teachers were also urged to promote loyalty to the principles of democracy in various ways. Endorsing the emotional nature of patriotism, Chase

(1943) advised social studies educators to use flag salutes, pledges, rituals, the singing of the national anthem, patriotic music, exhibits, bulletin boards, posters, artistic creations, motion pictures, radio programs, assembly programs, stories of heroes, and slogans as part of their daily classroom rituals. As World War II progressed, school children were encouraged to participate in various citizenship-related activities and projects to benefit the war effort and to maintain a high morale on the home front including many activities such as war bond and stamp sales campaigns, scrap collection drives, field trips to army camps, learning patriotic songs, making posters, participating in plays and pageants, and learning how to take more responsibility at home (Field, 1994, 1995, and 1996; Davis, 1993 and 1996).

By war's end, a move toward peacetime education with an emphasis on tolerance and world citizenship occurred. Citizenship education as a primary morale-builder on the home front gave way to an emphasis upon preventing the spread of communism. The socio-political atmosphere of the United States and the status of education during the late 1940s and early 1950s were open to widespread criticism from the general public. Among various problems often mentioned were a lack of money to build new schools, increased enrollments in schools caused by war babies born after 1945, a concern on the part of industry for a well-educated work force, the increased criticism of the school curriculum, and a pervasive fear of the spread of communism, advanced in large part by McCarthy advocates. Some critics of education believed that a continuation of progressive pedagogy indicated 'subversive plots that would lead to communist takeover of the United States' (Hepburn, 1990, p. 156). Demands were made for 'patriotic assemblies in the schools and more "Americanism" in the civic education curriculum' and for 'classroom recitation(s) of the traits of a "good citizen"' (Hepburn, 1990, p. 156).

The twenty-second NCSS yearbook (Carey, 1951) noted efforts being made in schools across the country to increase citizenship education. Various curriculum projects and teacher education efforts were reported. One hundred and thirty-five behaviors indicative of a good citizen were identified, and a bibliography of journal articles on citizenship education was provided, while over 1000 organizations with stated intentions to promote citizenship education were also recognized (Carey, 1951). The American Association of School Administrators publication, *Educating for American Citizenship* (1954), cautioned teachers and administrators to be mindful of the dangers of communism and to promote devotion to democracy with an informed citizenry. Along with calls to advocacy for teaching the merits of good citizenship were calls for educational reform.

By 1956, teachers in many parts of the country were burdened with the oppressiveness of overt and self-censorship (Foster, 1996) and attacks on teacher loyalty were widely reported, as were accusations against Americans in other professional fields. The National Council for the Social Studies' Committee on Academic Freedom vehemently opposed such attacks. Other social studies educators 'argued that the distinction must be made between indoctrination, which is the authoritarian method of social studies education, and reflective thinking, which is the democratic method' (Hepburn, 1990, pp. 156–157).

The schizophrenic nature of citizenship education also merited attention during the 1950s. A concern for the lack of an accepted definition of 'citizenship' was advanced by Niemeyer (1957) when he wrote,

> Current writers seem to have gone beyond the earlier acceptance of citizenship as merely synonymous with personal virtues, such as honesty, friendship, and responsibleness. Many of these educators think of citizenship as being concerned with all human relationships, while others urge us to limit our definitions lest we fail to educate for better citizenship simply because our goals are too broad. (1957, p. 214)

Paul Hanna addressed a concern for a reassessment of what it means to be a 'good citizen' when he noted,

> the development of [the] understanding and behavior of the good citizen cannot be left to chance; the stakes of cultural survival and progress are too high to permit anything less than a careful and comprehensive selection of those generalizations and values which are thought to give the greatest assurance of sound social arrangements and progress. (Hanna, 1957, pp. 27–28)

The new social studies movement of the 1960s suggested a more selective structure for social studies instruction. It included key decision-making skills to help students engage in 'public and private matters of social concern' (Engle, 1982, p. 301), as well as decision-making and problem-solving exercises. The movement focused on streamlined purposes for teaching social studies: 1) to prepare children to be good citizens, 2) to teach children how to think, and 3) to pass on cultural heritage (Fenton, 1967, p. 1). Fenton also noted that by the early 1960s 'the curricular reform movement reached the social studies' only with the realization that the 'social studies had failed to keep pace with curricular reform in science and mathematics' (p. 3). Social studies education also benefited from new information about how children learn, requiring that new textbooks and curriculum materials be written, and from an influx of money available to fund research in science, math, and social sciences. Localized examples of specific, hands-on citizenship education have been reported from this period, such as the education programs utilized by the Mississippi Freedom Schools (Chilcoat and Ligon, 1994). In 1971, the American Political Science Association Committee on Pre-Collegiate Education (1971) recommended that political science and civics education in the United States should emphasize 'knowledge about political behavior and processes, . . . skill in the process of social science inquiry, and . . . skills needed to participate effectively and democratically in the life of the society' (pp. 4–5).

As selected aspects of the 'new social studies' became a part of many school social studies curriculum offerings, a shift in educational trends and philosophies occurred in the 1970s. Politically split apart as a result of the crises of the unpopular Vietnam War and a growing lack of confidence in the government, partially resulting from the Watergate scandal, Americans were also divided about the nature of citizenship education. Many schools across the nation became involved in creative 'open classroom' experiments intended to revolutionize the curriculum and teaching practice, while others began to promote democratic concepts of pluralism (Hepburn, 1993). In spite of a wave of innovative approaches to education, and the celebration of the nation's bicentennial whose events spread over many months, a grave concern about the status of citizenship education in America was voiced:

> despite the conscientious efforts of many educators, citizenship education is in disarray. There is little evidence to indicate that the school's citizenship education efforts have affected generally the quantity or quality of adult citizen participation, and social studies programs and school environments often appear to be inconsistent with the demands of 'adult citizenship'. (Shaver, 1977, pp. vi–vii)

After the Conference on Citizenship Education, sponsored by the National Council for the Social Studies in March 1976, NCSS Bulletin 52: *Building Rationales for Citizenship Education* (Shaver, 1977) was published. In it, important theoretical issues about citizenship education, such as varying approaches to achieving civic competence, and the problems inherent in a problem-solving, consciousness raising approach to teaching civics, were raised.

Newmann's (1977) lead chapter in the Bulletin focused on the 'conceptual problem' of civic education and described eight approaches to achieving civic competence, including the following:

- Academic Disciplines: This approach assumes that learning 'scholarly material will help the citizen understand any civic problems that might come about and advocates the human search for truth'.

- Law Related Education: In the past, this approach has been characterized in civics classes by studying the Bill of Rights or the Constitution. This interpretation of the civics curriculum strives to help students learn how the legal system applies to them. The goal of this approach is to preserve and make more just the role of law in a democracy.

- Social Problems: This approach concentrates on issues that relate to students' lives, such as war, crime, and poverty, and strives to understand, and therefore, solve the problems.

- Critical Thinking: This approach is seen to be a cornerstone of civic competence. It involves learning a thinking process for assessing various issues and for testing, evaluating, valuing, and inferring.

- Values Clarification: When using values clarification processes, students investigate their central values through nonjudgmental questioning and interpretations. The goal is to help students become 'purposeful, enthusiastic, and positive'.

- Moral Development: Kohlberg's moral reasoning levels are the emphases of this approach. It differs from values clarification, in that it recognizes that certain levels of reasoning are advantageous.

- Community Involvement: This approach supports students' learning by doing. It advocates any real world experiences of citizenship, such as volunteering at a hospital or for a political campaign.

- Institutional School Reform: This approach is based on the assumption that school life has more impact than anything taught in a classroom and that students should be allowed more responsibility and involvement in decision-making at their school. (Newmann, 1977, pp. 4–8)

Berlak (1977) posited that the goal of citizenship education, or political education, was that of consciousness-raising. This goal was to be manifested by increasing students' capacities to see themselves from the perspective of others and to explore and pursue alternatives. Students should gain awareness and understanding of life situations, physical, social, and historical contexts, acquire the language and concepts necessary for thinking about social structures, and use skills to analyze life situations (p. 42).

Participatory citizenship projects were also advanced during the 1970s (Conrad and Heidin, 1977; Remy, 1979; Stahl, 1979) and attempts were made to identify the processes and practices necessary to achieve good citizenship. In the *Handbook of Basic Citizenship Competencies*, Remy (1979) developed a set of seven universal competencies needed by citizens, which included acquiring and using information, assessing involvement and stake in political situations, making decisions, making judgments, communicating, cooperating, and promoting interests. Suggestions for teacher use were provided for primary, intermediate, junior high, and high school levels of instruction. Similarly, educators were advised to incorporate the use of problem-solving and decision-making processes in order to help students 'comprehend and apply content, clarify their values and moral reasoning, and learn to make rational decisions in the contemporary world' (Stahl, 1979).

The 'Back to the Basics' curriculum movement of the 1980s seemed to secure the place of civics and political science education in the high school curriculum, while teaching civics declined in middle schools and junior high schools. In 1986, the completion of a high school government or civics course was required for graduation by 70 per cent of states, and only about 20 per cent of middle schools required a civics course (Patrick and Hoge, 1991). Also during the 1980s, a trend to include law-related education (LRE) in the curriculum was noticed. Law-related education's inclusion as a social studies topic or its introduction as a new, independent course was considered to be a high priority by state social studies specialists. Various other curriculum reform movements of the 1980s supported the requirement of a government course in high school and the promotion of government, civics, and law-related education as an integral part of the social studies curriculum content in elementary and middle schools was evident, as well (Butts, 1980; Bennett, 1986 and 1987). Two civics-related projects, CIVITAS and the *Our Democracy: How America Works*, began on a large scale in 1988. CIVITAS was developed by the Council for the Advancement of Citizenship and the Center for Civic Education and provided high school teachers with sophisticated, well-planned lessons and a cohesive framework for citizenship education. *Our Democracy: How*

America Works was developed by the Foundation for Teaching Economics and the Constitutional Rights Foundation and combined government, civics, and law into meaningful units of instruction. These and other, less publicized curriculum projects paved the way for the development of a set of standards by which to gauge civics instruction and a call toward considering pluralism, interdisciplinary opportunities, the democratic ideal, global perspective, cultural diversity, and participatory citzenship (Hepburn, 1993; Wraga, 1993; Parker, 1991) as important tenets of citizenship education in the 1990s.

Goals 2000: Educate America Act of 1994, clearly delineated the civic mission of schools. Two goals were most closely linked to citizenship education: Goal 3, Student Achievement and Citizenship, affirmed that 'by the year 2000, all students will leave grades 4,8, and 12 having demonstrated competency over challenging subject matter including . . . civics and government . . . so that they may be prepared for responsible citizenship, further learning, and productive employment'; Goal 6, Adult Literacy and Lifelong Learning, noted that 'by the year 2000, every adult American will be literate and will possess the knowledge and skills necessary to . . . exercise the rights and responsibilities of citizenship'. The United States Center for Civics Education developed comprehensive, voluntary *National Standards for Civics and Government*. The Standards are content-based and were not intended to serve as course outlines, instead, they were designed as 'exit standards', to signify what students should know at the fourth, eighth, and twelfth grade levels.

The *National Standards for Civics and Government* emphasize the civic mission of schools and the need for increased attention to civic education. At each of the three highlighted grades, several overarching content questions are provided, along with content summaries and rationales, content standards, and evaluative measures. For example, a grade 4 organizing content question is, 'What is government and what should it do?' that might lead to an investigation of the question 'What is government?' The accompanying content standard is that of 'defining government' (a working definition is provided), and

> students should be able to . . . describe government in terms of the people and groups who make, apply, and enforce rules and laws for others in their family, school, community, and nation and who manage disputes about them, e.g., 1) adult family members make, apply, and enforce rules for their children and manage disputes about them, 2) teachers, principals, and school boards make, apply, and enforce rules and laws for their schools and manage disputes about them, 3) city councils and mayors make, apply, and enforce rules for their communities, 4) governors and state legislatures make, apply, and enforce rules and laws for their states, 5) tribal governments make, apply, and enforce rules and laws for tribal members in Indian country, 6) the national government makes, applies and enforces rules and laws for the nation, and 7) courts at all levels apply laws, manage disputes, and punish lawbreakers.

For fourth grade students, seven other content standards accompany this question, including: defining power and authority, necessity and purposes of government, functions of government, purposes of rules and laws, evaluating rules and laws, limited and unlimited governments, and importance of limited government. (Center for Civics Education, 1994, pp. 15–40). The Center for Civics Education (1994) recognized that 'standards alone cannot improve student achievement, teacher performance, or schools quality, but they can be an important stimulus for change' (94, p. vi). The overall effect of the Civics and Government Standards upon the American students' achievement of civic competence has not yet been determined. Clearly, the Standards hold promise as a framework for educators.

Citizenship education, enacted eagerly as public schooling began in this country, has undergone periods of highlighting and blurred shadowing, from the 1700s to the present. From the earliest organized schooling, which emphasized citizenship education as a moral imperative; to a move toward shaping students' character in the early 1900s; to the unwavering citizenship education tactics undertaken during World War II; to the critical thinking, problem solving strategies taught during the New Social Studies movement of the 1960s; to the development of a set of *National Standards for Civics and Government Education* in the 1990s, citizenship education has adapted to the perceived needs of the society. Citizenship education has always, and likely will continue, to hold a place of prominence in the American school curriculum.

References

ADAMS, D. and GOTTLIEB, E.E. (1993) *Education and Social Change in Korea*, New York: Garland.

ALLEN, J.W. (1977) *A History of Political Thought in the Sixteenth Century*, London: Methuen.

AMERICAN ASSOCIATION OF SCHOOL ADMINISTRATORS (1954) *Educating for Democracy*, Arlington, VA: American Association of School Administrators.

AMERICAN POLITICAL SCIENCE ASSOCIATION OF PRE-COLLEGIATE EDUCATION (1971) *Political Education in the Public Schools: The Challenge for Political Science*, Washington, DC: American Political Science Association.

AMIN, M. and CALDWELL, M. (Eds) (1977) *Malaya: The Making of a Neo-Colony*, Nottingham: Russell Press Limited.

AMSDEN, A. (1992) *Asia's Next Giant: South Korea and Late Industrialization*, Oxford: Oxford University Press.

ANDERSON, B. (1983) *Imagined Communities*, London: Verso.

ANDERSON, P. (1974) *Lineages of the Absolutist State*, London: Verso.

ANDERSON, R.D. (1975) *Education in France, 1848–1870*, Oxford: Oxford University Press.

ANDREWS, G. (Ed) (1991) *Citizenship*, London: Lawrence and Wishart.

APPELBAUM, R. and HENDERSON, J. (Eds) (1992) *States and Development in the Asia Pacific Rim*, London: Sage.

ARCHER, M. (1979) *The Social Origins of Education Systems*, London: Sage.

ARCHER, M. and VAUGHAN, M. (1971) *Social Conflict and Educational Change in England and France, 1789–1848*, Cambridge: Cambridge University Press.

ARISTOTLE (1981) *The Politics*, (Rev. edn.), SAUNDERS, T.J. (Ed), Harmondsworth: Penguin.

ARTZ, F.B. (1966) *The Development of Technical Education in France, 1500–1850*, Cambridge, Massachusetts: M.I.T. Press.

ASHCRAFT, R. (1986) *Revolutionary Politics and Locke's Two Treatises of Government*, Princeton: Princeton University Press.

ASHTON, D.N. and SUNG, J. (1994) *The State, Economic Development and Skill Formation: A New Asian Model, Centre for Labour Market Studies*, University of Leicester.

AUSTRALIAN EDUCATION COUNCIL (AEC) (1989) *Common and Agreed National Goals for Schooling in Australia*, Melbourne: Australian Education Council.

AUSTRALIAN EDUCATION COUNCIL (AEC) (1992) *Listening to Girls*, Melbourne: Australian Education Council.

BACCHI, C. and EVELINE, J. (1996) 'The politics of incorporation', in BACCHI, C.L. *Affirmative Action in Context: Category Politics and the Case for 'Women'*, London: Sage.

BAHMUELLER, C. (1991) *Civitas: A Framework for Civic Education*, Calabasas, CA: Center for Civic Education.

BAIROCH, P. (1993) *Economics and World History*, London: Harvester Wheatsheaf.

BARBALET, J. (1988) *Citizenship*, Open University Press, Milton Keynes.

BARBER, B. (1984) *Strong Democracy: Participatory Politics for a New Age*, Berkeley: University of California Press.

BARR, R.D., BARTH, J.L. and SHERMIS, J.L. (1977) *Defining the social studies*, Bulletin 51, Washington, DC: National Council for Social Studies.

BARTH, J.L. (1996) 'NCSS and the nature of social studies', in DAVIS, JR., O.L. (Ed) *NCSS in Retrospect*, Bulletin 92, Washington, DC: National Council for the Social Studies.

BATHO, G. (1990) 'The history of the teaching of civics and citizenship in English Schools', *The Curriculum Journal*, **1**, 1, pp. 91–107.

BAUDRILLARD, J. (1983) *In the Shadow of the Silent Majorities . . . or the End of the Social, and Other Essays*, New York: Semiotexte(E), Inc.

BAUDRILLARD, J. (1986) *L'Amérique*, Paris: B. Grasset.

BECK, U. (1992) *Risk Society: Towards a New Modernity*, London: Sage.

BEILHARZ, P., CONSIDINE, M. and WATTS, R. (1992) *Arguing About the Welfare State: The Australian Experience*, Sydney: Allen & Unwin.

BENDIX, R. (1964) *Nation-Building and Citizenship*, Sanford University of California Press.

BENHABIB, S. (1992) *Situating the Self: Gender, Community and Postmodernism in Contemporary Ethics*, Cambridge UK: Polity Press.

BENHABIB, S. (1993) 'Feminist theory and Hannah Arendt's concept of public space', *History of the Human Sciences*, **6**, 2, pp. 97–114, London: Sage.

BENNETT, J. (1986) *First Lessons: A Report on Elementary Education in America*, Washington, DC: US Department of Education.

BENNETT, J. (1987) *James Madison High School: A Curriculum for American Students*, Washington, DC: US Department of Education.

BENTHAM, J. (1943) 'Constitutional code book 1', in *The Works of Jeremy Bentham Vol IX*, Edinburgh: W. Tait.

BERLAK, H. (1977) 'Human consciousness, social criticism and civic education', in SHAVER, J.P. *Social Studies in the Elementary School*, (The fifty-six yearbook of National Society for the Study of Education), Chicago: Chicago University Press, pp. 34–47.

BERLIN, I. (1969) *Four Essays on Liberty*, Oxford: Oxford University Press.

BERRELL, M. (1993) 'Classrooms as sites for citizenship education', in KENNEDY, K., WATTS, O. and McDONALD, G. (Eds) *Citizenship Education for a New Age*, Toowoomba: University of Southern Queensland Press, pp. 62–77.

BEST, R. (1994) 'Care, control and the community', in LANG, P., BEST, R. and LICHTENBERG, A. (Eds) *Caring for Children: International Perspectives on Pastoral Care and PSE*, London: Cassell.

BIGGS, J. (1995) 'Quality in education: A perspective from learning, research and theory', in SIU, P.K. and TAM, T.K. (Eds) *Quality in Education: Insights from Different Perspectives*, Hong Kong: Hong Kong Educational Research Association, pp. 50–69.

BITTMAN, M. (1995) 'Recent changes in unpaid work', ABS Catalogue No. 4154.0, Canberra.

BODIN, J. (1962) 'Six Books of the Commonwealth', McRAE, K. (Ed) Cambridge, Mass: Harvard University Press.

BOLI, J. (1989) *New Citizens for a New Society: The Institutional Origins of Mass Schooling in Sweden*, Oxford: Pergamon.

BOND, M.H. (1993) 'Between the yin and yang: the identity of the Hong Kong Chinese', Professorial Inaugural Lecture Series, No. 19, Chinese University Bulletin.

BOSTON, K. (1996) 'Civics and citizenship: Priorities and directions', *Unicorn*, **22**, 1, pp. 84–88.

BOTTERY, M. (1992) 'Education for citizenship in the 21st century', *Curriculum*, **13**, 3, pp. 196–201.

BOWES, J. (1995) 'Adolescents' ideas about citizenship and democracy', Paper presented at the annual conference, Australian Association for Research in Education, Hobart.

BRAY, M. and HUI, P. (1991) 'Macau', in MARSH, C. and MORRIS, P. (Eds) *Curriculum Development in East Asia*, London: Falmer, pp. 181–201.

BRAY, M. and LEE, W.O. (1993) 'Education, democracy and colonial transition: The case of Hong Kong', *International Review of Education*, **39**, 6, pp. 541–566.

BRENNAN, M. (1996) 'Sustaining new forms of school life? A response to Stuart Macintyre', in KENNEDY, K. (Ed) *New Challenges for Citizenship Education*, Canberra: Australian Curriculum Studies Association.

BRUBACHER, R. (1992) *Citizenship and Nationhood in France and Germany*, Cambridge: Harvard University Press.

BRUNE, F. (1993) 'Les Médias pensent comme moi!': Fragments du Discours Anonyme, Paris: L'Harmattan.

BRUNT, R. (1989) 'The politics of identity', in HALL, S. and JACQUES, M. (Eds) *New Times: The Changing Face of Politics in 1990s*, London: Lawrence and Wishart.

BURCHELL, D. (1994a) 'The virtuous citizen and the commercial society: The unhappy prehistory of citizenship and modernity', *Communal/Plural*, **2**.

BURCHELL, D. (1994b) 'Civic virtue, civic advice: Genealogies of citizenship and modernity', *Political Theory Newsletter*, **6**, 1.

BURCHELL, D. (1995a) 'The attributes of citizens: Virtue, manners and the activity of citizenship', *Economy and Society*, **24**, 4, August.

BURCHELL, D. (1995b) 'Just citizens? Dialects of citizenship and justice', *Melbourne Studies in Education*, **2**, 36.

BURCHELL, G. (1991) 'Peculiar interests: Civil society and governing the system of natural liberty', in BURCHELL, G., GORDON, C. and MILLER, P. (Eds) *The Foucault Effect: Studies in Governmentality*, Hemel Hempstead: Harvester Wheatsheaf.

BURKES, A.W. (Ed) (1985) *The Modernizers: Overseas Students, Foreign Employees, and Meiji Japan*, Boulder, USA: Westview Press.

BUTTS, R.F. (1980) *The Revival of Civic Learning: A Rationale for Citizenship Education in American Schools*, Bloomington IND: Phi Delta Kappa Education Foundation.

CAPPO, D. and CASS, B. (1994) 'Reworking Citizenship and Social Protection: Australia in the 1990s', Paper presented to the 26th World Conference of the International Council on Social Work, Global Welfare '94, Tampere, Finland, July.

CAREY, R.W. (Ed) (1951) *Education for Democratic Citizenship*, Washington, DC: National Council for Social Studies, 22nd Yearbook.

CARTER, J. (1993) 'Parliamentary education — A strategy for teaching about politics in school', in KENNEDY, K. et al. (Eds) *Citizenship for a New Age*, Toowoomba: USQ Press.

CASS, B. (1994) 'The state and economy in Australia. An overview of work, welfare and the position of women', *Social Politics*, No. 1.

CASTELLS, M. (1992) 'Four Asian Tigers with a dragon's head: A comparative analysis of the state, economy and society in the Asian Pacific Rim' in APPELBAUM, R. and HENDERSON, J. (Eds) *States and Development in the Asia Pacific Rim*, London: Sage.

CASTLES, F. (1985) *The Working Class and Welfare*, Sydney: Allen & Unwin.

CENTER FOR CIVIC EDUCATION (1994) *National Standards for Civics and Government*, Calabasas, CA: Center for Civic Education.

CENTER FOR CIVIC EDUCATION (1994) 'The Role of Civic Education: A Report of the Task Force on Civic Education', Paper prepared for the Second Annual White House Conference on Character Building for a democratic, Civil Society, 19–20 May.

CHANG, P. (1973) *Educational Development in a Plural Society: A Malaysian Case Study*, Singapore: Academia Publications.

CHARLESWORTH, H. (1992) *Has the United Nations Forgotten the Rights of Women? Research and Information Series*, Canberra: Australian Council for Overseas Aid.

CHASE, W.L. (1943) *Wartime Social Studies in the Elementary School*, Washington, DC: The National Council for the Social Studies.

CHEN, Y.T. (1994) 'School citizenship education in the Republic of China of Taiwan', *Journal of the Middle States Council for the Social Science*, **15**, 1, pp. 21–33.

CHILCOAT, G.W. and LIGON, J.A. (1994) 'Developing democratic citizens: The Mississippi freedom schools as a model for social studies instruction', *Theory and Research in Social Education*, **22**, 2, pp. 128–175.

CHILDREN'S SOCIETY (1991) *Education for Citizenship*, London: Children's Society.

CHOLI, P.K. (1980) 'A search for cultural identities: The students' movements of the early seventies', in SWEETING, A.E. (Ed) *Differences and Identities: Educational Argument in Late Twentieth Century Hong Kong*, Hong Kong: Faculty of Education, University of Hong Kong, pp. 81–107.

CIVICS EXPERT GROUP (1994) *Whereas The People . . . Civics and Citizenship Education*, Canberra: Australian Government Publishing Service.

CLARK, A. (1996) 'Civics and citizenship and the teaching of values', *Unicorn*, **22**, 1, pp. 54–58.

COCKBURN, C. (1991) *In The Way of Women: Men's Resistance to Sex Equality in Organisations*, Basingstoke: Macmillan.

COHEN, J. and ARATO, A. (1992) *Civil Society and Political Theory*, Cambridge, Mass: MIT Press.

COLLINS, H. (1985) 'Political Ideology in Australia: The Distinctiveness of a Benthamite Society', *Daedalus*, **114**.

COMMISSION ON CITIZENSHIP (1990) *Encouraging Citizenship*, London: HMSO.

CONNELL, R.W. (1987) 'Curriculum politics, hegemony and strategies of social change', Unpublished paper.

CONNELL, R.W. (1987) *Gender and Power*, Stanford: Stanford University Press.

CONNELL, R. (1971) *The Child's Construction of Politics*, Melbourne: Melbourne University Press.

CONNELL, R. (1994) 'Knowing about masculinity teaching boys and men: Education implications on the new sociology of masculinity and the old sociology of schools', Paper presented at the Annual Conference of the Pacific Sociological Association, San Diego.

CONRAD, D. and HEIDIN, D. (1977) 'Learning and earning citizenship through participation', in SHAVER, J.P. *Social Studies in the Elementary School*, The fifty-six yearbook of National Society for the Study of Education, Chicago: Chicago University Press, pp. 48–73.

CONSTANT, B. (1988) 'The liberty of the ancients compared to that of the modern', in FONTANA, B. (Ed) B. *Constant, Political Writings*, New York: Cambridge University Press.

CORRIGAN, P. and SAYER, D. (1985) *The Great Arch: English State Formation as Cultural Revolution*, Oxford: Blackwell.

CRAVEN, R. (1995) 'Incorporating Aboriginal studies and perspectives into citizenship education', *The Social Educator*, **14**, 3, November.

CRITTENDEN, B. (1995) 'The revival of civics in the school curriculum: Comments on the Report of the Civics Expert Group', *Melbourne Studies in Education*, **36**, 2, pp. 21–30.

CROOK, S., PAKULSKI, J. and WATERS, M. (1992) *Postmodernization: Change in Advanced Society*, London: Sage.

CUBAN, L. (1992) 'Curriculum stability and change', in JACKSON, P. (Ed) *Handbook of Research on Curriculum*, New York: Macmillan.

CUMMINGS, W.K. (1980) *Education and Equality in Japan*, Princeton: Princeton University Press.

CUMMINGS, W., GOPINATHAN, S. and TOMODA, Y. (1988) (Eds) *The Revival of Values Education in Asia and the West*, Oxford: Pergamon.

CURRICULUM DEVELOPMENT COMMITTEE (1985) *Guidelines on Civic Education in Schools*, Hong Kong Government.

CURRICULUM DEVELOPMENT COUNCIL (1986) *Guidelines on Sex Education in Schools*, Hong Kong Government.

CURRICULUM DEVELOPMENT COUNCIL (1987) *The School Based Curriculum Project Scheme*, Hong Kong Government, paper 11/87.

CURRICULUM DEVELOPMENT COUNCIL (1992) *Guidelines on Environmental Education in Schools*, Hong Kong Government.

CURRICULUM DEVELOPMENT INSTITUTE (1994) *A Study on Knowledge and Attitudes of Secondary School Pupils on Sex and Sex Education*, Hong Kong: Curriculum Development Council.

CURRICULUM DEVELOPMENT INSTITUTE (1995) *A Study on the Development of Civic Awareness and Attitudes of Pupils of Secondary Schools in Hong Kong*, Hong Kong: Hong Kong Government.

CURTIS, B. (1988) *Building the Educational State: Canada West, 1836–1871*, London, Ontario: Falmer Press.

DAHL, R. (1989) *Democracy and Its Discontents*, Yale University Press: New Haven.

DAVEY, I. and MILLER, P. (1990) 'Family formation, schooling and the patriarchal state', in THEOBALD, M. and SELLECK, D. (Eds) *Family, School and State in Australian History*, London: Allen and Unwin.

DAVEY, I. and MILLER, P. (1993) 'Patriarchal Transformations, Schooling and State Formation', Paper for Social Science History Association Conference, New Orleans.

DAVIES, I. (1994) 'The nature of education for citizenship', *Social Science Teacher*, **24**, 1, pp. 2–4.

DAVIS, G., WANNA, J., WARHURST, J. and WELLER, P. (1993) *Public Policy in Australia*, 2nd edn, Sydney: Allen & Unwin.

DAVIS, O.L., JR. (1993) 'Citizenship education as the central purpose of the social studies: The heavy load of a dead metaphor', *The International Journal of Social Education*, **6**, pp. 33–36.

DAVIS, O.L., JR. (1996) 'Toward celebration and continuance: An invitation to reflection', in DAVIS, O.L. JR. (Ed) *NCSS in Retrospect*, Bulletin 92, Washington, DC: National Council for the Social Studies.

DE TOCQUEVILLE, A. (1956) *The Old Regime and the French Revolution*, translated by Stuart Gilbert, New York.

DEAN, M. (1994a) *Critical and Effective Histories: Foucault's Methods and Historical Sociology*, London: Routledge.

DEAN, M. (1994b) 'A social structure of many souls: Moral regulation, government and self formation', *Canadian Journal of Sociology*, **19**, 12.

DEARING, R. (1994) *The National Curriculum and Its Assessment*, SCAA.

DEPARTMENT OF EDUCATION AND SCIENCE (DES) (1963) *Half Our Future: A Report of the Central Advisory Council for Education (England)*, (The Newsom Report), London: HMSO.

DEPARTMENT OF EDUCATION AND SCIENCE (DES) (1980) *Framework for the Curriculum*, London: HMSO.

DEYO, F. (1992) 'The political economy of social policy formation: East Asia's newly industrialized countries', in APPELBAUM, R. and HENDERSON, J. (Eds) *States and Development in the Asia Pacific Rim*, London: Sage.

DIAMOND, L. (1994) 'Rethinking civil society: Towards democratic consolidation', *Journal of Democracy*, **5**, 3, pp. 4–17.

DOIG, B., PIPER, K., MELLOR, S. and MASTERS, G. (1994) *Conceptual Understanding in Social Education*, Melbourne: Australian Council for Educational Research.

DORE, R. (1984) *Education in Tokugawa Japan*, London: Athlone.

DORE, R. and SAKO, M. (1989) *How the Japanese Learn to Work*, London: Routledge.

DURKHEIM, E. (1956) *Education and Sociology*, trans. FOX, S.D. Illinois: Glencoe.

DWORKIN, R. (1981) 'What is equality? Part 2: Equality of resources', *Philosophy and Public Affairs*, **10**.

DYNNESON, T. (1992) 'What's hot and what's not in effective citizenship instruction', *The Social Studies*, Sept/Oct.

DYNNESON, T. and GROSS, R. (1991) 'Citizenship education in American society', in GROSS, R. and DYNNESON, T. (Eds) *Social Science Perspectives on Citizenship Education*, New York: Teachers College Press, pp. 1–42.

DYNNESON, T., GROSS, R. and NICKEL, J. (1992) 'Can student perceptions be used to improve citizenship education?', *International Journal of Social Education*, **7**, 1.

EDUCATION AND MANPOWER BRANCH AND EDUCATION DEPARTMENT (EMB ED) (1991) *The School Management Initiative: Setting a Framework for Quality in Hong Kong Schools*, Hong Kong: Government Printer.

EDUCATION BILLS (1995) *Percetakan National Malaysia* BHD, Kuala Lumpur: Percetakan Nasional Malaysia BHD.

EDUCATION DEPARTMENT (1981) *General Guidelines on Moral Education in Hong Kong*, Hong Kong Government.

EDUCATION DEPARTMENT (1996) *Guidelines on Civic Education in Schools*, Hong Kong Government.

EDWARDS, J. and FOGELMAN, K. (1991) 'Active citizenship and young people' in FOGELMAN, K. (1991b) *Citizenship in Schools*, London: David Fulton Publishers.

EDWARDS, J. and FOGELMAN, K. (1993) *Developing Citizenship in the Curriculum*, London: David Fulton Publishers.

EDWARDS, J. and PATHAN, L. (Eds) (1993) *Cross-Curricular Resources and INSET Pack*, Cambridge: Pearson Publishing.

ELGQVIST-SALTZMAN, I. (1995) *Personal Communication*, 28 June.

ELGQVIST-SALTZMAN, I., PRENTICE, A. and MACKINNON, A. (in press) *Dangerous Terrain for Women? Education into the Twenty-first Century*, London: Falmer Press.

ELIAS, N. (1978) *The Civilising Process, Vol. 1, The History of Manners*, New York: Pantheon.

ELSON, R.M. (1964) *Guardians of Tradition: American Schoolbooks of the Nineteenth Century*, Lincoln, Nebraska: University of Nebraska Press.

ENGLE, S.H. (1982) 'Defining the social studies: What is the problem?', *The Social Studies Teacher*, **3**, 5, pp. 1, 4, and **3**, 6, pp. 3–5.

ENGLE, S. and OCHOA, A. (1988) *Education for Democratic Citizenship: Decision-making in the Social Studies*, New York: Teachers College Press.

EVELINE, J. (1994) 'The politics of advantage', *Australian Feminist Studies*, **19**, pp. 129–154.

EVELINE, J. (1995) 'The (Im)possible reversal: Advantage, education and the process of feminist theorising', in *Lararuitbildning och forskning i Umea* (Teacher Education and Research in Umea) **2**, 3–4, pp. 29–46.

FEDERATION OF MALAYA (1956) *Report of the Education Committee 1956*, Kuala Lumpur: Government Press.

FEDERATION OF MALAYA (1960) *Report of the Education Committee 1960*, Kuala Lumpur: Government Press.

FEDERATION OF MALAYA (1961) *Education Act 1961*, Kuala Lumpur: Government Press.

FENTON, E. (1967) *The New Social Studies*, New York: Holt, Rinehart and Winston, Inc.

FIELD, S.L. (1991) 'Doing their bit for victory: Elementary school social studies during World War II', unpublished doctoral dissertation, The University of Texas at Austin.

FIELD, S.L. (1992) 'Old Glory, the Constitution, and responsible Americanism: Elementary school citizenship education during World War II', *Citizenship as Social Studies Education*, Foundations of the Social Studies Special Interest Group, Bulletin 4, pp. 4–13.

FIELD, S.L. (1994) 'Scrap drives, stamp sales and school spirit: Examples of elementary social studies during World War II', *Theory and Research in Social Education*, **23**, 1, pp. 441–460.

FIELD, S.L. (1995) 'Intercultural education, a wartime recognition of oversight, and Negro history in Chicago schools', *Midwest History of Education Society*, **22**, pp. 75–85.

FIELD, S.L. (1996a) 'Roosevelt's World War II army of community service workers: Children and their teachers', *Social Education*, **60**, 5, pp. 280–283.

FIELD, S.L. (1996b) 'Character education: A historical perspective', *The Educational Forum*, **60**, 2, pp. 118–123.

FLIEGELMAN, J. (1982) *Prodigals and Pilgrims. The American Revolution Against Patriarchal Authority, 1750–1800*, Cambridge: Cambridge University Press.

FOGELMAN, K. (1990) 'Citizenship in secondary schools: A national survey', (Appendix E) in *Speaker's Commission on Citizenship*.

FOGELMAN, K. (1991a) 'Citizenship in secondary schools: The national picture', in FOGELMAN, K. *Citizenship in Schools*, London: David Fulton Publishers.

FOGELMAN, K. (Ed) (1991b) *Citizenship in Schools*, London: David Fulton Publishers.

FOSTER, S. (1996) 'Red alert! The National Education Association's National Commission for the Defense of Democracy through Education confronts the "Red Scare" in American Schools', unpublished doctoral dissertation, University of Texas at Austin.

FOSTER, V. (1989) 'Is "gender-inclusive" curriculum the answer for girls?', in LEDER, G.C. and SAMPSON, S.N. (Eds) *Educating Girls: Practice and Research*, Sydney: Allen & Unwin, pp. 26–38.

FOSTER, V. (1992) 'Different but equal? Dilemmas in the reform of girls' education', *Australian Journal of Education*, **36**, 1, pp. 53–67.

FOSTER, V. (1994a) 'Making women the subject of educational change: An interdisciplinary and comparative study', unpublished doctoral dissertation, Macquarie University.

FOSTER, V. (1994b) 'What about the boys! Implications of the theory/policy/curriculum nexus for the education of girls and boys', *Education Links*, **48**, pp. 4–7.

FOSTER, V. (1995) '"What about the boys!" Presumptive equality as the basis for policy change in the education of girls and boys', in published proceedings of the 1995 National Social Policy Conference, 'Social Policy and the challenges of Social Change', University of New South Wales, 5–7 July.

FOSTER, V. (1996a) 'Space Invaders: Desire and threat in the schooling of girls', *Discourse: Studies in the Cultural Politics of Education*, **17**, 1, pp. 43–63.

FOSTER, V. (1996b) '*Whereas the People* and civics education: Another case of "add women and stir?"' *Curriculum Perspectives*, **16**, 1, pp. 52–56.

FOUCAULT, M. (1977a) *Discipline and Punish*, trans. SHERIDAN, A. New York: Pantheon.

FOUCAULT, M. (1977b) *Language, Counter-Memory, Practice*, BOUCHARD, D. (Ed) Ithaca: Cornell University Press.

FOUCAULT, M. (1978) *The History of Sexuality, Vol. 1, An Introduction*, trans. HURLEY, R. New York: Pantheon.

FOUCAULT, M. (1980) *Power/Knowledge*, GORDON, C. (Ed) New York: Pantheon.

FOUCAULT, M. (1986a) *The History of Sexuality, Vol. 2, The Use of Pleasure*, New York: Pantheon.

FOUCAULT, M. (1986b) *The History of Sexuality, Vol. 3, The Care of the Self*, New York: Pantheon.

FOUCAULT, M. (1988) 'Politics and Reason', in KRITZMAN, L. (Ed) *Michel Foucault: Politics, Philosophy, Culture*, New York: Routledge.

FOUCAULT, M. (1991) 'Governmentality', in BURCHELL, G., GORDON, C. and MILLER, P. (Eds) *The Foucault Effect: Studies in Governmentality*, Hemel Hempstead: Harvester Wheatsheaf.

FRANKLIN, J. (1973) *Jean Bodin and the Rise of Absolutist Theory*, Cambridge: Cambridge University Press.

FRANKLIN, J. (1978) *John Locke and the Theory of Sovereignty: Mixed Monarchy on the Right Resistance in the Political Thought of the English Revolution*, Cambridge: Cambridge University Press.

FRANKLIN, J. (1992) *Bodin: On Sovereignty*, Cambridge: Cambridge University Press.

FRANKLIN, J. (1993) *Jean Bodin and the Sixteenth-century Revolution in the Methodology of Law and History*, New York: Harper.

FUNG, Y.W. and LEE, C.K. (1993) 'Environmental education in Hong Kong Secondary Schools', Paper presented at the UNESCO Conference: Overcoming the barriers to environmental education through teacher education, Australia: Griffith University.

FURNIVALL, J.S. (1948) *Colonial Policy and Practice: A Comparative Study of Burma and India*, Cambridge: Cambridge University Press.

GAMBLE, A. (1981) *Britain in Decline*, London: Macmillan.

GAVISON, R. (1992) 'Feminism and the public/private distinction', *Stanford Law Review*, **45**, 1, pp. 1–5.

GELLNER, E. (1983) *Nations and Nationalism*, Oxford: Blackwell.

GELLNER, E. (1993) *Postmodernism, Reason and Religion*, London: Routledge.

GIBBINS, J. (1989) 'Contemporary political culture: An introduction', in GIBBINS, J. (Ed) *Contemporary Political Culture: Politics in a Postmodern Age*, London: Sage.

GIDDENS, A. (1981) *A Contemporary Critique of Historical Materialism, Vol. 1, Power, Property and the State*, Berkeley: University of California Press.

GIDDENS, A. (1982) 'Class division, class conflict and citizenship rights', in *Profiles and Critiques in Social Theory*, London: Macmillan.

GIERKE, O. (1959) *Political Theories of the Middle Ages*, Boston: Beacon Press.

GILBERT, R. (1992) Citizenship, education and postmodernity, *British Journal of Sociology of Education*, **13**, 1, pp. 51–68.

GILBERT, R. (1993) 'Citizenship and the problem of identity', in KENNEDY, K., WATTS, O. and McDONALD, G. (Eds) *Citizenship Education for a New Age*, Toowoomba: University of Southern Queensland Press, pp. 87–100.

GILBERT, R. (in press) 'Identity, culture and environment: Education for citizenship for the twenty-first century', in DEMAINE, J. and ENTWISTLE, H. (Eds) *Citizenship, Politics and Education*, London: Paul Chapman.

GIROUX, H.A. (1980) 'Critical theory and rationality in citizenship education', *Curriculum Inquiry*, **10**, 4, pp. 327–366.

GOLDMAN, R. and PAPSON, S. (1994) 'The postmodernism that failed', in DICKENS, D. and FONTANA, A. (Eds) *Postmodernism and Social Inquiry*, London: UCL Press.

GOPINATHAN, S. (1994) 'Educational Development in a Strong-Developmentalist State: The Singapore Experience', Paper presented at the Australian Association for Research in Education Annual Conference.

GORDON, C. (1987) 'The soul of the citizen: Max Weber and Michel Foucault on rationality and government', in LASH, S. and WHIMSTER, S. (Eds) Max Weber: Rationality and Modernity, London: Allen & Unwin.

GORDON, C. (1991) 'Governmental rationality: an introduction', in BURCHELL, G., GORDON, C. and MILLER, P. (Eds) *The Foucault Effect: Studies in Governmentality*, Hemel Hempstead: Harvester Wheatsheaf.

GRAYCAR, R. (1992) 'Before the high court: Women's work, Who cares?' *14 Sydney Law Review*, **86**, pp. 8–105.

GRAYCAR, R. (1993) 'Legal categories and women's work: Explorations for a cross-doctrinal feminist jurisprudence', *Canadian Journal of Women and the Law*, **6**.

GREEN, A. (1990) *Education and State Formation: The Rise of Education Systems in England, France and the USA*, London: Macmillan.

GREEN, A. (1991) *Education and State Formation*, Macmillan: London.

GREEN, A. (1994) 'Postmodernism and state education', *Journal of Education Policy*, **9**, 1, pp. 67–83.

GROVES, M. (1983) *Sevenoaks VSU*, Sevenoaks Voluntary Service Unit.

GUTMANN, A. (1987) *Democratic Education*, Princeton: Princeton University Press.

HABERMAS, J. (1991) *The Structural Transformation of the Public Sphere*, trans. BURGER, T., Cambridge, Mass: MIT.

HALL, S. (1989) 'The meaning of new times', in HALL, S. and JACQUES, M. (Eds) *New Times: The Changing Face Of Politics in the 1990s*, London: Lawrence And Wishart.

HAMILTON, V.L., BLUMENFELD, P.C., AKOH, H. and MIURA, K. (1984) Citizenship and scholarship in Japanese and American fifth grades', *American Educational Research Journal*, **26**, 1, pp. 44–72.

HANCOCK, W. (1930) *Australia*, London: Ernest Benn.

HANNA, P. (1957) 'Generalizations and universal values: Their implications for the social studies program', in HENRY, N.B. (Ed) *Social Studies in the Elementary School: The Fifty-sixth yearbook of National Society for the Study of Education*, Chicago: Chicago University Press, pp. 22–47.

HANSENNE, M. (1992) 'Women fail to make gains in workplace: Percentage in workforce expected to decline', *International Labor Organisation: Press Release*, 6 September.

HARIS, M.J. (1993) 'Implementing a national Curriculum: Tradition vs. Change', *Pacific-Asian Education*, **5**, 2, pp. 1–9.

HARIS, M.J. and AHMAD, K. (1987) *Values Education in Malaysia: State-of-the-Practice* Review. SEARRAG.

HARTSHORNE, H. and MAY, M.A. (1928–1930) *Studies in the Nature of Character*, Vols. 1–3, New York: Macmillan.

HARVEY, D. (1989) *The Condition of Postmodernity: An Enquiry into the Origins of Cultural Change*, Oxford: Blackwell.

HARVEY, D. (1990) *The Condition of Post-Modernity*, Oxford: Blackwell.

HEATER, D. (1990) *Citizenship: The Civic Ideal in World History, Politics and Education*, London: Longman.

HEBDIGE, R. (1990) 'Fax to the future', *Marxism Today*, January, pp. 18–23.

HELD, D. (1987) *Models of Democracy*, Cambridge: Polity Press.

HELD, D. (1989) *Political Theory and the Modern State*, Cambridge: Polity Press.

HELD, D. (1989) *Political Theory and the Modern State*, Stanford: University of California Press.

HEPBURN, M.A. (1990) 'Education for democracy: The years following World War II', *The Social Studies* (July/August), pp. 153–160.

HEPBURN, M.A. (1993) 'Concepts of pluralism and the implications for citizenship education', *The Social Studies* (January/February), pp. 20–26.

HERTZBERG, H.W. (1981) *Social studies reform, 1880–1980*, A Project Span Report. Boulder, CO: Social Studies Education Consortium.

HILL, B. (1996) 'Civics and citizenship and the teaching of values', *Unicorn*, **22**, 1, pp. 34–43.

HILL, M. and FEE, L.K. (1995) *The Politics of Nation-Building and Citizenship in Singapore*, London: Routledge.

HINDESS, B. (1986) *Discourses of Power: From Hobbes to Foucault*, Oxford: Blackwell.

HMI (1977) *Curriculum 11–16*, London: HMSO.

HOBBES, T. (1978) 'The citizen (De Cive): Philosophical rudiments concerning government and society', in GERT, B., SMITH, P. (Ed) *T. Hobbes, Man and Citizen*, Mass: Gloucester.

HOBBES, T. (1962) *Leviathan*, OAKESHOTT, M. (Ed) New York: Collier Books.

HOBSBAWM, E.J. (1969) *Industry and Empire*, Harmondsworth: Penguin.

HOBSBAWN, E.J. (1977) *The Age of Capital 1848–1875*, London: Abacus.

HOBSBAWM, E.J. (1990) *Nations and Nationalism since 1780: Programme, Myth, Reality*, Cambridge: Cambridge University Press.

HOBSBAWM, E.J. (1994) *The Age of Extremes: The Short Twentieth Century, 1914– 1991*, London: Michael Joseph.

HOGAN, D. (1990) 'Modes of discipline: The New England pedagogy, 1820–1850', *Journal of American Education*, November, 1–56.

HOGAN, D. (1996) 'Before virtue: A study in the theory of interests and civics education', *Australian Educational Researcher*, **22**, 3, pp. 45–70.

HOGAN, D. (1996a) 'The liberty of the moderns: Interests, justice and civic education', *Melbourne Studies in Education*, **37**, 1, May, pp. 57–88.

HOGAN, D. (1996b) 'Liberal Democracy: From Citizenship to Civics', Paper presented to the Culture and Citizenship Conference, Australian Key Centre for Cultural and Media Policy, Griffith University, October 1.

HOGAN, D., FEARNLEY-SANDER, M. and LAMB, S. (1996) 'From civics to citizenship: Whereas the people and civic education', in KENNEDY, K. (Ed) *New Challenges for Citizenship Education*, Canberra: Australian Curriculum Studies Association.

HORIO, T. (1988) *Educational Thought and Ideology in Modern Japan*, edited and translated by PLATZER, S., Tokyo: University of Tokyo Press.

HOY, A. (1925) *Civics for Australian Schools*, Melbourne: Lothian Publishing Co.

HUBBACK, E.M. and SIMON, E.D. (1934) *Education for Citizenship*, Morley College for Working Men and Women.

HUME, D. (1948a) 'Of the first principles of government', in AIKEN, H. (Ed) *Hume's Moral and Political Philosophy*, New York: Hafner Press.

HUME, D. (1948b) 'Of the social contract', in AIKEN, H. (Ed) *Hume's Moral and Political Philosophy*, New York: Hafner Press.

HUME, D. (1978) *A Treatise on Human Nature*, NIDDITCH, P.H. (Ed) Oxford: Clarendon Press.

HUNTER, I. (1993) 'Culture, bureaucracy and the history of popular education', in MEREDYTH, D. and TYLER, D. (Eds) *Child and Citizen: Genealogies of Schooling and Subjectivity*, Brisbane: Griffith University Press.

HUNTER, I. (1994) *Rethinking the School*, Sydney: Allen & Unwin.

HUTCHINS, W.J. (1917) *Children's Code of Morals for Elementary Schools*, Washington, DC: Character Education Institution.

ICHILOV, I. (1994) 'Political education', in HUSEN, T. and PASTLEWAITE, T.N. (Eds) *The International Encyclopaedia of Education*, 2nd edition, Oxford: Pergamon.

IDEAS FOR AUSTRALIA PROGRAM (1993) *Issues for Citizenship Education*, Melbourne: The Author.

IGNATIEFF, M. (1987) 'The myths of citizenship', *Queens Law Journal, 12, 399–420*.

JAMESON, F. (1984) 'Postmodernism, or the cultural logic of late capitalism', *New Left Review*, **146**, pp. 53–92.

JAROLIMEK, J. and PARKER, W.C. (1991) *Social Studies in Elementary Education* (9th Ed), New York: Macmillan.

JOHNSON, C. (1982) *MITI and the Japanese Miracle: The Growth of Industrial Policy, 1925–1975*, Stanford: Stanford University Press.

JOINT STANDING COMMITTEE ON MIGRATION (JSCM) (1994) *Australians All: Enhancing Australian Citizenship*, Canberra: Australian Government Publishing Service.

KAESTLE, C.F. (1983) *Pillars of the Republic: Common Schools and American Society, 1780–1860*, New York: Hill and Way.

KALANTZIS, M. (1994) 'Republicanism and cultural diversity', in HUDSON, W. and CARTER, D. (Eds) *The Republican Debate*, Sydney: University of New South Wales Press.

KANT, I. (1991) *Kant: Political Writings*, REISS, H. (Ed) Cambridge: Cambridge University Press.

KEATING, P. (1994) 'Membership of the Civics Expert Group', statement by the Prime Minister, Canberra, 23 June.

KELLNER, D. (1992) 'Popular culture and the construction of postmodern identities', in LASH, S. and FRIEDMAN, J. (Eds) *Modernity and Identity*, Oxford: Blackwell.

KENNEDY, K. (1993) 'Why citizenship education for Australian schools?', in KENNEDY, K., WATTS, O. and McDONALD, G. (Eds) *Citizenship Education for a New Age*, Toowoomba: USQ Press.

KENNEDY, K. (1995) 'Conflicting conceptions of citizenship and their relevance for the school curriculum', in PRINT, M. (Ed) *Civics and Citizenship Education: Issues from Practice and Research*, Canberra, Australian Curriculum Studies Association.

KENNEDY, K. (1996) (Ed) *New Challenges for Citizenship Education*, Canberra, Australian Curriculum Studies Association.

KENNEDY, K. (1996) 'Best Practice Programs in Civics and Citizenship Education', Commissioned paper, Canberra, Curriculum Corporation.

KENNEDY, K. (1993) 'Why citizenship education for Australian schools?', in KENNEDY, K., WATTS, O. and McDONALD, G. (Eds) *Citizenship Education for a New Age*, Toowoomba: USQ Press, pp. 1–3.

KENNEDY, K. (1995) 'Civics education as a component of the school curriculum: The Australian experience in early twentieth century Australia', Paper presented for the Annual Meeting of the Society for the Study of Curriculum History, San Fransisco, 17–18 April.

KENNEDY, K. (1995) 'Conflicting conceptions of citizenship and their relevance for the school curriculum', in PRINT, M. (Ed) *Civics and Citizenship Education: Issues from Practice and Research*, Canberra: Australian Curriculum Studies Association, pp. 13–18.

KENNEDY, K. (1995a) 'Civics education in the US is near universal but may be short on values', *ACE News*, **14**, 2, pp. 7–8.

KENNEDY, K. (1996) 'Civics and Citizenship Education: A New Priority for the School Curriculum', Keynote address prepared for the Canberra Summer School for Teachers of Studies of Society and the Environment, University of Canberra, 24 January.

KENNEDY, K. and PRINT, M. (1994) 'Citizenship education for a new age', Keynote address, National Council for the Social Studies annual conference, Phoenix, Arizona.

KING, D. and WALDRON, J. (1988) 'Citizenship, social citizenship and the defence of welfare provision', *British Journal of Political Science*, **18**, pp. 415–443.

KIRSCHENBAUM, H. (1994) *100 Ways to Enhance Values and Morality in Schools and Youth Settings*, Boston: Allyn and Bacon.

KITSON, N. (1993) 'Drama', in Edwards J. and Fogelman K. *Developing Citizenship in the Curriculum*, London: David Fulton Publishers.

KOIKE, K. and INOKI, T. (Eds) (1990) *Skill Formation in Japan and South East Asia*, Tokyo, University of Tokyo Press.

KOREAN EDUCATION DEVELOPMENT INSTITUTE (1985) *Korean Education 2000*, Seoul: KEDI.

KOREAN EDUCATION DEVELOPMENT INSTITUTE (1984) *Schooling and Social Achievement*, Seoul: KEDI.

KROKER, A. and COOK, D. (1986) *The Postmodern Scene: Excremental Culture and Hyper-Aesthetics*, New York: St Martin's Press.

LANDES, D. (1969) *The Unbound Prometheus: Technological Change and Industrial Development in Western Europe from 1750 to the Present*, Cambridge: Cambridge University Press.

LASH, S. and URRY, J. (1987) *The End of Organised Capitalism*, Cambridge: Polity Press.

LASH, S. and URRY, J. (1994) *Economies of Signs and Space*, London: Sage.

LASH, S. (1990) *Sociology and Postmodernism*, London: Routledge.

LAU, S.-K. and KUAN, H.-C. (1988) *The Ethos of the Hong Kong Chinese*, Hong Kong: The Chinese University Press.

LECA, J. (1992) 'Questions on citizenship', in MOUFFE, C. (Ed) *Dimensions of Radical Democracy: Pluralism, Citizenship, Community*, London: Verso.

LEE, W.O. and BRAY, M. (1995) '*Education: Evolving Pattern and Challenges*', in CHENG, Y.S. and LO, S.H. *From Colony to SAR: Hong Kong's Challenges Ahead*, Hong Kong: The Chinese University Press.

LEE, W.O. (1991) *Social Change and Educational Problems in Japan, Singapore and Hong Kong*, London: Macmillan.

LEECH, M. (1994) 'Women, the State and Citizenship: "Are women in the building or in a separate annex?"', *Australian Feminist Studies*, **19**.

LEPANI, B. (1996) 'Education in the information society', in KENNEDY, K. (Ed) *New Challenges for Citizenship Education*, Canberra: Australian Curriculum Studies Association.

LEUNG, S.W. (1995) 'Depoliticization and trivialization of civic education in secondary schools: Institutional constraints on promoting civic education in transitional Hong Kong', in SIU, P.K. and TAM, T.K. (Eds) *Quality in Education: Insights from Different Perspectives*, Hong Kong: Hong Kong Educational Research Association.

LLOYD, G. (1984) *The Man of Reason: 'Male' and 'Female' in Western Philosophy*, London: Methuen.

LOCKE, J. (1963) *The Two Treatises of Government*, LASLETT, P. (Ed) New York: Mentor.

LOCKE, J. (1964a) *An Essay Concerning Human Understanding*, WOOZLEY, A.D. (Ed) New York: Meridan.

LOCKE, J. (1964b) *John Locke on Education*, GAY, P. (Ed) New York: Teachers College Press.

LOH, P. (1975) *Seeds of Separatism: Educational Policy in Malaya 1874–1940*, Kuala Lumpur: Oxford University Press.

LOH, P. (1983) 'Ethnicity, Politics and Education: A Study in the Development of Malayan education and its policy implementation process', unpublished thesis, University of Keele.

LONGSTREET, W.S. (1985) 'Citizenship: The phantom core of social studies curriculum', *Theory and Research in Social Education*, **13**, 2, pp. 21–29.

LUK, H.K. (1991) 'Chinese culture in the Hong Kong curriculum, heritage and colonialism', *Comparative Education Review*, **34**, 4.

LUKE, C. (1992) 'Feminist politics in radical pedagogy', in LUKE, C. and GORE, J. (Eds) *Feminisms and Critical Pedagogy*, New York: Routledge, pp. 25–53.

LUKE, T. (1986–7) 'Televisual democracy and the politics of democracy', *Telos*, **70**, pp. 59–79.

LYOTARD, J. (1984) *The Postmodern Condition: A Report on Knowledge*, Manchester: Manchester University Press.

MACINTYRE, A. (1981) *After Virtue: A Study in Moral Theory*, Notre Dame: University of Notre Dame Press.

MACINTYRE, S. (1985) *Winners and Losers: The Pursuit of Social Justice in Australian History*, Sydney: Allen & Unwin.

MACINTYRE, S. (1994) 'Concerns about Citizenship Education', paper to the Prime Minister and Cabinet, Melbourne: The Author.

MCINTYRE, S. (1996) 'Diversity, citizenship and the curriculum', in KENNEDY, K. (Ed) *New Challenges for Citizenship Education*, Canberra: Australian Curriculum Studies Association.

MACINTYRE, S. (1991) *A Colonial Liberalism: The Lost World of Three Victorian Visionaries*, Melbourne: Oxford University Press.

MACINTYRE, S. (1995) 'Diversity, citizenship and the curriculum', Keynote address, Biennial Conference of the Australian Curriculum Studies Association, The University of Melbourne, 13 July 1995.

MCNALLY, D. (1989) 'Locke, levellers and liberty: Property and democracy in the thought of the first whigs', *History of Political Thought*, **X**, 1, Spring.

MacPherson, C.B. (1977) *The Life and Times of Liberal Democracy*, Oxford: Oxford University Press.

Madison, J. ' "Federalist #10" and "Federalist #51" ', in Hamilton, A., Jay, J. and Madison, J. (Eds) *The Federalist: A Commentary on the Constitution of the United States*, New York: E.M. Earle.

Malaysia (1970) *Federal Constitution*, Kuala Lumpur: Government Press.

Malaysia (1971) *Second Malaysia Plan 1971–1975*, Kuala Lumpur: Government Press.

Mann, M. (1987) 'Ruling strategies and citizenship', *Sociology*, **21**, 3, pp. 339–54.

Manning, D.J. (1976) *Liberalism*, New York: St Martin's Press.

Marquand, D. (1988) *The Unprincipled Society: New Demands and Old Politics*, London: Cape.

Marsh, C. and Morris, P. (Eds) (1991) *Curriculum Development in East Asia*, London: Falmer Press.

Marshall, T. (1964) *Class, Citizenship and Social Development*, Doubleday, New York.

Marshall, T.H. (1950) *Citizenship and Social Class*, Cambridge: Cambridge University Press.

Marshall, T.H. (1964) 'Citizenship and Social Class', in Marshall, T. *Class, Citizenship and Social Development*, Chicago: Chicago University Press.

Martin, J.R. (1981) 'The ideal of the educated person', *Educational Theory*, **31**, 2, pp. 97–109.

Martin, J.R. (1985) *Reclaiming a Conversation. The Ideal of the Educated Woman*, New Haven NY: Yale University Press.

Martin, J.R. (1991) 'The contradiction and the challenge of the educated woman', *Women's Studies Quarterly*, **1** and **2**, pp. 6–27.

Martin, J.R. (1996) 'The wealth of cultures and the poverty of curriculum; or, education and our great unmooring', 1996 John Dewey Lecture, American Education Research Association, New York, April.

Marx, K. (1967) *Capital, Vol. 1*, New York: International Publishers.

Marx, K. (1975) 'On the Jewish question', in *Karl Marx: Early Writings*, Harmondsworth: Penguin.

Massey, D. (1994) *Space, Place and Gender*, Cambridge: Polity Press.

Mayer Report (1992) *Employment-related Key Competencies: A Proposal for Consultation*, Melbourne: Owen King.

Mead, L. (1986) *Beyond Entitlement: The Social Obligations of Citizenship*, New York: Free Press.

Mellor, S. (1996) 'What can history contribute to the development of citizenship curriculum', *Unicorn*, **22**, 1, pp. 72–81.

Melton, J. Van Horn (1988) *Absolutism and the 18th-Century Origins of Compulsory Schooling in Prussia and Austria*, Cambridge: Cambridge University Press.

Metcalf, L.E. (1963) 'Research on teaching the social studies', in Gage, N.L. (Ed) *Handbook of Research on Teaching*, Chicago: Rand McNally.

MEYER, J. (1988) 'A subtle and silent transformation: Moral Education in Taiwan and the PRC', in CUMMINGS, W., GOPINATHAN, S. and TOMODA, Y. (Eds) *The Revival of Values Education in Asia and the West*, Pergamon: Oxford.

MILL, J. (1967) *Essays on Government, Jurisprudence, Liberty of the Press and Law of Nations*, New York: Augustus M. Kelley.

MILL, J.S. (1958) *Considerations on Representative Government*, SHIELDS, C.V. (Ed) Indianapolis: Bobbs Merril.

MILL, J.S. (1970) 'The subjection of women', in ROSSI, A.S. (Ed) *Essays on sex equality*, Chicago and London, The University of Chicago Press. Originally published 1869, pp. 123–242.

MILL, J.S. (1989) 'On liberty', in COLLINI, S. (Ed) *J.S. Mill: On Liberty and Other Writings*, Cambridge: Cambridge University Press.

MILLER, D. (1995) *Acknowledging Consumption: A Review of New Studies*, London: Routledge.

MINISTRY OF EDUCATION (1979) *Report of the Cabinet Committee on the Implementation of Education*, Kuala Lumpur: Dewan Bahasa dan Pustaka.

MINISTRY OF EDUCATION (1983) *New Primary School Curriculum* (in Malay language), Kuala Lumpur: Dewan Bahasa dan Pustaka.

MINISTRY OF EDUCATION (1985) *Report of the Cabinet Committee: To Review*, Kuala Lumpur: Dewan Bahasa dan Pustaka.

MINISTRY OF EDUCATION (1987) *Integrated Curriculum for Secondary Schools* (in Malay language), Kuala Lumpur: Dewan Bahasa dan Pustaka.

MINISTRY OF EDUCATION (1990) *Moral Education Syllabus for Secondary Schools* (in Malay language), Kuala Lumpur: Dewan Bahasa dan Pustaka.

MINISTRY OF EDUCATION (1990) *History Syllabus for Lower Secondary School* (in Malay language), Kuala Lumpur: Dewan Bahasa dan Pustaka.

MINISTRY OF EDUCATION (1990) *History Syllabus for Upper Secondary School* (in Malay language), Kuala Lumpur: Dewan Bahasa dan Pustaka.

MINISTRY OF EDUCATION (1990) *Moral Education Syllabus for Primary Schools* (in Malay language), Kuala Lumpur: Dewan Bahasa dan Pustaka.

MINSON, G. (1993) *Questions of Conduct: Sexual Harassment, Citizenship and Government*, Macmillan: London.

MOON, D. (1988) 'The moral basis of the democratic welfare state', in GUTMANN, A. (Ed) *Democracy and the Welfare State*, Princeton: Princeton University Press.

MOORE, B. JR. (1967) *Social Origins of Dictatorship and Democracy*, Boston: Beacon Press.

MORGAN, E. (1988) *Inventing the People: The Rise of Popular Sovereignty in England and America*, New York: W.W. Norton.

MORLEY, D. and ROBINS, K. (1995) *Spaces of Identity: Global Media, Electronic Landscapes and Cultural Boundaries*, London: Routledge.

MORRIS, P. (1988) 'The effect on the school curriculum of Hong Kong's return to Chinese sovereignty in 1997', *Journal of Curriculum Studies*, **20**, 6, pp. 509–520.

MORRIS, P. (1995) 'Introduction', in MORRIS, P. and SWEETING, A. (Eds) *Education and Development in East Asia*, New York: Garland Press.

MORRIS, P. (1996) *The Hong Kong School Curriculum: Development, Issues and Policies*, Hong Kong: Hong Kong University Press, 2nd revised edition and Chinese translation.

MORRIS, P. and CHAN, K.K. (1996) 'Cross-curricular themes and curriculum reform: Policy as text and discourse', Paper presented at AERA conference Boston, USA 1996.

MORRIS, P. and SWEETING, A. (1991) 'Education and politics: The case of Hong Kong from an historical perspective', *Oxford Review of Education*, **17**, 3, pp. 249–267.

MORRISON, K. (1994) *Implementing Cross-Curricular Themes*, London: David Fulton Publishers.

MORT, F. (1989) 'The politics of consumption', in HALL, S. and JACQUES, M. (Eds) *New Times: The Changing Face of Politics in the 1990s*, London: Lawrence and Wishart.

MOUFFE, C. (Ed) (1992) *Dimensions of Radical Democracy*, London: Verso.

MOUFFE, C. (1993) *The Return of the Political*, London: Verso.

MURDOCH, W. (1916) *The Australian Citizen*, Melbourne: Whitcome and Tombs.

MURRAY, C. (1984) *Losing Ground: American Social Policy 1950–1980*, New York: Basic Books.

MUSGRAVE, P. (1994) 'How should we make Australians?' *Curriculum Perspectives*, **14**, 3, pp. 11–18.

NAIRN, T. (1981) *The Break-up of Britain: Crisis and Neo-Nationalism*, London: Verso.

NATIONAL COMMISSION ON EDUCATION (1993) *Learning to Succeed*, London: Heinemann.

THE NATIONAL COUNCIL FOR THE SOCIAL STUDIES (1942) *The Social Studies Mobilize for Victory*, Washington, DC: The National Council for the Social Studies.

THE NATIONAL COUNCIL FOR THE SOCIAL STUDIES (1944) *The Social Studies Look Beyond the War: A Statement of Postwar Policy*, Washington, DC: The National Council for the Social Studies.

THE NATIONAL EDUCATION ASSOCIATION (1943) *The Wartime Handbook of Education*, Washington, DC: National Education Association.

NATIONAL CURRICULUM COUNCIL (NCC) (1989) *Circular Number 6. The National Curriculum and Whole Curriculum Planning: Preliminary Guidance*, York: National Curriculum Council.

NATIONAL CURRICULUM COUNCIL (NCC) (1990a) *Curriculum Guidance Number 3: The Whole Curriculum*, York: National Curriculum Council.

NATIONAL CURRICULUM COUNCIL (NCC) (1990b) *Curriculum Guidance Number 8: Education for Citizenship*, York: National Curriculum Council.

NEWELL, S. (1995) 'Real life experiences for practising citizenship', *The Primary Educator*, **1**, 5, pp. 5–7.

NEWMAN, F. (1977) 'Building a rationale for citizenship education', in SHAVER, J.P. (Ed) *Building Rationales for Citizenship Education*, Bulletin 52, Washington, DC: National Council for the Social Studies.

NEWSPAPERS IN EDUCATION (1995) *Citizenship through Newspapers: National Edition*, The Newspaper Society.

NG, M.-I. (1994) 'Sexuality in Hong Kong', in MCMILLER, D. and MAU, S. (Eds) *The Other Hong Kong Report*, Hong Kong: The Chinese University Press, pp. 415–28.

NIEMEYER, H.J. (1957) 'Education for citizenship', in HENRY, N.B. (Ed) *Social Studies in the Elementary School: The Fifty-sixth Yearbook of National Society for the Study of Education*, Chicago: Chicago University Press, pp. 214–37.

NOVACK, M. (1987) *The New Consensus on the Family and Welfare*, Washington, DC: American Enterprise Institute for Public Policy Research.

NOZICK, R. (1974) *Anarchy, State and Utopia*, Oxford: Blackwell.

NSW DEPARTMENT OF SCHOOL EDUCATION (1994) *Evaluation of Educational Outcomes for Girls in NSW Government Secondary Schools*, NSW Department of School Education.

NUSSBAUM, M. (1990) 'Aristotelian Social Democracy', in DOUGLASS, R., MARA, G. and RICHARDSON, H. (Eds) *Liberalism and the Good*, New York: Routledge Kegan Paul.

OESTREICH, G. (1983) *Neo-Stoicism and the Early Modern State*, trans. MCLINTOCK, D. Cambridge: Cambridge University Press.

OFFICE OF THE PRIME MINISTER (1995) *Government Response to the Report of the Civics Expert Group*, Canberra: The Author.

OFSTED (1995) *Guidance on the Inspection of Secondary Schools*, London: HMSO (there are separate handbooks for nursery and primary schools, and special schools).

OKIN, S.M. (1988) *Justice, Gender and the Family*, New York: Basic Books.

O'NEILL, W.F. (1981) *Educational Ideologies: Contemporary Expressions of Educational Philosophy*, California: Goodyear Publishing Company Inc.

ORGANISATION FOR ECONOMIC COOPERATION AND DEVELOPMENT (OECD) (1996) *Girls and Women in Education. A Cross-national Study of Sex Inequalities in Upbringing and in Schools and Colleges*, Paris: OECD.

OZMENT, S. (1980) *The Age of Reform, 1250–1550*, New Haven: Yale University Press.

PARKER, W. (1991) *Renewing the Social Studies Curriculum*, Alexandra, VA: Association for Supervision and Curriculum Department.

PASCOE, S. (1996) 'Civics and citizenship education: The Australian context', *Unicorn*, **22**, 1, pp. 18–29.

PASSIN, H. (1965) *Society and Education in Japan*, New York: Teachers' College Press.

PATEMAN, C. (1970) *Participation and Democratic Theory*, Cambridge: Cambridge University Press.

PATEMAN, C. (1988) *The Sexual Contract*, Cambridge UK: Polity Press.

PATEMAN, C. (1988a) *The Sexual Contract*, Stanford: Stanford University Press.

PATEMAN, C. (1988b) 'The patriarchal welfare state', in GUTMANN, A. (Ed) *Democracy and the Welfare State*, Princeton: Princeton University Press.

PATEMAN, C. (1989) 'The Fraternal Social Contract', in *The Disorder of Women*, Stanford: University of California Press.

PATEMAN, C. (1989) 'Feminist critiques of the public/private dichotomy', in PATEMAN, C. (Ed) *The Disorder of Women: Democracy, Feminism and Political Theory*, Cambridge UK: Polity Press, pp. 118–40.

PATEMAN, C. (1992) 'Citizen male', *Australian Left Review*, **137**, March.

PATRICK, J. and HOGE, J. (1991) 'Teaching government, civics, and the law', in SHAVER, J. (Ed) *Handbook of Research on Social Studies Teaching and Learning*, New York: Macmillan.

PERKIN, H. (1985) *Origins of English Society*, London: Ark.

PHILLIPS, A. (1991) 'Citizenship and feminist theory', in Andrews, G. (Ed) *Citizenship*, London: Lawrence and Wishart.

PHILLIPS, A. (1995b) *The Politics of Presence*, Oxford: Clarendon Press.

PHILLIPS, H. (1989) 'Political education in Australia: Well-being for youth', *Australian Journal of Teacher Education*, **14**, 2, pp. 21–34.

PHILLIPS, H. (1995) 'The ideas of citizenship: Perceptions of Western Australian youth', in PRINT, M. (Ed) *Civics and Citizenship Education: Issues from Practice and Research*, Canberra, Australian Curriculum Studies Association.

PHILLIPSON, N. and SKINNER, Q. (Eds) (1993) *Political Discourse in Early Modern Britain*, Cambridge: Cambridge University Press.

PIXLEY, J. (1992) 'Citizen, worker or client', in MUETZELFEDT, M. (Ed) *Society, State and Politics in Australia*, Leichardt: Pluto Press.

PIXLEY, J. (1993) *Citizenship and Employment*, Melbourne: Cambridge University Press.

PLAMENATZ, J. (1961) *Man and Society*, Vol. 1, London: Longman.

PLANT, R. (1988) 'Needs, agency and rights', in MOON, D. (Ed) *Responsibility, Rights and Welfare*, Boulder, Colorado: Westview Press.

PLANT, R. (1991) 'Social rights and the reconstruction of the welfare state', in ANDREWS, G. (Ed) *Citizenship*, London: Lawrence and Wishart.

PLANT, R. (1992) *Modern Political Thought*, Oxford: Blackwell.

POCOCK, J.G.A. (1975) *The Machiavellian Moment*, Princeton: Princeton University Press.

POCOCK, J.G.A. (1985) 'Virtue, rights and manners: A model for historians of political thought', in *Virtue, Commerce and History*, Cambridge: Cambridge University Press.

POCOCK, J.G.A. (1993) 'The ideal of citizenship since classical times', in BEINER, R. (Ed) *Theorising Citizenship*, Albany: State University of New York Press.

POLYANI, K. (1957) *The Great Transformation*, Boston: Beacon Press.

PORTER, M.E. (1990) *The Competitive Advantage of Nations*, London: Macmillan.

PRINT, M. (1994) 'Civics and citizenship education: Research findings and directions for schooling', Keynote address, Political Education Conference, Parliament House, Canberra.

PRINT, M. (1995a) 'Research on political literacy as a basis for civics education', in PRINT, M. (Ed) *Civics and Citizenship Education: Issues from Practice and Research*, Canberra: Australian Curriculum Studies Association.

PRINT, M. (1995b) *Political Understanding and Attitudes of Secondary Students*, Canberra, Commonwealth of Australia.

PRINT, M. (1995c) 'Introduction: context and change in civics education', in PRINT, M. (Ed) *Civics and Citizenship Education: Issues from Practice and Research*, Canberra, Australian Curriculum Studies Association.

PRINT, M. (1996) *Pedagogical Strategies for Civics and Citizenship Education*, Commissioned paper, Melbourne, Curriculum Corporation.

PROST, A. (1968) Histoire de l'Enseignement en France, 1800–1967, Paris: Armand Colin.

PUSEY, M. (1991) *Economic Rationalism in Canberra*, Melbourne: Cambridge University Press.

QUAH, J.S.T. (1984) 'The public policy-making process in Singapore', *Asian Journal of Public Administration*, **6**, 2, pp. 108–126.

RABINOW, P. (Ed) (1985) *The Foucault Reader*, New York: Pantheon.

RANSON, S. (1994) *Towards a Learning Society*, London: Cassell.

RAWLS, J. (1991) *A Theory of Justice*, Cambridge: Harvard University Press.

RAWLS, J. (1993) *Political Liberalism*, New York: Columbia University Press.

REICH, R. (1991) *The Work of Nations: A Blueprint for the Future*, New York: Vintage.

REID, A. (1986) 'Political education — of what kind?', *Curriculum Concerns*, August.

REISENBERG, P. (1992) *Citizenship in the Western Tradition*, Chapel Hill: The University of North Carolina.

REMY, R.C. (1979) *Handbook of Basic Citizenship Competencies*, Alexandria, VA: Association for Supervision and Curriculum Development.

REPORT OF THE CIVICS EXPERT GROUP (1994) *Whereas the People . . . Civics and Citizenship Education*, Canberra: Australian Government Publishing Service.

REPORT OF THE EDUCATION COMMITTEE (1956) *Razak Report*, Kuala Lumpur: Government Press.

REPORT OF THE EDUCATION COMMITTEE (1960) *Rahman Talib Report*, Kuala Lumpur: Government Press.

RHEE, JONG-CHAN (1994) *The State and Industry in South Korea*, London: Routledge.

RINGER, F. (1979) *Education and Society in Modern Europe*, Bloomington: Indiana University Press.

ROCHE, M. (1987) 'Citizenship, social theory and social change', *Theory and Society*, **16**.

ROCHE, M. (1992) *Rethinking Citizenship: Welfare, Ideology and Change in Modern Society*, Cambridge: Polity Press.

ROFF, W.R. (1967) *The Origins of Malay Nationalism*, Kuala Lumpur: University of Malaya Press.

ROSE, N. and MILLER, P. (1992) 'Political power beyond the State: Problematics of government', *British Journal of Sociology*, **43**, 2, June.

Ross, S. (1990) 'Worldview address', Delivered at the Edinburgh International Television Festival, 26 August.

Rousseau, J.J. (1913) 'A discourse on political economy', in *The Social Contract and Discourses*, London: J.M. Dent.

Rousseau, J.J. (1953) 'Considerations on the Government of Poland and its proposed reformation', in Watkins, F. (Ed) *Rousseau: Political Writings*, New York: Nelson.

Rousseau, J.J. (1967) 'The social contract', in Crocker, L. (Ed) *The Social Contract and Discourse on the Origin of Inequality*, New York: Pocket Books.

Rowe, D. and Thorpe, T. (1993) *Living with the Law*, London: Hodder and Stoughton.

Rowe, G. and Whitty, G. (1993) 'Five themes remain in the shadows', *Times Educational Supplement*, April 9th.

Rudnitski, R.A. (1995) 'Nineteenth century readers and the changing conception of reading', Paper presented at the Annual Meeting of the Society for the Study of Curriculum History, San Francisco.

Rust, V. (1991) 'Post-modernism and its comparative education implications', *Comparative Education Review*, **35**, 4, pp. 610–626.

Sabine, G.H. (1937) *A History of Political Theory*, 3rd edn, London: George Harrap.

Said, E.W. (1978) *Orientatism*, New York: Pantheon.

Sandel, M. (1984b) 'Morality and the Liberal Ideal', *The New Republic*, May 7.

Sandel, M. (1982) *Liberalism and the Limits of Justice*, New York: Cambridge University Press.

Sandel, M. (1984a) 'The Procedural Republic and the Unencumbered Self', *Political Theory*, **12**, 1 (Feb).

Sarup, M. (1994) 'Home and identity', in Robertson, G., Mash, M., Tickner, L., Bird, J., Curtis, B. and Putnam, T. (Eds) *Travellers' Tales: Narratives of Home and Displacement*, London: Routledge.

Saunders, C. (1996) 'Challenges for citizenship', *Unicorn*, **22**, 1, pp. 30–34.

Saunders, L., MacDonald, A., Hewitt, D. and Schagen, S. (1995) *Education for Life: The Cross-Curricular Themes in Primary and Secondary Schools*, Slough: NFER.

Schools Commission (1975) *Girls, School and Society: Report of a Study Group to the Schools Commission*, Canberra: Schools Commission.

Schoppa, J. (1991) *Education Reform in Japan: A Case of Immobilist Politics*, London: Routledge.

Schuster, M. and Van Dyne, S. (1984) 'Placing women in the liberal arts: Stages of curriculum transformation', *Harvard Educational Review*, **54**, pp. 413–428.

Scott, I. (1989) *Political Change and the Crisis of Legitimacy in Hong Kong*, Hong Kong: Oxford University Press.

Scott, I. (1996) 'The State and Civil Society in Hong Kong', paper presented at International Conference on Political Development in Taiwan and Hong Kong, University of Hong Kong.

SEARS, A. and HUGHES, A. (1995) 'Citizenship education and current educational reform', *Canadian Journal of Education*.

SENATE LEGAL AND CONSTITUTIONAL REFERENCES COMMITTEE (SLCRC) (1995) *A System of National Citizenship Indicators*, Canberra: Australian Government Publishing Service.

SENATE STANDING COMMITTEE ON EMPLOYMENT, EDUCATION AND TRAINING (1989) *Education for Active Citizenship in Australian Schools and Youth Organisations*, Canberra: Australian Government Publishing Service.

SENATE STANDING COMMITTEE ON EMPLOYMENT, EDUCATION AND TRAINING (SSCEET) (1991) *Active Citizenship Revisited*, Canberra: Australian Government Publishing Service.

SHANLEY, M.L. (1991) 'Marital Slavery and Friendship, John Stuart Mill's The Subjection of Women', in SHANLEY, M.L. and PATEMAN, C. (Eds) *Feminist Interpretations and Political Theory*, Cambridge UK: Polity Press.

SHAVER, J.P. (Ed) (1977) *Building Rationales for Citizenship Education*, Bulletin 52; Washington, DC: National Council for the Social Studies.

SHAVER, J.P. (1996) 'NCSS and citizenship education', in DAVIS, JR., O.L. (Ed) *NCSS in Retrospect*, Bulletin 92, Washington, DC: National Council for the Social Studies.

SHAVER, J.P. and KNIGHT, R.S. (1986) 'Civics and government in citizenship education', WRONSKI, S.P. & BRAGAW, D.H. (Eds) *Social Studies and Social Sciences: A Fifty-Year Perspective*, Bulletin No. 78, Washington, DC: The National Council for the Social Studies.

SINGH, M. (1993) 'Teaching social education from the viewpoint of active citizens', in KENNEDY, K., WATTS, O. and MACDONALD, G. (Eds) *Citizenship Education for a New Age*, Toowoomba: USQ Press, pp. 101–122.

SITI HAWA (1986) 'Implementing a New Curriculum for Primary Schools: A case study for Malyasia', Unpublished Thesis, University of London.

SKINNER, Q. (1978a) *The Foundations of Modern Political Thought, Vol. 1, The Renaissance*, Cambridge: Cambridge University Press.

SKINNER, Q. (1978b) *The Foundations of Modern Political Thought, Vol. 2, The Age of the Reformation*, Cambridge; Cambridge University Press.

SMITH, A.D. (1995) *Nations and Nationalism in the Global Era*, Cambridge: Polity Press.

SOMERS, M. (1994) 'Rights, relationality, and membership: Rethinking the making and meaning of citizenship', *Law and Social Inquiry*, pp. 63–112.

SOMMERVILLE, J.P. (1986) *Politics and Ideology in England, 1603–1640*, London: Longman.

SOON TECK WONG (1992) 'Development of Human Resources and Technological Capability in Singapore', working paper, The Economic Development Institute of the World Bank.

SPEAKER'S COMMISSION ON CITIZENSHIP (1990) *Encouraging Citizenship*, London: HMSO.

STAHL, R.J. (1979) 'Developing values dilemmas for content-centered social studies instruction: Theoretical construct and practical applications', *Theory and Research in Social Education*, **7**, 2, pp. 50–74.

STANDING SENATE COMMITTEE ON SOCIAL AFFAIRS, SCIENCE AND TECHNOLOGY, THE SENATE OF CANADA (1993) *Canadian Citizenship: Sharing the Responsibility*, Ottawa: Minister of Supply and Services Canada.

STEPHENS, M. (1991) *Education and the Future of Japan*, Sandgate, UK: Japan Library.

STONE, L. (1977) *The Family, Sex and Marriage in England, 1500–1800*, New York: Harper & Row.

STOURZH, G. (1970) *Alexander Hamilton and the Idea of Republican Government*, Stanford: Stanford University Press.

STRADLING, R. (1987) *Education for Democratic Citizenship*, Council of Europe.

STUBBS, B. (1995) 'Civics and citizenship education: How can primary schools contribute?' *The Primary Educator*, **1**, 5, pp. 1–5.

SUH, S. (1988) 'Ideologies in Korea's morals and social studies texts: A content analysis', in CUMMINGS, W., GOPINATHAN, S. and TOMODA, Y. *The Revival of Values Education in Asia and the West*, Oxford: Pergamon.

SWEETING, A. (1995) 'Hong Kong', in MORRIS, P. and SWEETING, A. (Eds) *Education and Development in East Asia*, New York: Garland Press.

SWEETING, A. and MORRIS, P. (1993) 'Educational reform in post-war Hong Kong: Survival and crisis intervention', *International Journal of Educational Development*, **13**, 1, pp. 1–16.

TANG and MORRIS, P. (1989) 'The abuse of educational evaluation: a study of the evaluation of the civic education guidelines', *Educational Research Journal*, **4**, 1.

TAPPER, M. (1986) 'Can a feminist be a liberal?' in THOMPSON, J. (Ed) *Australasian Journal of Philosophy, Supplement to Volume 64*, Bundoora, Vic: Australasian Association of Philosophy, pp. 3747.

TAYLOR, C. (1985) *Philosophy and the Human Sciences: Philosophical Papers*, Cambridge: Cambridge University Press.

TAYLOR, C. (1989a) *Sources of the Self: The Making of Modern Identity*, Cambridge, Mass: Harvard University Press.

TAYLOR, C. (1989b) 'Cross purposes: The Liberal-Communitarian debate', in ROSENBLUM, N. (Ed) *Liberalism and the Moral Life*, Cambridge, Mass: Harvard University Press.

TAYLOR, C. (1994) 'The Politics of Recognition', in GUTMANN, A. (Ed) *Multiculturalism*, Princeton: Princeton University Press.

TEN DAM, G. and VOLMAN, M. (1996) 'Women's history and the subject "Care"', *The High School Journal*, **79**, 3, pp. 262–70.

THERBORN, G. (1977) 'The rule of capital and the rise of capitalism', *New Left Review*, 103.

THOMAS, J. (1994) 'The history of civics education in Australia', in *Civics Expert Group, Whereas the People . . . Civics and Citizenship Education*, Canberra: Australian Government Publishing Service, 161–171.

THOMPSON, P. (1996) 'Citizenship and values', *Unicorn*, **22**, 1, pp. 44–53.

THORN, F. and RIGG, E. (1923) *Handbook of Civics*, Melbourne: Oxford University Press.

TODD, M. (1987) *Christian Humanism and the Puritan Social Order*, Cambridge: Cambridge University Press.

TSANG, W.K. (1985) 'Analyzing the direction and approach of guidelines on civic education in schools', *Chung Pao Monthly*, December, pp. 47–52 (in Chinese).

TSANG, W.K. (1996) 'The Constitution of a Defiant Electorate: The Case of Hong Kong', paper presented at the International Conference on Political Development in Taiwan and Hong Kong, The University of Hong Kong, February 8–9.

TUCK, R. (1979) *Natural Rights Theories: Their Origin and Development*, Cambridge: Cambridge University Press.

TUCK, R. (1993) *Philosophy and Government, 1572–1651*, Cambridge: Cambridge University Press.

TULLY, J. (1989) 'Governing conduct', in LEITES, E. (Ed) *Conscience and Casuistry in Early Modern Europe*, Cambridge: Cambridge University Press.

TURNER, B. (1990) 'Outline of a theory of citizenship', *Sociology*, **24**, 2, May.

TURNER, B. (1989) 'From postindustrial society to postmodern politics: The political sociology of Daniel Bell', in GIBBINS, J. (Ed) *Contemporary Political Culture: Politics in a Postmodern Age*, London: Sage.

TURNER, B. (1986) *Citizenship and Capitalism*, London: Allen and Unwin.

ULLMAN, W. (1965) *A History of Political Thought: The Middle Ages*, Harmondsworth: Penguin.

UNICEF — SAVE THE CHILDREN (1990) *The Rights of the Child UNICEF-UK*: The Author.

USHER, R. and EDWARDS, R. (1994) *Postmodernism and Education: Different Voices, Different Worlds*, London: Routledge.

VE, H. (1989) 'Educational planning and rational ambiguity', Paper presented at the VIIth World Congress of Comparative Education, Montreal, 25–30 June.

VISITING PANEL (1982) *A Perspective on Education in Hong Kong*, Hong Kong: Government Printer.

VON ALBERTINI, R. (1982) *Decolonization: The Administration and Future of the Colonies, 1916–1960*, translation, GARVIE, F., New York: Africana Publishing Company.

WADE, R. (1990) *Governing the Market: Economic Theory and the Role of Government in East Asian Industrialization*, Princeton: Princeton University Press.

WALZER, M. (1970) *Obligations: Essays on Disobedience, War and Citizenship*, Cambridge, Mass: Harvard University Press.

WALZER, M. (1983) *Spheres of Justice: A Defence of Pluralism and Equality*, New York: Basic Books.

WALZER, M. (1989) 'Citizenship', in BALL, T., FARR, J. and HANSON, R. (Eds) *Political Innovation and Conceptual Change*, Cambridge: Cambridge University Press.

WATTS, R. (1995b) 'Rethinking the Employment/Citizenship Link', *Political Expressions*, **1**, 1.

WATTS, R. (1995a) 'Educating for citizenship and employment in Australia', *Melbourne Studies in Education*, **36**, 2, pp. 83–106.

WEALE, A. (1983) *Political Theory and Social Policy*, London: Macmillan.

WEBER, E. (1979) *Peasants into Frenchmen: The Modernization of Rural France, 1870–1914*, London: Chatto.

WEXLER, P. (1990) 'Citizenship in the semiotic society', in TURNER, B. (Ed) *Theories of Modernity and Postmodernity*, London: Sage.

WHITTY, G., ROWE, G. and AGGLETON, P. (1994) 'Subjects and themes in the secondary school curriculum', *Research Papers in Education*, **9**, 2, pp. 159–181.

WIELEMANS, W. and CHOI-PING CHAN, P. (Eds) (1994) *Education and Culture in Industrializing Asia. The Interaction between Industrialization, Cultural Identity and Education*, Leuven University Press.

WILLIAMSON-FIEN, J. (1994) 'Facing the Tiger: The problematics of Asian studies education', *Discourse*, **15**, 1.

WOLCOTT, I. and GLEZER, H. (1995) *Work and Family Life: Achieving Integration*, Melbourne: Australian Institute of Family Studies.

WOLIN, S. (1960) *Politics and Vision: Continuity and Innovation in Western Political Thought*, Boston: Little, Brown & Company.

WOODHOUSE, A.S.P. (Ed) (1938) *Puritanism and Liberty: Being the Army Debates (1647–49)*, Chicago: The University of Chicago Press.

WOODS, D. (1996) 'Aboriginality, Citizenship and the Curriculum — A response to Stuart MacIntyre's "Diversity, Citizenship and the Curriculum"', in KENNEDY, K. (Ed) *New Challenges for Citizenship Education*, Canberra: Australian Curriculum Studies Association.

WORLD BANK (1984) *East Asian Economic Miracle*, Geneva: World Bank.

WORLD COMMISSION ON ENVIRONMENT AND DEVELOPMENT (1987) *Our Common Future*, Oxford: Oxford University Press.

WRAGA, W. (1993) 'The inter-disciplinary imperceptive for citizenship education', *Theory and Research in Science Education*, **21**, 3, pp. 201–31.

WRINGE, C. (1992) The ambiguities of education for active citizenship, *Journal of Philosophy of Education*, **26**, 1, pp. 29–38.

WYN, J. (1995) '"Youth" and citizenship', *Melbourne Studies in Education*, **36**, 2, pp. 45–64.

YATES, L. (1995) 'Citizenship and Education', *Melbourne Studies in Education*, **36**, 2.

YATES, L. (1991b) 'Gender inclusive curriculum', Keynote address to Post-Primary Teacher's Association of New Zealand National Conference: Christchurch.

YATES, L. (1993) 'Feminism and Australian state policy: Some questions for the 1990s', in ARNOT, M. and WEILER, K. (Eds) *Feminism and Social Justice in Education: International Perspectives*, London: Falmer Press, pp. 167–85.

YATES, L. (1991a) 'A tale full of sound and fury — signifying what? Feminism and curriculum policy in Australia', paper presented to the annual conference of the American Educational Research Association, Chicago, Symposium on *Feminist Politics and the Struggle for Social Justice in Education: Comparative Perspectives*, April.

YEATMAN, A. (1994) *Postmodern Revisionings of the Political*, London: Routledge.

YEATMAN, A. (1990) *Bureaucrats, Technocrats, Femocrats: Essays on the Contemporary Australian State*, Sydney: Allen and Unwin.

YOUNG, C. (1996) 'Civics and citizenship education and the teaching of history', *Unicorn*, **22**, 1, pp. 64–71.

YOUNG, I. (1987) 'Impartiality and the civic public: Some implications of feminist critiques of moral and political theory', in BENHABIB, S. and CORNELL, D. (Eds) *Feminism as Critique*, Cambridge: Polity Press.

YOUNG, I.M. (1989) 'Polity and group difference: A critique of the ideal of universal citizenship', *Ethics*, **99**, pp. 250–274.

YOUNG, I.M. (1990) *Justice and the Politics of Difference*, Princeton: Princeton University Press.

YOUNG, YI-RONG (1994) 'Education and Social Change in Taiwan', Paper to 16th Congress of the Comparative Education Society in Europe, Copenhagen in June 1994.

YULISH, S.M. (1980) *The Search for a Civic Religion: A History of the Character Education Movement in America, 1890–1935*, Washington, DC: University Press of America.

Notes on Contributors

Sherry L. Field is Associate Professor in the Department of Social Science Education at The University of Georgia. She is a graduate of The University of Texas at Austin. Her teaching and research interests include the history of social studies education, elementary and middle school social studies teaching methods, children's historical thinking, and global education. She has published articles in *Theory and Research in Social Education*; *Social Education, Journal of Social Studies Research*; *The Social Studies*; and *Journal of Curriculum Supervision*. Dr Field consults with school districts across the nation on updating social studies curricula. She currently serves as President of Society for the Study of Curriculum History, co-chair of the 10th Conference on Qualitative Education, chair of the Textbooks and Teaching AERA SIG, and as editor of *Social Studies and the Young Learner*.

Ken Fogelman is Professor of Education at the University of Leicester, UK. After a period as a secondary maths teacher, his early career was as a researcher, with the National Foundation for Educational Research and the National Children's Bureau. For sixteen years he led the team undertaking the National Child Development Study, a longitudinal study of some 15,000 people born in 1958. He moved to Leicester in 1988, and in 1991 established the Centre for Citizenship Studies in Education, which carries out research and development to promote and support citizenship education in schools. His publications include *Citizenship in Schools* and (with J. Edwards) *Developing Citizenship in the Curriculum*, both published by David Fulton.

Victoria Foster is Visiting Scholar in the Faculty of Education at the University of Canberra, Nepean, Australia. Her research interests focus on interdisciplinary and comparative studies of gender and equality issues in education, with a particular interest in the foundations of education and curriculum design and implementation. She has directed several Australian curriculum projects on gender and education. She is the author of many published research articles and books, including the best-selling *Changing Choices: Girls, School and Work*. Her forthcoming book is *Space Invaders: Barriers to Equality in the Schooling of Girls* (Allen and Unwin) and *Contemporary Issues in Education Series*. In 1995 she was appointed Adviser on gender issues to the Hon. John Aquilian, New South Wales Minister for Education and Training.

Rob Gilbert is Associate Professor at James Cook University. After teaching geography, history, social science, and English at secondary school, he moved to the university to teach social science and geography curriculum studies. He has considerable experience in secondary school curriculum development and evaluation in this field, and has published widely in social, geographical, citizenship, legal and history education, as well as in educational research methods and social justice issues.

Andy Green is a Reader in Education at London University Institute of Education. He has written widely on comparative education history and policy and his books include: *Education and State Formation*, (Macmillan, 1990); *Education Limited: Schooling and Training and the New Right Since 1979*, (Unwin Hyman, 1991) (with other is Cultural Studies); *Education, Youth and Work: World Yearbook on Education*, (Kogan Page, 1995) (edited with L. Bash); *Education, Globalization and the Nation State*, (Macmillan, 1997).

David Hogan is Professor of Education and Director of the Centre for Citizenship and Education at the University of Tasmania. Prior to the end of 1993 he taught at the University of Pennsylvania in the USA. He has written extensively about the history of education in the United States and won a series of awards and honours for his work, including the AERA Outstanding Book Award for 1986, the Henry Barnard Prize and the History of Education Society Award of the History of Education Society of the United States, and Spencer and National Endowment of the Humanities Fellowships. In 1993–4 he was elected President of the History of Education Society. Currently, he is engaged in two broad areas of research, one on citizenship and civic education in Australia, and the other on the relationship between social demography, school organization and governance, and student achievement in Tasmania. He lives in Hobart, Tasmania, with his wife, daughter, the sea, the bust and several incomplete manuscripts.

Haris Md Jadi is Associate Professor of Education at the School of Educational Studies, University Sains Malaysia, Penang. He obtained his B.A from USM, Malaysia; M.A from Teachers College, Columbia University, New York; Ph.D. from Keele University, England. Areas of interest include History and Philosophy of Education, Education and Development, and Curriculum Studies. He has authored a book *Ethnicity, Politics and Education* which explored the development of Malaysian Education from 1955–1970. Currently serving as Chief Educator, Journal of Higher Education, University Sains Malaysia, Penang.

Kerry J. Kennedy is a Professor of Education and Dean of the Faculty of Education at the University of Canberra. He is also the President of the Australian Curriculum Studies Association. He was formerly the director of the Centre for Continuing Education at the Australian National University. His research interests include curriculum-policy development and the impact of curriculum policy on educational practice.

Paul Morris is a Reader in the Department of Curriculum Studies, Faculty of Education, the University of Hong Kong, where he has worked in various capacities since 1976. From 1986 until 1992 he was Dean of the Faculty, and from 1988 to 1993 he was a member of the Government's Education Commission. He has published extensively in areas of curriculum analysis and comparative education. His recent books include: *The Hong Kong School Curriculum: Development, Issues and Policy*, 1996 and (co-edited with Anthony Sweeting) *Education and Development in East Asia*, (New York: Garland Press, 1995).

Murray Print is a leading participant in the civics and citizenship education within Australia. He has advised both the Australian Government and the country's national curriculum agency, the Curriculum Corporation, on civics education. He has published extensively in the field as well as conducted research on student civic literacy. Currently he is director of Civics Education Assessment and Benchmark Project funded by the Australian Research Council.

Index